AF698790

GEORGE MASON UNIVERSITY
UNIVERSITY LIBRARIES

CHINA IN THE 21ST CENTURY

THIRTY YEARS OF CHINA'S ECONOMIC REFORM: INSTITUTIONS, MANAGEMENT ORGANIZATIONS AND FOREIGN INVESTMENT

CHINA IN THE 21ST CENTURY

China in World Affairs
V. Clarence (Editor)
ISBN: 1-56072-359-9

China's Relations with Japan in an Era of Economic Liberalisation
Dong Dong Zhang (Editor)
ISBN: 1-56072-625-3

Bicoastal China: A Dialectical, Paradigmatic Analysis
Peter Kien-hong Yu
ISBN: 1-56072-640-7

Crisis and Reform in China
E. Bliney
ISBN: 1-56072-416-1

The Political Dynamics of Hong Kong Under the Chinese Sovereignty
Jermain T.M. Lam
ISBN: 1-56072-806-X

US China Policy: Interest Groups and Their Influence
H. Comet
2001. ISBN: 1-59033-044-7

FDI in China: Contributions to Growth, Restructuring and Competitiveness
Jiang Xiaojuan
2003. ISBN: 1-59033-894-4

China: Possible Missile Technology Transfers
Shirley A. Kan (Editor)
2003. ISBN: 1-59033-758-1

Government and Market in China: A Local Perspective
Jian Zhang
2004. ISBN: 1-59033-883-9

China's Telecommunications Reforms: From Monopoly towards Competition
Yunxiang (Scott) Guan
2007. ISBN: 1-59033-540-6

China and Antiterrorism
Simon Shen (Editor)
2007. ISBN: 1-60021-344-8

Congress and US China Policy
Jian Yang
2008. ISBN: 1-56072-844-2

China-U.S. Economic and Geopolitical Relations
Jerald D. Finn (Editor)
2008. ISBN: 978-1-60456-052-7

Education in China
James U. Landowe (Editor)
2008. ISBN: 978-1-60456-309-2

Trade Barriers and China
Martha B. Kessler
2008. ISBN: 978-1-60456-686-4

China Naval Modernization: Implications for U.S. Navy Capabilities
Ronald O'Rourke
2008. ISBN: 978-1-60456-709-0

Is China A Threat to the U.S. Economy?
Craig K. Elwell, Marc Labonte and Wayne M. Morrison
2008. ISBN: 978-1-60456-843-1

Is China A Threat to the U.S. Economy?
Craig K. Elwell, Marc Labonte and Wayne M. Morrison
2008. ISBN: 978-1-61668-067-1 (E-book)

China: Has the Last Opportunity Passed By?!
Guang Wu
2009. ISBN: 978-1-60741-538-1

Human Rights in China
Lee R. Massingdale (Editor)
2009. ISBN: 978-1-60741-116-

China's Foreign Policy and Soft Power Influence
Alice V. Monroe (Editor)
2010. ISBN: 978-1-60692-994-0

China's Foreign Policy and Soft Power Influence
Alice V. Monroe (Editor)
2010. ISBN: 978-1-61668-791-5 (E-book)

China and the U.S.: Comparing Global Influence
Thomas Lum, Christopher M. Blanchard, Nicolas Cook and Kerry Dumbaugh
2010. ISBN: 978-1-60692-995-7

Business, Finance and Economics of China
Lian Guo and Fai Zong (Editors)
2010. ISBN: 978-1-60741-299-1

China's Agricultural Modernization
Russell H. Jeffries (Editor)
2010. ISBN: 978-1-60876-088-6

China's Political and Economic Transformation: Theory and Case Studies
Rongxing Guo
2010. ISBN: 978-1-60876-321-4

Measuring China's Military Might
Samuel E. Fleischer (Editor)
2010. ISBN: 978-1-60876-846-2

Thirty Years of China's Economic Reform: Institutions, Management Organizations and Foreign Investment
Yue Wang and Prem Ramburuth (Editors)
2010. ISBN: 978-1-60876-908-7

The Chinese Economy
Benjamin A. Tyler (Editor)
2010. ISBN: 978-1-60876-937-7

The Chinese Economy
Benjamin A. Tyler (Editor)
2010. ISBN: 978-1-61668-648-2 (E-book)

The Rhetoric and Reality of Culture-Led Urban Regeneration: A Comparison of Beijing and Shanghai, China
Jun Wang and Shaojun Li
2010. ISBN: 978-1-61668-686-3

CHINA IN THE 21ST CENTURY

THIRTY YEARS OF CHINA'S ECONOMIC REFORM: INSTITUTIONS, MANAGEMENT ORGANIZATIONS AND FOREIGN INVESTMENT

YUE WANG
AND
PREM RAMBURUTH
EDITORS

Nova Science Publishers, Inc.
New York

Copyright © 2010 by Nova Science Publishers, Inc.

All rights reserved. No part of this book may be reproduced, stored in a retrieval system or transmitted in any form or by any means: electronic, electrostatic, magnetic, tape, mechanical photocopying, recording or otherwise without the written permission of the Publisher.

For permission to use material from this book please contact us:
Telephone 631-231-7269; Fax 631-231-8175
Web Site: http://www.novapublishers.com

NOTICE TO THE READER

The Publisher has taken reasonable care in the preparation of this book, but makes no expressed or implied warranty of any kind and assumes no responsibility for any errors or omissions. No liability is assumed for incidental or consequential damages in connection with or arising out of information contained in this book. The Publisher shall not be liable for any special, consequential, or exemplary damages resulting, in whole or in part, from the readers' use of, or reliance upon, this material. Any parts of this book based on government reports are so indicated and copyright is claimed for those parts to the extent applicable to compilations of such works.

Independent verification should be sought for any data, advice or recommendations contained in this book. In addition, no responsibility is assumed by the publisher for any injury and/or damage to persons or property arising from any methods, products, instructions, ideas or otherwise contained in this publication.

This publication is designed to provide accurate and authoritative information with regard to the subject matter covered herein. It is sold with the clear understanding that the Publisher is not engaged in rendering legal or any other professional services. If legal or any other expert assistance is required, the services of a competent person should be sought. FROM A DECLARATION OF PARTICIPANTS JOINTLY ADOPTED BY A COMMITTEE OF THE AMERICAN BAR ASSOCIATION AND A COMMITTEE OF PUBLISHERS.

LIBRARY OF CONGRESS CATALOGING-IN-PUBLICATION DATA

Thirty years of China's economic reform : institutions, management
organizations and foreign investment / editors, Yue Wang, Prem Ramburuth.
p. cm.
Includes index.
ISBN 978-1-60876-908-7 (hardcover)
1. China--Economic policy--1976-2000. 2. China--Economic policy--2000- 3. Investments, Foreign--China. I. Wang, Yue. II. Ramburuth, Prem.
HC427.92.T483 2010
330.951'05--dc22
2009054182

Published by Nova Science Publishers, Inc. ✝ New York

HC
427.92
.T483
2010

CONTENTS

PREFACE

The rise of China as an economic superpower is one of the most dramatic developments in the history of capitalism. Despite a large amount of research on a variety of topics related to Chinese business and management, the effect of China's economic reform cannot be fully understood unless its components are identified and analyzed. The transformation of the country from a closed planning economy to a dynamic capitalist society in the past 30 years can be broadly attributed to the changes in three inter-related areas: institutional reforms (especially at the level of governments), organizational innovations (especially the emergence of various private and hybrid management organizations), and foreign investment (both the huge influx of inward FDI into China and the increasingly aggressive outflow FDI by Chinese firms).

The book collects some of the recent scholarly projects that review the path the country's institutions and organizations have taken and the role of foreign investment has played during the reform era. Linking together research in the three distinctive areas (institutional reforms, management organizations and foreign direct investment), the 12 chapters contained in this book provide a complete picture of the changes that have occurred in the areas of business and management in China. The chapters are organized into the three themes:

The first theme (Chapters 1-4) examines institutional reforms at various levels of Chinese governments, the features of these institutional reforms, and the impact of these reforms on business strategies and performance of Chinese enterprises and Chinese entrepreneurs.

In Chapter 1, through historical reviews and case studies, Wenxian Zhang and Ilan Alon seek to understand why some initially successful entrepreneurs failed in the economic boom of past decades. Among various factors contributed to their downfalls are a unique political and business environment, fragile financial systems, traditional cultural influences and personal characteristics. Notwithstanding that these factors should be further tested through empirical studies, those high-profile entrepreneurs are oblivious but essential actors in the grand theater of China's economic transformation, and their failures have contributed to the swift development of the Chinese entrepreneurship over the last thirty years.

In Chapter 2, Cherrie Jiuhua Zhu, Mingqiong Zhang, Bruce Thomson, Chris Nyland, and Yue Guo investigate the significant changes in the available workforce in Chinese cities due to the influx of millions of migrant workers as the consequence of economic reforms. Drawing on institutional theory, this chapter discusses the emergence of the *'institution of mingongzhi'* (*mingong* means farmer-turned workers and *zhi* means system in Chinese) and provides a justification for applying the label of institution. Based on the empirical evidence from the case studies and surveys conducted in Changsha and Haerbin, the authors found the existence of the institution of *mingongzhi* even after many of the barriers for rural migrants were removed by the central government. The authors argue that *mingongzhi* needs to be deinstitutionalized if China is to establish a unified labour market as advocated by the International Labour Organization and the World Trade Organization.

In Chapter 3, Peter Sheldon, David Morgan, and Benard Gan discuss the management and organization of three public sector joint ventures (JVs) between Singaporean and Chinese government and other public sector bodies developed during the 1990s. Examination of the three projects – industrial parks at Suzhou and Wuxi, and a port development at Dalian – identifies contrasting experiences and outcomes resulting from the interplay of issues of economic, social and political control. The comparative analysis suggests the importance of the type of public sector JV, its scale, and particular dimensions of local institutional context. Knowledge transfer faced fewer political and institutional impediments where it focused predominantly on technical and managerial systems, was defined as more commercially oriented and took place within – rather than apart from – existing Chinese infrastructure and administrative structures. In particular, tensions with local Chinese authorities emerge over prioritising administrative 'software' transfer at arm's length from those authorities. These results point to the importance of institutional distance in the context of conflicting indications from the literatures on JVs and knowledge transfer.

In Chapter 4, Romie Littrell and Elisabeth Montgomery compare the individual cultural values of two types of entrepreneurs with a random sample of businesspeople in South China. The findings indicate that the individual cultural values of the types of businesspeople from 2004 and 2005 samples are similar, and are different from results of studies conducted in the mid-1990s. The results show businesspeople in South China are on average less adhering to tradition and valuing self-direction, indicating openness to innovation, but still expressing typical values of conformity, benevolence, and universalism, achievement oriented, and highly value security, perhaps seeing the business sector as a path to enhancement of personal and family security.

The second theme (Chapters 5-8) examines organizational changes and innovations in various types of Chinese enterprises, the emergence of new modes of management organization in response to institutional reforms, and the adoption of new management practices in Chinese enterprises.

In Chapter 5, Akira Tanaka and Yue Wang provide a pioneering study on the governance of business groups in China. Despite the rapid development of business groups in China and their ability to compete in the world market, little is known about their governance structures in comparison to their Asian counterparts. This chapter examines one of the key features of business group governance, namely inter-firm relationship, in one of China's major automobile groups Tianjin Automotive Group (TAG). Compared to the established practices of Japanese automobile groups, the authors found that TAG's inter-firm relationship is characterized by top-down hierarchical administration rather than a truly quasi-market quasi-hierarchy network structure typically found in Japan. The chapter shows that the emerging Chinese business groups are in essence administratively-driven rather than economically-driven industrial organizations, which explains why their governance structures are fundamentally different from the common features of business groups in Japan and the rest of the world.

In Chapter 6, Putai Jin examines the economic progress of China using historical comparisons, analyzes the psychological capital of China's workforces, and highlights emerging issues associated with Chinese human resource management for sustainable development. The four-stage cycle "Turbulent times – Concessions, constraints, and reforms of the new regime – Recovery of social productive forces – Prosperity of economy and associated aspects" (TCRP) can be identified in the Chinese history, such as the golden age of the West Han and Tang Dynasties. It is argued that, whereas the catalytic functioning of a series of policy changes initiated by the current Chinese government should be acknowledged, the relatively emancipated Chinese social productive forces in various types of enterprises need to be regarded as one of the crucial factors of recent remarkable economic growth in China. During the rapidly changing period, Chinese workers' positive motivational states, such as hope, resiliency, and realistic optimism, provide an invaluable psychological capital for coping with work stress and attaining high performance. Although China is faced with a number of problems associated with the global economic crisis, the positive psychological capital of Chinese workers will play a constructive role in the reforming and opening-up processes.

In Chapter 7, Snejina Michailova explores how Chinese executive elites' demographic attributes shape their companies' strategic behavior during the reform era. The chapter utilizes upper echelon theory to examine the demographic attributes of executive elites (Chief Executive Officers and/or Presidents) of the 15 largest companies across the manufacturing and services sectors in China. These companies are all state-owned enterprises, have long history and all, but one, are engaged in cross-border business activities. The author examines executive elites' age, functional track, career experience and formal education, and suggests that executives' political affiliation is an attribute relevant in the Chinese context although not considered by the original (Western) upper echelon theory. The findings show that the executives of the target companies have a high level of formal education and are strongly affiliated with the Communist Party. This study indicates that large Chinese firms' strategic innovative behavior (in terms of international expansion) can partly be attributed to their executives' demographic characteristics.

In Chapter 8, through historical review and case studies, Wenxian Zhang and Ilan Alon examine the development of female entrepreneurship in the People's Republic of China and argue that women entrepreneurs have been playing an increasingly significant role in the Chinese economic reform of the past thirty years. Faced with both challenges and opportunities, aspiring Chinese women must have a clear vision, sheer determination and perseverance to move forward, and they must also possess a sense of aggressiveness and decision-making competence in order to achieve desirable business objectives. In addition, successful female entrepreneurs in China appear to be well educated, mostly married and politically shrewd, they seem to enjoy strong family support and benefit greatly from extensive personal networks.

The third theme (Chapters 9-12) focuses on a relatively new phenomenon, namely the increasingly important role of outward foreign direct investment made by Chinese firms. The chapters in this theme analyze the impact of the outward FDI on China's economic reform as well as on the host countries' and regions' economies and firms.

In Chapter 9, Prem Ramburuth, Paul Buatsi and Richard Owusu explore the extent of China's economic engagement in Africa, its intentions and strategies. The Chapter examines the growing presence of Chinese SOEs and private sector enterprises, and implications for

African development. Adopting an interpretative approach, the author provides a comprehensive review of current literature and recent data to highlight China's activities in Africa and provide insights into areas of expansion and development. China's intentions seem to be divided between acting as a facilitator for Africa's development and an extractor of resources. It has adopted a 'soft diplomacy' strategy in its pursuit of global growth, and is supporting the increased presence of Chinese SOEs and privately owned enterprises in Africa. In weighing the benefits and challenges to Chinese firms' expansion and growth in Africa, the author argues African countries must adopt strategies to leverage the benefits of their rich resources and consider issues of sustainability for long term economic development.

In Chapter 10, Dylan Sutherland and Ning Lutao examine the extent to which China's large business groups have engaged in outward foreign direct investment (OFDI) and, more generally, their overall development trajectory to date. Chinese business groups have grown rapidly in recent years. To date, however, few studies have noted the concentration of assets, sales, profits and R&D expenditures in a small number of super-large trial business groups. These groups are now also responsible for a large share of China's outward foreign direct investment. This is no coincidence as top leaders have long harbored plans to create internationally competitive business groups, following their East Asian neighbors. In recent years, with rapidly growing OFDI from China, it is of interest to ask what progress these groups have made in internationalizing their operations. There is also a growing interest in the idea of 'strategic-asset-seeking' OFDI from China. This type of OFDI is found to be associated with rapid firm-level catch-up.

In Chapter 11, Gaston Fornes and Guillermo Cardoza study the international expansion of small-to-medium enterprises (SMEs) in China. The authors collected data from around 500 SMEs and then analysed using multivariate regressions. The results showed (1) several factors are hindering the expansion of Chinese SMEs, (2) finance does not seem to be a barrier to their expansion, (3) different barriers apply to cross the regional and national boundaries, and (4) ownership by the state does not seem to play a relevant role in the international expansion.

In Chapter 12, William Choy reviews the historical development of bilateral trade and foreign direct investment between China and the Association of the Southeast Asian Nations (ASEAN) since the 1970s till the present day. China's economic reform since 1979 has served as a great incentive for the ASEAN member countries to engage in continuous political and economic dialogues with the economic giant. The extensive political and economic efforts initiated by the ASEAN and Chinese governments have played a pivotal role in promoting bi-lateral trade and foreign direct investment. The institutional building at the macro-level between Chinese and ASEAN governments which shape the pattern of economic cooperation is different from those observed between China and Hong Kong/Taiwan. The case of Sino-Singapore Suzhou Industrial Park (SIP) illustrates the central roles of governments in driving the process of bi-lateral cooperation between China and the ASEAN member countries, leading to micro-level cooperation and business networking between firms.

By identifying and analyzing these three main components and factors contributing to China's economic reform (Chinese institutions, Chinese management organizations and foreign direct investment) in terms of their workings and interactions, this book helps us understand the successes and failures of China's market-oriented reform in the past, as well as enable us to better predict how "the market economy with Chinese characteristics" will continue to shape up in the future. The chapters contained in this book offer valuable insights into various aspects of Chinese institutions and organizations, and reveal enduring implications for theory development and management practices in the Chinese context. Aiming at marking the 30th anniversary of China's economic reform, the book makes an incremental yet important contribution to the emerging field of Chinese management research.

Yue Wang
Prem Ramburuth
September, 2009

CONTRIBUTORS

Akira Tanaka	Faculty of Economics, Nagoya City University, Nagoya, Japan
Bernard Gan	School of Organisation and Management, Australian School of Business, University of New South Wales, Sydney, Australia
Cherrie Jiuhua Zhu	Department of Management, Monash University, Melbourne, Australia
Chris Nyland	Department of Management, Monash University, Melbourne, Australia
David Morgan	School of Organisation and Management, Australian School of Business, University of New South Wales, Sydney, Australia
Dylan Sutherland	School of Contemporary Chinese Studies, Nottingham University
Elisabeth P. Montgomery	Regional General Manager - Pacific Rim, InterLangua.com
Gaston Fornes	University of Bristol (UK) and ESIC Business and Marketing School (Spain), Bristol, United Kingdom
Guillermo Cardoza	Instituto de Empresa Business School, Madrid, Spain
Ilan Alon	Rollins College, Winter Park, Florida, USA
Mingqiong Zhang	Department of Management, Monash University, Melbourne, Australia
Ning Lutao	East Asian Studies, University of Cambridge, UK
Paul N. Buatsi	Office of the Chief Director, Ministry of Education, Accra, Ghana
Peter Sheldon	School of Organisation and Management, Australian School of Business, University of New South Wales, Sydney, Australia
Prem Ramburuth	School of Organisation and Management, Australian School of Business, University of New South Wales, Sydney, Australia
Putai Jin	Faculty of Arts and Social Sciences, University of New South Wales, Sydney, Australia

Richard Owusu	Swedish School of Economics and Business Administration, CERS-Department of Marketing and Corporate Geography, Helsinki, Finland
Romie Littrell	AUT Business School, Auckland University of Technology, Auckland, New Zealand
S. Bruce Thomson	Department of Management, Monash University, Melbourne, Australia
Snejina Michailova	Department of Management and International Business, University of Auckland Business School, New Zealand
Wenxian Zhang	Rollins College, Winter Park, Florida, USA
William K. W. Choy	Policy and Leadership Studies Academic Group, National Institute of Education, Nanyang Technological University, Singapore
Yue Guo	Institute of Labour & Social Security, Chinese Academy of Social Sciences, Beijing, China
Yue Wang	School of Strategy and Entrepreneurship, Australian School of Business, University of New South Wales, Sydney, Australia

Part I. Institutional Reforms, Business Strategies and Performance

In: Thirty Years of China's Economic Reform
Editors: Yue Wang and Prem Ramburuth

ISBN: 978-1-60876-908-7
© 2010 Nova Science Publishers, Inc.

Chapter 1

A PRELIMINARY STUDY ON THE FACTORS THAT CONTRIBUTED TO THE DOWNFALL OF HIGH-PROFILE ENTREPRENEURS DURING THE CHINESE ECONOMIC REFORM

***Wenxian Zhang** and Ilan Alon*+**
Rollins College, Winter Park, Florida, USA

Man of noble character is keen on wealth and takes no money but in a moral way.
Confucius (551-479 BCE)

ABSTRACT

Through historical reviews and case studies, this research seeks to understand why some initially successful entrepreneurs have failed in the economic boom of past decades. Among various factors contributing to their downfalls are a unique political and business environment, fragile financial systems, traditional cultural influences and personal characteristics. Notwithstanding that these factors should be further tested through empirical studies, these high-profile entrepreneurs are oblivious but essential actors in the grand theater of China's economic transformation, and their failures have contributed to the swift development of Chinese entrepreneurship over the last thirty years.

Keywords: Chinese entrepreneurs, entrepreneurship, economic reform, corruption, business environment, cultural influence, personal characteristics.

---

* Email: wzhang@rollins.edu.Wenxian Zhang is Professor and Head of Archives & Special Collections at Rollins College, Winter Park, Florida, USA
+ Email: ialon@rollins.edu. Ilan Alon is Petters Chair of International Business, Executive Director of China Center at Rollins College, and Visiting Scholar of the John F. Kennedy School of Government at Harvard University.

INTRODUCTION

In any competitive business environment, both success and failure are expected. Of all new businesses launched, a great majority will fail sooner or later, as entrepreneurs will need not only luck and timing but also vision and perseverance to succeed. So failure is not something of which to be ashamed, but a great motivation factor for some new innovations and future undertakings.

China's economic transformation over the last thirty years is filled with stories of success and failure. Just as an old Chinese adage on human endeavors summarized - while winners were hailed as king, losers generally ended up as criminals - many of the failed entrepreneurs discussed in this paper have been allegedly involved in economic crimes of some sort. Whether publicly acknowledged or not, capitalist crimes have been growing as fast as the country's economy. According to a survey by the Political & Economic Risk Consultancy, China is considered to be among the three most corrupt countries in Asia (*Economist*, 1995). Despite the continuing efforts by the Chinese Communist Party (CCP) to crack down, corruption in China has grown both in frequency and scope. Corrupt acts that qualify as crimes include embezzlement, bribery, misappropriation, illegal earnings and illegal profiteering, but not squandering, privilege seeking, violation of accounting rules, and moral decadence (Shieh, 2005). In order to have a better-defined scope, however, this study will not cover the high-rank officials involved in bribery and corruption scandals, such as Chen Liangyu of Shanghai, Liu Zhihua of Beijing and Wang Xuebing of Bank of China, although their cases are closely related to the Chinese economic reform of the last thirty years.

This is China's Gilded Age, a period of growing wealth and industrialization, and a time of great ups and downs. Distinctive of capitalism in its early, exuberant stage of development, as noted by Mihm (2007), this period is one in which technology has improved dramatically and markets have burst their older boundaries. Yet the country is still relying on outdated regulations to control its booming commerce. Consequently when the lines between legitimate and fraudulent means of making money become blurry, laws will be broken and the downfall of many entrepreneurs will be inevitable, and more will follow in their paths, until China's regulatory institutions catch up with its economic ambitions.

Since there are so many failed entrepreneurs, this study will try to focus on private or collective businesses, and those cases that have a profound impact on Chinese economic development. Compared to the state-owned companies, the private sector in China is extremely dynamic, growing at around 20 percent a year, more than twice as fast as the economy as a whole. It has grown to contribute about two-thirds of China's gross domestic product and fixed capital investment, 70 to 80 percent of tax revenue for local government, and is responsible for most of the country's job creation by employing more than 75 percent of people in urban areas (James, 2005). Therefore, focusing on private entrepreneurs will likely present a more accurate and realistic picture of the Chinese economic reform.

Listed below are ten cases of high-profile failures of Chinese entrepreneurs. They range from an elementary school dropout to post-graduates of China's elite colleges, from a village leader and street vendor to a PLA officer and inventor. They were not only dreamers and reformers, but also *guanxi* builders, risk takers and gamblers. All in all, they are important actors on the grand stage of China's dramatic economic transformation over the past three decades, and through their ultimate downfall the glories and misfortunes of Chinese economic reform have been vividly documented.

TEN CASES OF HIGH-PROFILE FAILURES OF CHINESE ENTREPRENEURS

According to *Forbes* in 2001, Gu Chujun (1959-), a prominent Chinese entrepreneur, was China's 20th richest person with 236 million dollars of wealth. Born in Yangzhou, Jiangsu Province, Gu received his college education from Tianjin University. After he patented chlorofluorocarbon-free refrigerant technology in 1990, Gu formed Greencool Technologies, which served as the base for his corporate expansion ambitions. His crown jewel was Guangdong Kelon Electrical Holdings, then one of the largest refrigerator companies in China. However, in 2005 Gu was accused of overstating revenue, falsifying registered capital and embezzling company money. Gu denied the accusations, claiming that his alleged crimes were "common practices" in an "unfriendly environment" where authorities only supported state-owned enterprises and foreign investment.

Huang Guangyu (Wong Kwong Yu 1969-), known as "the Price Butcher" and one of the country's most dynamic young entrepreneurs, is a classic rags-to-riches story. Huang is, in many ways, the physical embodiment of China's economic miracle of the last three decades. As a high school dropout he moved to Beijing at age 16 with his brother and began selling radios and gadgets from a small shop. With $500 and a vision that an increasing level of income would go along with an increasing demand for household appliances, they eventually formed the nation's largest electronics retailing chain Gome, or Best Buy of China. As of June 2008, the company had a 12% share of China's electrical retail market, with 828 stores in 198 Chinese cities, selling everything from Dell computers to Apple I-Pods. *Hurun Report* in 2008 listed Huang as the richest person in China, worth about $6.3 billion. In November 2008 Huang was detained by police for alleged security fraud on the Shanghai Stock Exchange.

A self-made businessman and China's "most wanted" fugitive, Lai Changxing (1958-) was the head of Yuanhua Group based in Xiamen, a coastal city located in Fujian Province. In the late 1990s Lai was indicted in the largest smuggling and corruption case in the history of the People's Republic of China. Beginning by trading imported goods in the 1980s, Lai later built a smuggling monopoly in Xiamen. In a four-year period from 1996 to 1999, Lai's company smuggled in an estimated 53 billion yuan (US$6.38 billion) worth of goods, resulting in the loss of an estimated 30 billion yuan (US$3.6 billion) in taxes, which amounted to about half of national revenues from tariffs in 1998. When the dust finally settled, more than 600 people were involved in the smuggling operation, of which more than half were put on trial by 2001. While Lai fled to Canada upon being tipped by corrupt officials, Yuanhua's case has led to death sentences for 18 people - seven of them have been executed and at least 12 individuals are currently serving life sentences.

Mou Qizhong (1941-), one of China's richest entrepreneurs in the 1990s, is the former president of Nande Economic Group based in Tianjin. Once hailed as China's reform hero, Mou started out with only 500 yuan, but like an alchemist he transformed that into millions. His magic was to profit from an economy that in those days had huge demand but little cash.

Mou was known for swapping 500 railway cars full of surplus Chinese goods for four Soviet-built aircrafts, which netted him tens of millions of dollars in 1992. A man of ambition and imagination, Mou was full of dreams. He intended to purchase a Russian aircraft carrier for the Chinese navy, and considered blowing an opening through the Himalayas so that moist air from the Indian Ocean could be diverted to the dry regions of northern China. He also wanted to become China's king of privatization, setting up overseas holding companies to acquire state-owned assets, taking advantage of tax concessions for foreigners (*Economist*, 2000). However in a few short years, because of those multiple undertakings, his company accumulated major debts and was unable to resume normal operations. In 1999 Mou was charged with defrauding banks of $75 million by using fraudulent letters of credit and sentenced to 18 years behind bars.

Once known as the "king of Chinese capital", Tang Wanxin (1964-) was the president of D'Long Strategic Investments. Founded in 1986, D'Long Group first branched out into entertainment, computers, tourism and agriculture. In the early 1990s Tang jumped into China's burgeoning stock market and quickly made tens of millions. Only a decade later D'Long grew to become the controlling partner of 200 firms worth billions of yuan listed on the Shanghai and Shenzhen Stock Exchanges. Tang had aggressively sought to acquire companies both in China and abroad, leveraging his buyouts with borrowed money that carried annual interest rates as high as 20 percent. Although initially impressive, D'Long became an unsustainable stock market bubble. In 2004 when the central government ordered tightening of lending to stave off a looming bad loan crisis in China's banking system, the value of D'Long collapsed, resulting in the loss of billions of yuan and an eight-year prison sentence for Tang.

Yang Bin (1963-) was once listed by *Forbes* as the second richest man in China, with an estimated $900 million in assets in 2001. Born in Nanjing, Yang was orphaned at age five, but later attended the Chinese Naval Academy and served as a PLA officer. With a scholarship he went to study in the Netherlands, where he made a fortune with a Dutch company. Upon returning he launched horticulture and real estate business in northeast China. His Euro-Asia Group was one of the first private Chinese enterprises to list shares on the Hong Kong Stock Exchange. During his brief business career Yang had developed a reputation for his keen ability to generate large investment capitals from various international banks. However his fortunes shifted after a corruption scandal in Shenyang toppled the mayor, who had supported him. Under pressure, Yang traveled to Pyongyang, donated millions of dollars and developed ties to North Korean leaders. However just days after being appointed by North Korean leader Kim Jon Il to be the head of a new special economic zone near the border with China, Yang was arrested in China for economic crimes and tax evasion. He was sentenced to 18 years for bribery, forgery, contract fraud and illegal use of agricultural land.

Yang Rong (1956-) has contributed both fame and infamy to the Chinese economic reform. From a humble background he achieved a milestone by leading a Chinese company to the first global stock listing. His reputation and ability for wheeling and dealing brought him both fortune and risks during his entrepreneurial career. Using his connections at the highest levels of the central bank, he helped Brilliance China Automotive to become the first Chinese company listed on the New York Stock Exchange in 1992, and by 2001 he was ranked number three of the richest Chinese by *Forbes*, with an estimated net worth of $840 million. However, his fame also brought unwanted attention to the supposedly state-owned company, and the provincial officials were further irritated when he incorporated his holding company in Bermuda, and attempted to relocate its operations out of Shenyang. As the government began to investigate the potentially illegal financial dealings he was alleged to have conducted with Brilliance stock, Yang left China and sought refuge in the United States, where he claimed he was wrongly prosecuted.

Famous peasant boss of Daqiu Village, Yu Zuomin (1930-1999) was one of the pioneering entrepreneurs in the rural economic reform. Realizing from early on that agriculture could not serve as the source of wealth, he began to build factories in the late 1970s, one of first villages to do so in China. Within a year, his small steel mill earned more money than the village profits combined over the past three decades. Thus more factories were established, and Yu incorporated them into a village holding company in which he served as the president of the new rural conglomerate. By 1992, Daqiu was noted as the richest village in China, and its steel output constituted three percent of national production. However, Yu's arrogance grew along with wealth and fame, as his behavior became increasingly dictatorial, with little tolerance for different opinions or criticisms. In 1993 Yu was arrested and found guilty of harboring criminals, obstructing justice, bribery, unlawful detention and unlawful control of people. After being sentenced to twenty years in prison, he died of a heart attack while on parole a few years later.

A pharmacist and former PLA officer, Zhao Xinxian (1941-) was the chairman of Sanjiu Enterprise Group, a large state-owned enterprise based in Guangdong. After receiving his degree in pharmacology, Zhao went to work for a military hospital in Guangzhou. In 1985 he founded Nanfang Pharmaceutical with several colleagues, and two years later began to produce a traditional medicine for treating gastric disorders. It became an instant hit and the firm quickly grew to be the best-known and most profitable pharmaceutical company in Chinese medicine. Encouraged by this initial success, Zhao undertook a massive expansion drive in the mid-1990s, diversifying into eight lines of business including pharmaceutical and agricultural products, tourism and real estate development. During its peak the group controlled over 100 companies with combined assets of nearly 20 billion yuan. However due to unsustainable expansion strategies, the group collapsed a few years later and Zhao was arrested for alleged economic crimes.

Former head of Nongkai Development, Zhou Zhengyi (Chau Ching-ngai 1961-) was the self-proclaimed richest man in Shanghai. Although he did not complete high school, Zhou had a very quick mind and was a risk-taker. At age 17 he went to work cooking dumplings at a small restaurant and later sold clothes at a street stall. Taking advantage of China's shift to a market economy, he began trading in goods between provinces, and later playing the stock market by buying shares issued to employees of state firms at low prices before they were listed, allowing him to reap huge gains. By capitalizing on numerous ventures, he became a major investor of stock markets in both Hong Kong and Shanghai. Considered an eccentric, Zhou symbolized the term *Baofahu* -"explosively rich", which refers to China's unique breed of nouveau riche: uneducated but enormously wealthy and not afraid to flaunt it. In 2003 Zhou was accused of illegally purchasing bank loans and state land; shortly after serving a three-year sentence, Zhou was again accused of forgery of business documents that resulted in an illegal gain of millions of dollars. He was convicted of embezzlement, bribery and forgery in 2007, this time with a 16-year jail term.

It should be noted that not all failed Chinese entrepreneurs are involved with economic crimes. Some of their misfortunes are more associated with the underdeveloped systems instead of individual reasons, such as in the cases of Li Jingwei of Jianlibao Group and Pan Ning of Kelon Holdings. The underlying truth is that there is always a human face behind every successful or devastating story of the Chinese economic reform, such as Shi Yuzhu of Giant Group who experienced both triumph and collapse and then came back reinventing himself, or Sun Hongbin who fell first at Lenovo and tried and crashed again with his real estate firm Sunco. There are just too many tales to tell them all here. In any event, in order to have a more comprehensive understanding of Chinese entrepreneurial development, the following sections of this study will attempt to address various factors that might contribute to those high-profile failures mentioned above.

UNIQUE POLITICAL AND BUSINESS ENVIRONMENT

Most people agree that over the past thirty years China has been experiencing one of the most turbulent transformational periods in its long economic history. Under the so-called socialist market economy, the country has had a unique business environment with Chinese characteristics. After changing gear from planned to market economy, while the rules and regulations were being gradually established and continually improved, they generally lagged behind the reality of business practices. Enterprises and entrepreneurs have been facing enormous challenges both in and outside the business environment. On many occasions they have to go through grey areas, and break some legal boundaries in order to move forward. Notable among all risks faced by Chinese entrepreneurs are swift changes in political policies, because of their substantial impact on business operations. As numerous examples have illustrated, a simple miscalculation could spell doom for the businesses that entrepreneurs have built up over years. When confronting government authorities, private entrepreneurs generally lose, as with Li Jingwei of Jianlibao Group and Pan Ning of Kelon Holdings in their respective struggles over company ownership reforms.

Unlike the more developed Western economies, in the transition period of China the government still controls many scarce resources such as access to capital, the authority to examine and approve projects, government purchasing, the authority to examine and to approve firms listing on the stock market, the authority to use land, etc. Private entrepreneurs must gain the government's support in order to get those resources. According to Tian (2007), there are around 2000 authorities to examine and approve economic activities just at the central government level. As noted by Dalglish (1993), China has a history of allowing officials to profit from their positions of authority; the mandarins of the dynasties expected to be paid for services rendered. More recently, during the chaos of the Cultural Revolution when there were chronic shortages of many goods, the Chinese became accustomed to using the so-called "back door" to get things done. Clearly an inefficient bureaucracy is one of the key factors that supports corruption, which was one of the main objections voiced by the student protests in Tiananmen Square in 1989. It is precisely the difficulty of getting bank loans that fosters a gambling instinct and creative approach to the law among ambitious Chinese entrepreneurs.

As Savadove (2007) pointed out, the rise of street-smart entrepreneurs like Lai Changxing and Zhou Zhengyi in many ways embodies the growth of private companies in China and illustrates how political connections can bring success in the country's freewheeling business environment. Politics, as well as crime, are the real story behind virtually every high-profile case. Business people, for their part, pay bribes to buy political protection for misdeeds, such as tax evasion or misappropriation of public assets. Bribes secure lucrative land deals, government contracts, and rights to buy state enterprises at cut-rate prices. For businessmen, an official on the take is what Chinese call "a mountain to lean against." The overlap between business and party in an authoritarian system makes a "red-collar crime" (Lague and Lawrence, 2002). Among all the high-profile entrepreneurs mentioned above, Yang Bin's case stands out. Allegedly Yang was close to Vice Premier Li Lanqing, as well as to Liaoning Governor Bo Xilai, one of the stars of the so-called Fifth Generation of Chinese leaders. This would certainly explain his initial phenomenal success. However Yang made one fatal mistake when he failed to keep the Chinese government properly informed of his proposed plan for a special economic zone with North Korea. Yang was seen as a victim of the complex relationship between China and North Korea, of his own political naivety, and of a management style that ran his company as family business.

Within the enterprises discussed above, the issue of corporate structure and governance may be one important factor that contributed to their eventual downfall. As in Chinese society, patriarchy prevails in the business world, especially in private enterprises. For example, Yu Zuomin ran his Daqiu conglomerate like a feudal dictatorship, and Yuanhua's board consisted mainly of Lai's close family members, including his wife, three brothers and brother-in-law, with Lai serving as chairman. The Tendency toward having a "weak board and strong chairman" is common in China, and boards tend to be tight-knit groups built on business or personal networks (*PR Newswire*, 2007). Independent directors are mostly brought in to fulfill legal requirements and are limited to advisory roles. Personal networks and connections are largely what bind those boards together. Although this is very much in line with the Chinese cultural tradition of *guanxi*, it also opens the door for cozy relationships that can breed corporate corruption. As noted by Sun and Zhang (2006), the corporate governance restructuring of China's publicly listed companies has been opaque with one-sided outcomes in favor of mangers and local officials. To be a fully-fledged member and effectively compete in the global business environment, this will be one of the major challenges for Chinese entrepreneurs, companies and regulators in the near future. Looking forward, China will have to improve its legal and social systems in order to reduce further turmoil and avoid a fatal collapse of its remarkable economic transformation.

Fragile Financial System

Closely associated with the nation's political environment, the financial system that supports China's economic growth is very fragile. The country may have one of the fastest-growing economies in the world, but the financial infrastructures that support new businesses are rudimentary at best. Since bank loans tend to go to state-owned firms, private enterprises are at a particular disadvantage when it comes to financial growth. They are also in a weak position when competing with large international firms in terms of finance and taxation. As one expert summarized, if the private sector is China's brightest hope, the financial system is its weakest link (James, 2005). In recent years David Barboza of *New York Times* has written several reports on business scandals and corruption in China. According to Barboza (2005), in a country awash in speculative money intended to fuel its economic boom, many executives have turned greedy, and even low-level employees are engaging in self-serving transactions by funneling millions of dollars into offshore accounts. Weak regulation and oversight, deep-seated government corruption and poor risk-management practices are to blame for allowing fraud artists and looters to run off long before investigators discover that anything is missing.

This view is generally shared by other observers. As Lague and Lawrence (2002) point out, China's economic boom created almost ideal conditions for an explosion of financial crime, where loosely controlled privatization, poorly regulated equity markets, burgeoning foreign trade and huge flows of investment nourish rampant graft. In the absence of independent courts, effective investigating authorities and a free media, it is much easier to escape detection and punishment inside or outside the government and the ruling party. Looking at the high-profile cases mentioned above, financial fraud and embezzlement seem to be the main reasons for the downfall of the majority of those entrepreneurs including Tang Wanxin, Gu Chujun, Mou Qizhong, Yang Rong, Zhou Zhengyi and Huang Guangyu. Although China only has a brief history in stock market development, the recent rise of security fraud has been particularly alarming.

Unsurprisingly, China's large state-owned banks have been plagued by scandals over recent years. Consequently, thousands of people had been punished for misappropriating money or making unauthorized loans, and billions of dollars of bad debt had to be handled by the government by using its huge foreign currency reserves. Although various corruption cases are yet to slow down China's impressive economic growth, the country's banking and financial systems have to be modernized for China to be a truly economic superpower in the twenty-first century.

PERSONAL CHARACTERISTICS

Over the course of Chinese business reform, more than 10 million enterprises have been established; most of them are privately run. While a great majority of those enterprises were developed legally, some became wealthy by taking advantage of corrupt officials' greed, while others got rich by grasping market opportunities. Luck often goes with capability, as noted by Wang (2003); only those who are capable of grasping those opportunities can assert that they are lucky. While reviewing the individual backgrounds of the failed entrepreneurs listed above, certain personal characteristics are observed. Many of them had very humble beginnings, born in the countryside and growing up in dire poverty, which likely motivated them to seek a change of fate and move ahead at any cost. Whilst some graduated from elite universities in China, others did not even complete primary school. Regardless of their different educations, they all seem to be strong-minded and hard working individuals, who were street smart and willing to gamble and take risks, and have demonstrated high levels of social intelligence amongst the people around them.

However, in a number of instances, it is this personal greed and gambling mentality that led to their initial success and eventual downfall. With specific regard to Tang Wanxin, Sun Hongbin and Zhao Xinxian, it seems that their inflated egos prevented them from having a clear vision of the risks and benefits associated with their aggressive business expansion strategies. A strong determination is certainly a virtue in a competitive business environment.

Nevertheless, when a person cannot listen to different opinions or tolerate others' criticisms, it becomes pure madness. As the stories of Mou Qizhong, Yang Bin and Yu Zuomin confirmed, they gambled and lost dreadfully, along with their multi-million dollar businesses as sacrifices.

Perhaps the case of Lai Changxing is the best example to illustrate the impact of personal characteristics on business operations. Born in 1958 into a peasant family of eight in a village near the port city of Quanzhou, Lai was flamboyant and elusive, known for his generosity and thoughtfulness. With a magic charisma, he was respectful and gregarious. Lai was especially adept at identifying people's weaknesses, whether they be money, art or women, and exploiting them in a way that established a personal connection. He was a natural at setting up businesses, at engaging people, drawing them to his cause, charming and bribing them. Despite being an elementary school dropout, Lai enjoyed a growing reputation and status as a successful businessman and community leader. He was well known for his many charitable activities in the late 1990s. He was an honorary citizen of Xiamen, a member of the Fujian Political Consultative Committee, and received an award as a 'Famous National Private Entrepreneur' from the National Industrial and Commercial Association for his flood relief efforts. The fact that he managed to achieve all this, while still maintaining a near monopoly on smuggling operations in Xiamen, demonstrated his high social intelligence and criminal mastermind.

INFLUENCES OF CHINESE CULTURE

Beneath the role of strong personal characteristics lies a cultural tradition of thousands of years, which has a much deeper impact on how Chinese entrepreneurs behave and function in the business world. Despite its speed and volume of growth, the Chinese economy, and behind it Chinese culture, is still a fairly new player on the global stage; therefore its significance may not be as obvious to some outside observers. In reviewing the legacy of Chinese culture on its entrepreneurial development, it is clear that the concept of *guanxi* (关系) has a very profound influence on the establishment of personal relationships and business transactions. *Guanxi* has played a vital role in the evolution of Chinese society. The cultural emphasis on personal relationships means that Chinese business connections and deals are built on *guanxi* ties. Strongly influenced by Confucian teachings, Chinese view other individuals in terms of particular relationships. *Guanxi* is "an informal, unofficial relationship utilized to get things done, from simple tasks to major life choices" (Ruan, 1993). Simply put, *guanxi* is an interpersonal network that Chinese use as a crucial social resource to pursue their personal interests (Brown, 2002). *Guanxi* is not just something mechanical, or simply a Western version of networking. It is about "affectual relations" among people. *Guanxi* is an emotional bond, and requires cultivation over time (Gold, 2001). In the business world, *guanxi* practice has evolved into a powerful and flexible tool that allows people to create trustworthy, expansive business networks in the absence of adequate legal guarantees – a type of capitalism without contracts (Hsu, 2005). However *guanxi* is also a double-edged sword. If the social relationship is being developed without any boundaries; it may eventually jeopardize businesses and doom entrepreneurs. As the cases with Yang Bin and Lai

Changxing clearly illustrated, when the bottom line was crossed, and serious crime committed, even the so-called "mountain to lean on" would not be able to protect them.

In Chinese traditional ethics, according to Lu (1997), the relationship between *Yi* (义) and *Li* (利) is a very old and recurrent topic. *Li* means benefits and *Yi* refers to the principle of norms for obtaining and distributing benefits or profits. *Yi* as the core notion in Chinese traditional ethics has an indissoluble bond to *Li*. The connection between them is expressed by the deep-rooted Confucian view: "A person of noble character can understand *Yi*, but a low person only knows *Li*" (Lu, 1997). An individual who puts *Li* ahead of *Yi* (见利忘义) is not a true gentleman. As early as twenty-five hundred years ago Confucius had stated his personal belief that there was a *Tao* or right way of seeking wealth. According to him: man of noble character is keen on wealth and takes no money but in a moral way (君子爱财，取之有道). However, throughout the brief history of Chinese economic reform there are numerous cases of personal greed and total disregard for moral principles, as a number of entrepreneurs have demonstrated their lack of basic respect for the notion of fair play and an ethical bottom line. Focusing on a single goal of relentless pursuit of personal wealth, to them there is no right or wrong in business competition, only continual growth and eventual success. Although some of the entrepreneurs were well educated, their ego, greed and gambling instinct made them ignore the basic rules of business operation, thus leading their businesses on a dangerous path of self-destruction.

Faced with mounting pressure from the public to address this increasingly serious issue, China's ruling Communist Party has launched frequent crackdowns on government corruption and business fraud during the past thirty years, resulting in the exposure of numerous scandals involving high-ranked officials and the downfall of well-known entrepreneurs. While some have argued (Shieh, 2005) that without addressing the root causes of the problem, the Chinese government's approach was only a short-term solution, the simple truth is that over a history of thousands of years, China's legal culture has thrived on the principle of "killing the chicken to scare the monkeys." For many, high-profile businessmen like Zhou Zhengyi, Yang Bin and Yu Zuomin were conveniently those conspicuous "chickens" during show-time.

Burden of "Original Sins"

At the onset of the economic reform, many of the first entrepreneurs in the early 1980s had low social status because they lived on the margins of society. They were often ex-convicts who had no official connections and could not get respectable jobs in state-owned enterprises (Garnaut, 2008). After Deng Xiaoping made his audacious call for people to get rich ahead of others, common views toward wealth and business began to change. Entrepreneurs were hailed as reform heroes, who were brave enough to abandon the old system and chart their own destinies, and who would lead society out of poverty.

However, when a country is increasingly commercialized and income gaps drastically widened, people begin to question the legitimacy of large amounts of wealth accumulated by a few individuals over such a short period of time. The public generally believe that many of those private fortunes built through a process of primitive capital accumulation during the 1980s and 1990s were based largely on illegal means. "Original sin" refers to the way entrepreneurs flouted convention and laws to make the first "pot of gold" to fund their start-ups (Cai, 2007). As noted before, misconduct ranged from smuggling, bribery, speculation and theft to tax evasion, loan fraud, organized crime and subjecting workers to badly paid jobs in "sweat shops". Reviewing the brief history of the Chinese economic reform, one can observe at least three rounds of new wealth generation or private redistribution where the "original sins" were committed. According to Zang Xiaowei (2008), the first real wave of the well-connected new breed arrived with the government's dual-track pricing system in the mid-1980s. Referred to as official racketeering - the unscrupulous combination of speculation and political power - managers of state-owned enterprises pocketed government subsidies and sold surplus production on the private market at inflated prices. From the late 1980s, private real estate became the next and much greater source of wealth, as developers only had two main requirements: land and bank loans, both of which were allocated by officials. In Shanghai, well connected "princelings" control nine of the top ten real-estate development companies and 13 of the 15 largest building companies (Garnaut, 2008). A third source of private wealth was management buy-outs of state-owned companies in the late 1990s. Managers bought the companies at discount prices, fired excess workers and quickly made huge profits. Two glitzy examples were Gu Chujun's acquisition of Guangdong Kelon Electrical Holdings in 2001-02 and Yang Rong's play with Brilliance China Auto.

Today, wealthy Chinese are reviled as much as they are envied. Many Chinese see wealth as simply the newest manifestation of political power: a currency that is bought, stolen or inherited through *guanxi* connections with the government elite (Garnaut, 2008). As the widening income gap has sparked increased resentment toward rich people in China, even the government's official English paper *China Daily* (2007) has publicly acknowledged that it has been an open secret that many of today's successful entrepreneurs accumulated their wealth by smuggling, evading taxes, polluting the environment and bribing officials to land lucrative business deals. The issue of "original sin" has been hotly debated, not only by ordinary citizens but also among Chinese economists. A number of them believe that because many entrepreneurs initially built their wealth through illegal means, their honesty and credibility would always be in question; others believe that society should not place the full blame on those millionaires. Since China's current regulations have problems of their own, tightening supervision and changing regulations are the only solutions (Zou, 2003). If some "sins" were committed, they probably would be more appropriately categorized as a misdeed of the era or a broken system, instead of blaming certain individuals.

Notwithstanding the debate on the burden of "original sins", the fact of the matter is that successful entrepreneurs often come under much closer public and government scrutiny after they reach the pinnacle of wealth. This may be an important contributing factor in explaining the eventual downfall of those well-known entrepreneurs mentioned above. Some of the billionaires and millionaires got into trouble because of problems in capital flow caused by unlimited financial expansion and abuse. They bribed bank officials and conducted financial fraud when they could not get loans through normal procedures. While the government and the public usually pay scant attention to the tricks of small enterprises, as those enterprises develop more and more people will examine and scrutinize their operations, and any major mistake would be found out. In an efficient economy, an enterprise can never be successfully developed through crooked means over an extended period of time (Zou, 2003). Therefore, under the increasingly developed market-oriented economy it is not only possible, but necessary to run an enterprise through normal and standardized ways; and it is the moral responsibility for today's entrepreneurs to operate their businesses in a socially accepted manner. The upcoming challenge for China is to ensure that various measures are taken to rectify market order and strengthen laws and regulations so that a sound and efficient market economy can be established in the near future.

CONCLUSION

This is China's Gilded Age, a period of rising wealth and industrialization, and a time of great ups and downs. As Brown (2002) rightly points out, China is an extremely complex society due to its deep cultural heritage and its rapid transformation from an agrarian, plan-based economy to what the political leadership has called a "socialist market economy with Chinese characteristics." Along the turbulent course of economic reform since 1978, some brave entrepreneurs seized opportunities and succeeded, while many others tried and failed miserably. Regardless of their amazing triumphs or heartbreaking failures, their stories already touched the lives of hundreds of millions and they have inadvertently contributed to the swift development of Chinese entrepreneurship over the last three decades.

Many factors could contribute to the downfall of Chinese entrepreneurs. During the chaotic process of economic transformation, entrepreneurs have to face various challenges both in and outside the business environment. Notable among the risks are abrupt changes of political policies, owing to their significant impact on business operations. In the area of financing, private entrepreneurs are at a particular disadvantage. As *Economist* (2003) pointed out, it is precisely the difficulty of getting bank loans and listings that fosters a creative approach to the law among ambitious Chinese entrepreneurs. In terms of corporate structure and governance, patriarchy still prevailed in the business world, especially in private enterprises, which may be another important factor that contributed to their ultimate demise. With a history over thousands of years, the behavior of entrepreneurs has been deeply influenced by the Chinese cultural tradition. In addition, under the burden of "original sin" and with a changing attitude toward private wealth, Chinese entrepreneurs have been facing mounting scrutiny from the public and the government. Entrepreneurs themselves will certainly have to bear some personal responsibility. The strong individual determination, sheer greed and gambling mentality that contributed to their initial success could also lead to their eventual downfall. Due to all those compelling reasons, their corporate failures seem to be inevitable. If it were not them, somebody else would very likely play exactly the same, or very similar, roles. In a nutshell, high-profile entrepreneurs like Huang, Lai and Yang are oblivious but essential actors on the grand stage of China's economic transformation of the last thirty years.

From a historical standpoint, it is necessary to reflect on China's entrepreneurial growth from the global economic perspective. Over recent years it seems that public media have been filled with all kinds of negative views about Chinese business operations - from loan fraud, bribery, speculation, theft and tax evasion to smuggling and sacrificing safety in pursuit of profit. However, according to Mihm (2007), to see China today is to glimpse, in a distant mirror, the 19th-century American economy in all its corner-cutting, fraudulent glory. In many ways China is a younger version of the United States or early industrial Britain; its fast and loose brand of commerce is not an expression of national character, but a phase in the country's development. As Mihm suitably labeled it, China's "adolescent capitalism" is just like a typical teenager, bursting with energy, exuberant and dynamic, while reckless, irresponsible, and dangerous. Only with this understanding can the rest of world begin to work effectively with China on the best ways to deal with its growing pains.

Out of the chaos and failures, a new Chinese entrepreneurship is currently being developed. Among the lessons learned from those high-profile downfalls, aspiring Chinese entrepreneurs should always remember there is a *Tao* or right approach to seeking personal wealth. As Confucius noted over twenty-five hundred years ago, man of noble character is keen on wealth and takes no money but in a moral way. To succeed in the twenty-first century, entrepreneurs will have to work hard to gain the trust of both the Chinese and international communities. And on a broad scope, China in the coming years will have to improve its legal, financial and social systems to establish the institutions that will both support business development and clearly define corporate and personal ethics.

REFERENCES

[1] Barboza, D. (2005). Wave of corruption tarnishes China's extraordinary growth. *New York Times, 22* March, C1.

[2] Barboza, D. (2007). Scandal and suicide in China: A dark side of toys. *New York Times, 23* August, C1.

[3] Brown, B. (2002). Entrepreneurship and ethics in the Chinese context. *Ruffin Series in Business Ethics*, 219.

[4] Cai, J. (2007). Dangerous days for free market's 'original sinners'. *South China Morning Post*, 17 February, 5.

[5] *China Daily* (2007). 'Original Sin' debate rages on, 22 March.

[6] Cody, E. (2006). China's crackdown on corruption still largely secret. *Washington Post*, 31 December, A19.

[7] Dalglish, B. (1993). The cost of business. *Maclean's, 106* (19), 10 March, 29.

[8] *Economist* (1995). Business ethics: Hard graft in Asia. 27 May, 61.

[9] *Economist* (2000). Asia: An alchemist's downfall. 3 June, 42.

[10] *Economist* (2003). Scandal in Shanghai. 16 August, 58.

[11] Falconer, M. (2007). China's most wanted. *South China Morning Post*, 16 September, 5.

[12] Garnaut, J. (2008). Connections the currency for new rich. *The Age*, 31 March, 3 (Business).

[13] Gold, T. (2001). In China – bonding gone bad? *Christian Science Monitor*, 10 January, 6.

[14] Hsu, C. (2005). Capitalism without contract versus capitalists without capitalism: Comparing the influence of Chinese *guanxi* and Russian blat on marketization. *Communist and Post-Communist Studies, 38* (3), 309.

[15] James, G. (2005). Tao of innovation. *Electronic Business, 31* (8), 54.

[16] Lague, D., & Lawrence, S. (2002). Rank corruption. *Far Eastern Economic Review, 165* (43), 31 Oct., 32.
[17] Lu, X. (1997). Business ethics in China. *Journal of Business Ethics, 16* (4), 1509.
[18] Mihm, S. (2007). A nation of outlaws – A century ago, that wasn't China – it was us. *Boston Globe*, 26 August, 1 (Ideas).
[19] *PR Newswire* (2007). Heidrick & Struggles and Fudan University study calls for more independent board of directors in China, 7 February.
[20] Ruan, D. (1993). *Social Networks in Urban China* [dissertation]. New York: Columbia University, 19.
[21] Savadove, B. (2007). From cook, to tycoon to jailbird, again. *South China Morning Post*, 1 December, 5.
[22] Shieh, S. (2005). The rise of collective corruption in China: The Xiamen smuggling case. *Journal of Contemporary China, 14* (42), 67-91.
[23] Sun, P., & Zhang, Y. (2006). Is there penalty for crime? Corporate scandal and management turnover in China. *EFA 2006 Zurich Meetings Paper* [eLibrary]. http://ssrn.com/abstract=891096.
[24] Tian, Z., Gao, H. and Cone, M. (20007). A study of the ethical issues of private entrepreneurs participating in politics in China. *Journal of Business Ethics, 80*, 627-642.
[25] Toy, M. (2007). Wealth of suspicion; fairytale. *The Age*, 17 February, 6.
[26] Wang, S. (2003). Pointless debate. *Beijing Review, 46* (37), 11 September.
[27] Zang, X. (2008). Market transition, wealth and status claims. In D.S. Goodman (Ed.), *The New Rich in China: Future Rulers, Present Lives* (pp. 53-70). Abingdon, Oxon and New York: Routledge.
[28] Zou, L. and others (2003). Private entrepreneurs: Bad by nature? *Beijing Review, 46* (37), 11 September, 46.

In: Thirty Years of China's Economic Reform
Editors: Yue Wang and Prem Ramburuth

ISBN: 978-1-60876-908-7
© 2010 Nova Science Publishers, Inc.

Chapter 2

THE EMERGENCE OF THE INSTITUTION OF MINGONGZHI AND ITS IMPLICATIONS FOR A UNIFIED LABOUR MARKET IN CHINA

***Cherrie Jiuhua Zhu*[*,1], *Mingqiong Zhang*[+,1], *S. Bruce Thomson*[§,1], *Chris Nyland*[¥] and *Yue Guo*[2]**

[1]Department of Management, Monash University, Melbourne, Australia
[2]Institute of Labour & Social Security,
Chinese Academy of Social Sciences, Beijing, China

ABSTRACT

There have been significant changes in the available workforce in Chinese cities due to the influx of millions of migrant workers as the consequence of economic reforms. Drawing on institutional theory, this chapter discusses the emergence of the *'institution of mingongzhi'* (*mingong* means farmer-turned workers and *zhi* means system in Chinese) and provides a justification for applying the label of institution. *Mingongzhi* refers to a social-economic system under which certain people or social groups, known as *mingong* here, are socially excluded in urban areas of contemporary China. Based on the empirical evidence from the case studies and surveys conducted in Changsha and Haerbin, we found the existence of the institution of *mingongzhi* even after many of the barriers for rural migrants were removed by the central government. We argue that *mingongzhi* needs to be deinstitutionalized if China is to establish a unified labour market as advocated by the International Labour Organization and the World Trade Organization.

Keywords: China, institutionalism, labour market, rural migrant workers, the institution of *mingongzhi*

---

* Email: cherrie.zhu@buseco.monash.edu.au.
\+ Email: mingqiong.zhang@buseco.monash.edu.au.
§ Email: bruce.thomson@buseco.monash.edu.au.
¥ Email: chris.nyland@buseco.monash.edu.au.

Introduction

In the 1950s, in order to manage the movement of labour, the government of the People's Republic of China initiated a household registration system, *hukou*, which divided labour into two categories – urban workers (*gongren*) and rural farmers (*nongmin*). The system created a divided labour market, which considered rural farmers to be substandard and second-class citizens (Chan & Buckingham, 2008). The economic reforms of the last three decades have created labour shortages in many large urban areas which have been the primary recipients of economic growth. To fill the labour demand rural farmers streamed into the urban areas, creating one of the largest rural/urban migrations in history (Liang, 2001). These rural or farmer-turned–workers (*mingong*) have suffered from discrimination and unethical and unjust treatment by employers and government officials (Chan & Buckingham, 2008; Solinger, 1999 a and b).

In recognition of the plight of *mingong,* the central government has taken steps to ratify the system in order to create a unified labour market. Chan and Buckingham (2008) argue that while these steps may have achieved improvements in some areas, they have not been effective in creating a unified labour market. In fact, they contend the *hukou* system is so entrenched it is nothing less than an "institution". This paper endorses the arguments of Chan and Buckingham (2008) and argues that the *hukuo* system has indeed spawned another institution, which we have termed *mingongzhi.* This institution refers to the systematic social exclusion of *mingong* in urban areas based solely on their *hukuo* status.

As a unique institution in contemporary China, the institution of *mingongzhi* has influenced almost all aspects of Chinese society, including industrial relations. In the formation of Chinese industrial relations, the *mingongzhi* has weakened the standard of labour protection and hence created an unbalanced industrial relations (IR) system characterised by low levels of labour protection for employees and seemingly unchecked managerial power. In the evolution of the Chinese labour market, the *mingongzhi* has created a classic dual labour market as defined by Doeringer and Piore (1971). Rural migrants have mainly been confined to the bottom of a loosely structured secondary labour market which is characterized by low pay, long working hours, low labour protection, three-D jobs (dirty, dangerous and deeming), and high job uncertainty. It is also difficult for rural workers to move to the highly structured primary market which is characterised by high pay, high labour protection, high social status jobs, and high job certainty. As a result, the primary market is dominated by urban residents while rural migrants are over-represented in the secondary labour market.

The chapter has several aims. First, it examines the emergence of the institution of *mingongzhi*. Second, the chapter will provide a justification for labelling *mingongzhi* an institution. To achieve these goals we will examine the regulations, customs and norms related to *mingong* from an institutional perspective. Also, this chapter will provide empirical evidence to validate Chan and Buckingham's (2008) claim that the institution created by the *hukou* system still exists and is largely the result of the unwillingness of provincial and municipal governments to act. Another aim of the chapter is to explain why *mingongzhi* needs to be deinstitutionalized if China is to accelerate the establishment of a unified labour market as desired by the national government and advocated by global institutions such as the International Labour Organization (ILO) and the World Trade Organization (WTO).

To achieve these objectives, we initially review the changes in the urban workforce that are a consequence of economic reforms, focusing on the push and pull factors in rural and urban areas, as well as changes to government household registration (*hukou*) and migration policy. Next, we discuss the emergence of the institution of *mingongzhi* and explain why this should be deemed an unethical institution. The research methodology section outlines the data collection methods and the justification for the sample population. The empirical evidence is then presented and discussed utilising Scott's (2001) institutional model as a framework. A discussion of policy implications concludes the results and discussion section, and is followed by the Conclusion in which we present some final thoughts regarding the implications of our findings.

CHANGES IN URBAN WORKFORCE WITH THE INFLUX OF *MINGONG*

Since the early 1980s, millions of farmers have flooded into urban areas for work (Liang, 2001; Roberts, 2002; Solinger, 1999a). It is estimated that the number of *mingong* reached 62 million in 1989 and 134 million in 2006 (Hu & Zhang, 2007). This phenomenon is a consequence of 'push and pull' factors in rural and urban areas respectively. On the push side, the introduction of the household responsibility system in the late 1970s increased agricultural productivity and created a huge pool of excess agricultural workers. On the pull side, open-door policies, an influx of foreign direct investment (FDI), and the mushrooming of the private sector initially created job opportunities for migrants in the booming coastal cities and then in other parts of the country. Meanwhile, relaxed government controls on rural-urban migration (e.g. reforms in the *hukou* system and relevant policies) and the increased social status and lifestyle enjoyed by urbanites encouraged farmers to work in urban areas.

There has been extensive research conducted on the Chinese *hukou* system (e.g., CECOC, 2005; Chan & Buckingham, 2008; Chan & Zhang, 1999, Cheng & Selden, 1994, Wang 2005). Introduced in 1951 in cities and extended to rural areas in 1955, *hukou* has governed the movement of the Chinese population. The reforms to the system adopted by the Chinese government in the late 1990s and early 2000s have included relaxing limitations on migration to small towns and cities, streamlining *hukou* registration in some provinces and large cities, by granting *mingong* local *hukou* based on certain criteria such as a "stable place of residence" and a "stable source of income", and instituting many individual reforms that address the discrimination of *mingong* such as the limit of urban employment opportunities and differing reward practices (CECOC, 2005:4).

The *hukou* reforms have been accompanied by a set of policies that deal with surplus rural labour. For instance, in 1991 the State Council issued 'provisions on the recruitment of contract migrant workers by wholly state-owned enterprises' (COD, 2005: 1-9), which allows state-owned (also called entirely/wholly people-owned) enterprises to recruit *mingong,* albeit under many restrictions such as the state labour quota control and approval by local government. Some policies introduced by the central government between 2001 and early 2005 are selected in the following to indicate the central government's determination to facilitate rural-urban migration using the step-by-step or 'crossing river by feeling the stone' approach (see Table 1). The reason for selecting policies from this time period is mainly because China ratified the International Covenant on Economic, Social and Cultural Rights (ICESCR) in early 2001 and terminated all previous requirements that were imposed on *mingong* wishing to work in urban areas. The ratification in 2001 indicates the Chinese government's determination to undertake actions with 'a view to achieving progressively the full realization of the rights recognized in the Covenant by all appropriate means, including particularly the adoption of legislative measures' (ILO, 2000:29). These measures require China to respect and to provide for the social and economic rights of all its citizens regardless of their hukou status.

Table 1. Policies on improving employment environment for *mingong* (2001-5)

Item	Issued Date (dd/mm/yy) No. of Doc.	Issurer	Document
1	30/10/2001 No.2220	Ministry of Finance, State Planning Committee.	Notification on sorting out and rectifying charges over migrant workers by State Planning Committee and Ministry of Finance (国家计委，财政部关于全面清理整顿外出或外来务工人员收费的通知).
2	05/01/2003 No.1	General Office of State Council	Circular on the administration of and services for rural migrant workers in urban areas (国务院办公厅关于做好农民进城务工就业管理和服务工作的通知).
3	17/09/2003 No.78	General Office of State Council	State Council notice on approving the Ministry of Education and other Ministries' opinions on further implementing compulsory education for children of rural-migrant workers (国务院办公厅转发教育部等部门关于进一步做好进城务工就业农民子女义务教育工作的意见)
4	22/03/2004 No.4	Ministry of Agriculture, Ministry of Labour and Social Security, Ministry of Finance, Ministry of Science and Technology, Ministry of Education, and Ministry of Construction	Circular concerning the sunshine project on organizing and implementing the rural labour migration and training and the project management details (关于组织实施农村劳动力转移培训阳光工程的通知及附件)
5	18/09/2003 No.79	General Office of State Council	State Council notice on approving the 2003-2010 national training program for migrant workers prepared by Ministry of Agriculture and other departments (国务院办公厅转发农业部等部门2003-2010年全国农民工培训规划的通知)
6	25/12/2003 No.561	Ministry of Finance, Ministry of Labour and Social Security, Ministry of Public Security, Ministry of Education, State Population Planning Committee	Circular on including the administration and management expenses of rural migrant workers to the fiscal budget and Estimated expenditure. (关于将农民工管理等有关经费纳入财政预算支出范围有关问题的通知).
7	20/01/2004 No.21	Ministry of Labour and Social Security	Provisions on the minimum standard of wages (最低工资规定)

Table 1. Continued

Item	Issued Date (dd/mm/yy) No. of Doc.	Issurer	Document
8	28/05/2004 No.5	General Office of Ministry of Labour and Social Security	Opinions on facilitating and implementing medical insurance coverage for employees of all enterprises with mixed ownership types and economic organizations with non-public ownership (关于推进混合所有制企业和非公有制经济组织从业人员参加医疗保险的意见)
9	01/06/2004 No.18	Ministry of Labour and Social Security	Notice on the coverage of industrial injury insurance for rural migrant workers (关于农民工参加工伤保险有关问题的通知).
10	16/07/2004 No.1405	State Development and Reform Committee, Ministry of Finance, Ministry of Public Security, Ministry of Labour and Social Security, Ministry of Agriculture, Ministry of Public Health, Ministry of Education, General Office of State Council, State Population and Birth Control Committee.	Circular on further sorting out and abolishing discrimination against rural migrant workers and unreasonable charges across districts and industries (关于进一步清理和取消针对农民跨地区就业和进城务工歧视性规定和不合理收费的通知).
11	16/12/2004 No.280	Ministry of Labour and Social Security	Circular concerning the launch of spring campaign to further improve employment services for rural migrant workers (关于开展春风行动完善农民工就业服务的通知)
12	01/11/2004 No.368	General Offices of Ministry of Labour and Social Security, Ministry of Construction and ACFTU	Circular concerning the inspection of the wage payment for rural migrant workers (关于开展农民工工资支付情况专项检查活动的通知)
13	27/12/2004 No.92	General Office of State Council	Circular on further improving the employment environment for rural migrant workers in urban areas (国务院办公厅关于进一步做好改善农民进城就业环境工作的通知).

Table 1. Continued

Item	Issued Date (dd/mm/yy) No. of Doc.	Issurer	Document
14	07/02/2005 No.18	Ministry of Labour and Social Security	Circular concerning the abolishment of interim regulations on the administration of rural labour cross-province employment and related documents (关于废止"农村劳动力跨省流动就业管理暂行规定"及有关配套文件的通知).
15	03/2005	Ministry of Labour and Social Security, Ministry of Construction and ACFTU	Circular on strengthening labour contract management for rural migrant workers in the construction and other industries (关于加强建设等行业农民工劳动合同管理的通知)

Source: COD-Compilations of documents on improving urban employment environment for migrant workers (*guanyu kaishan nongmin jinchen jiuye huanjing wenjian huibian* 关于改善农民进城就业环境文件汇编), Ministry of Labour and Social Security, April 2005.

Documents in Table 1 show a series of changes in the central government's approach to *mingong* from 2001 to early 2005. These relate to various charges and levies, discriminatory employment policies, poor working environment, wage arrears, lack of social insurance coverage, lack of training and the education for *mingong's* children. For instance, the first document (Item 1 in Table 1) aimed to abolish many levies imposed upon *mingong,* such as fees relating to temporary residence, floating population administration, family-planning administration, infrastructure development, labour regulation, non-local employee administration and non-local construction firms' administration fees.

In the second document issued in 2003 (Item 2), the State Council recognized the necessity for workers to migrate to urban areas and consequently sought to abolish various licences or certificates. This document also offered guidelines to address a series of issues around *mingong* which included removing various unreasonable or excessive charges (Item 10); offering 9-year compulsory education to *mingong* children by local government where migrants and their children stay (Item 3); solving the problem of late or arrear payment by using labour contracts and establishing inspection mechanisms (Items 7 and 12); facilitating migration of rural labourers to work in urban areas by offering training (Items 4 and 5); extending social insurance coverage to migrants (Items 8 and 9); and strengthening the administration and management of work for migrants and their families (Items 11 and 13). The last two documents in Table 1 were released in 2005. One aimed to abolish the use of the *mingong* employment registration card required by the Ministry of Labour and the other to establish the labour contract system for *mingong* and to specify the details to be included in the contract. All these documents indicate significant changes in the central government's attitudes towards rural migrants.

According to China's fifth census conducted in 2000, *mingong* made up 52.6% of the commercial and restaurant labour force, 68.2% in manufacturing, and 79.8% of the construction sectors (Fan, 2006). *Mingong* have grown to be a major part of the urban workforce (Survey Team of Ministry of Labour and Social Security, 2006), and have been supporting vital sectors of the economy and keeping the cities functioning. However, few migrant workers have been granted the social status and the working/living conditions enjoyed by urbanites in spite of the reforms and changes in the *hukou* system and central government policies. They are still kept at the lowest social stratum, hence powerless, voiceless and vulnerable to discrimination and exploitation (Zhang, 1999; Li, 2005). Regardless of how long they stay and work in the urban areas, many migrants cannot escape the social label of farmers without official change of their *hukou* status (Guang, 2001; Solinger, 1999a).

In spite of the central government's initiatives the majority of *mingong* are not eligible for urban political rights, most urban welfare benefits such as subsidized housing and the minimum living allowance for the urban poor, and even some types of jobs (Zhan, 2005). They are primarily limited to a secondary labour market characterized by low skill, low pay and high job instability. They often have to work long hours and receive a very low piece-rate wage, even lower than the local legal minimum wage, and have to tolerate retained wages, fines, and payment in arrears (Association for Sustainable & Responsible Investment in Asia, 2002; Li, 2005). They enjoy few welfare benefits and little social protection (Chan, Madsen and Unger, 1992; Solinger, 1999b). Their living conditions are usually low-quality, crowded and isolated from the urban housing areas (Solinger, 1999b; Li, 2005). What is more, their health tends to be affected by noise, dust and exposure to poisons in bad working conditions. They have become the main victims of work-related injuries and illness, especially in the manufacturing and mining industries (Association for Sustainable & Responsible Investment in Asia, 2002; Xiang, 2003). The status of *mingong* has often been blamed on *hukou*-based rules, norms and related managerial practices that discriminate against migrants. The next section discusses this unique phenomenon in China from the perspective of institutionalism.

THE INSTITUTION OF *MINGONGZHI*: NATURE, AND PROBLEMS

In order to examine thoroughly the rural-urban migration and the consequent emergence of millions of *mingong* with the accompanying set of socially constructed formal and informal rules, norms and patterns of managerial practices we have employed institutional theory and created a new term: 'the institution of *mingongzhi*' or simply *mingongzhi*. *Mingongzhi*, like the term 'the institution of slavery', refers to a social-economic regime under which certain persons or a social group, known as *mingong* or rural migrant workers in this case, are socially excluded in urban areas of contemporary China, with their exclusion being founded legally on their household registration (*hukou*) status. The formulation of this term is based on Scott's integrated model of institutions (2008:48):

> *Institutions are composed of regulative, normative and cultural-cognitive elements that, together with associated activities and resources, provide stability and meaning to social life.*

Further, institutions can be contextualised through different methods, either formal or informal and they exhibit social structures which have attained a significant degree of resilience (Scott, 2001). As Scott states, an institution is composed of 'three pillars' - regulative, normative and cultural-cognitive (2008). The regulative pillar refers to a stable system of rules backed by surveillance and sanction. The normative pillar emphasises the centrality of norms and values in defining and explaining behaviour. The cultural-cognitive pillar refers to ''the shared conceptions that constitute the nature of social reality and the frames through which meaning is made'' (Scott, 2001:57).

The regulative pillar of the institution of *mingongzhi* is manifest in a set of complex rules such as the *hukou* system and relevant labour regulation. As discussed previously, the *hukou* system categorizes Chinese citizens into two groups and offers each different rights and public services. As a mechanism of social control, sustained for over half a century, the *hukou* system has made a profound mark on almost all aspects of contemporary China and has generated far-reaching social consequences. First, the *hukou* system creates *hukou*-based rural-urban inequality (Chan & Zhang, 1999; Cheng & Selden, 1994). The *hukou* system divides the population into "two 'castes', one (i.e., urban-*hukou* holders) economically and socially superior to the other (i.e., non-urban-*hukou* holders), with vastly different opportunities, obligations and socio-economic statuses" (Chan & Zhang,1999:830). Second, *hukou* has gained identity and even ethnic meaning. This administrative classification has solidified and evolved into a social identity that is passed across generations (CECOC, 2005). Third, it has given rise to a unique social group, *mingong*, providing them with few resources, restricting their citizenship rights, and limiting their opportunities for upward social mobility (CECOC, 2005; Ngai., 2004; Windrow & Guha, 2005). Finally, the *hukou* system has had a significant impact on the Chinese governance style with the responsibility and evaluation of local governments also being *hukou*-based; that is, local governments only take care of local-*hukou* holders.

From 1980 to 2000, the central government issued numerous employment regulations to restrict and control the employment of *mingong* in cities and to protect the employment privilege of urban residents (Huang and Pieke, 2003; Meng, 2002). Although not all labour regulations in China overtly discriminate against rural workers, discrimination is also implicit in labour regulations that ignore *mingong* and in doing so fail to provide them with proper protection available to those workers with an urban registration. For example, the Labour Law in China is not formulated to protect the legal entitlements of all employees, but rather the workers who have signed contracts with employers, whereas most rural migrants have no labour contract. The social insurance system is also designed for employees in the urban primary labour market characterized by high pay, stable income, and high job security, not for *mingong* who are confined to the secondary labour market characterized by low pay, unstable income and low job security. Although Table 1 listed regulations issued by the state, most of them have not been legislated, so enforcement is difficult.

Normatively, the institution of *mingongzhi* has developed a set of socially shared beliefs. After the rural-urban division of several decades, rural-urban *hukou* classification has solidified into *hukou*-based social identities with different social status. As a result, few urban residents are willing to socialize with *mingong*, let alone to make friends with them. Urban children also tend not to play with and make friends with rural children (Stockman & Ding, 1999). The *hukou*-based administrative classification has also evolved into a social norm of non-intermarriage between urbanites and *mingong* as well (Thakur, 2002; Xu, 2000; Zhu, 2003). Urban residents normally do not marry *mingong* and other non-urban-*hukou* holders if they can find an urban spouse, because marrying a *mingong* is regarded as a socially downward move due to the large rural-urban social and economic gap, and more so for women than men (Xu, 2000).

Cognitively, rural migrant workers are negatively labelled, stereotyped, separated from the urban community and treated differently. Due to their social attributes being deemed shameful, *mingong* have been linked to negative stereotypes by a dominant urban social belief. Numerous studies have shown that the urban public in China usually hold the view that *mingong* are poor, dirty, uneducated, slow-witted, and even uncivilized (ASRIA, 2002; Solinger, 1999b; Wang & Zuo, 1999; Wong et al., 2007; Xu, 2000). In a word, *mingong* are deemed to be of low quality and hence can be discriminated against (Wong et al., 2007). As a result, the stigmatization and social exclusion suffered by *mingong* is attributed to the low quality of their capabilities, rather than to prevalent discrimination and unjust social institutions.

A clear manifestation of the existence of *mingong* stigma is the *hukou*-based human resource management (HRM) system. *Mingong* are differently treated in firms due to their *hukou* status. This can be identified in terms of recruitment, rewards, training, promotion, and social insurance. In brief, there has been a clear division in firms between urbanites as core employees and *mingong* as peripheral workers. *Mingong* tend to suffer from job and wage discrimination in firms (Knight and Song, 1999; ROSC, 2006; Solinger, 1999b; Xu, 2000). They also tend to have less access to training, social insurances, welfare, and promotion than urban-*hukou* holders (Lu, 2006; ROSC, 2006). Consequently, job classification, wage, training, social insurance, welfare and promotion hierarchies based on *hukou* status have emerged in firms and *mingong* are usually at the low end of every hierarchy (Xu, 2000). Scholars describe this *hukou*-based managerial practice as ''one factory, two systems'' (Lu, 2006:492).

The examination of the three pillars of the institution of *mingongzhi* or *hukou*-based rules, norms and patterned managerial practices that discriminate against *mingong*, clearly indicate three major features of the institution - 1) widespread embodiment in a set of formal rules and regulations enforced by government, (especially before 2001 when numerous barriers were set up for farmers moving to cities); 2) wide acceptance that *mingong* are inferior to urbanites as appropriate and acceptable social values and norms; and 3) the prevalent *hukou*-based stigmatisation and managerial routine among organizations in the urban area. This institution has placed *mingong* in a disadvantageous situation, weakened the standard of labour protection and, hence, created a haven of low labour protection for organizations that employ *mingong*. The following section supplies empirical evidence to further highlight the manner in which the institution of *mingongzhi* influences and shapes labour management practices in China.

RESEARCH METHODOLOGY

In 2005/6, we conducted research on 'the integration of rural migrant workers into urban labour markets' in four regions, including one provincial level city and three provinces in China. The project was assisted by the Ministry of Labour and Social Security (MOLSS) and was supported by local governments. The project aimed to identify problems and difficulties that were encountered by *mingong* in their process of migration and working in cities. This included the impact of *hukou* identity with respect to employment and daily life. Implications for labour market reform were drawn from the data collected. The findings were also utilised to substantiate our claim regarding the existence of the institution of *mingongzhi* despite the removal of many barriers for *mingong* by the central government in early 2005.

Population Sample

Two cities, Changsha and Haerbin, were selected for this chapter due to their representativeness in terms of labour exporting and importing. The profile of these two cities is displayed in Table 2. Changsha, the capital city of Hunan province is located further inland. The arable land of this province is about 0.057 hectare per capita, and it has a large rural redundant labour force and is thus one of the major rural labour force exporting provinces. Unlike the coastal areas that have attracted massive FDI and rural labour since the early 1980s, Changsha started developing rapidly in the 1990s. Only one third of its population (6.02 million) were residents with urban *hukou*. Up until 2004 the city exported 1.2 million people to other parts of the country and imported 600,000 migrants; two thirds of migrants obtained temporary resident cards from the local bureau of public security.

Haerbin, the capital city of Heilongjiang province, is in northeast China. Heilongjiang was a heavy industry-based province and home to many large state-owned enterprises (SOEs) that were established in the 1950s with assistance from the former Soviet Union. This region is in decline due to the collapse of SOEs, insufficient FDI and a large number of laid-off workers. At the same time, Heilongjiang is rich in arable land, with each person having about 0.4 hectares of arable land. Among a population of 9.7 million people in Haerbin, 40.7 per cent were urban residents. The city exported nearly one million of its rural residents and imported about 300,000 migrants by the end of 2004.

Table 2 indicates that Changsha was better off than Haerbin in terms of urban residents' disposable income and rural net income per capita in 2004. Although the percentage of unemployed people was similar in both cities, Haerbin had nearly all its urban workers (1.807 million, i.e., 99 per cent) covered by unemployment insurance while in Changsha there were fewer (60,000). Furthermore, the number of urban residents in Haerbin who relied on a social safety net (i.e., received minimum living payments due to unemployment) were more than double that in Changsha (259,000 versus 110,000), and funding spent on social security was also much higher in Haerbin than in Changsha (183 million *yuan* versus 100 million *yuan*). Therefore, by choosing Changsha and Haerbin as case cities we can examine whether the situation of the local labour market has an impact on the attitude of urban governments and firms toward rural migrants. The primary reason we chose Changsha and Haerbin as case cities was because of accessibility received through MOLSS contacts that allowed access to personnel and records.

In the field study, focus group interviews were conducted first with representatives of local government departments and non-government organizations. Participating departments included the Bureau of Statistics; Bureau of Labour and Social Security; Bureau of Education; Bureau of Public Security; Bureau of Safety and Production; Bureau of Construction; Bureau of Health, and trade unions. The government policies and practices relevant to *mingong* and all related official data were obtained through the interviews. A small scale sample survey of both *mingong* and local residents with urban *hukou* was conducted with approximately 70 to 100 participants from each category and from both cities. The survey was designed to compare the use of labour contracts, working hours, and income levels among these two groups of employees. The survey participants were selected from various organizations. After the survey, in-depth interviews were carried out with 22 *mingong* (13 at Changsha and 9 at Haerbin).

Table 2. Profile of two case cities – Changsha and Haerbin

As of 2004		Changsha	Haerbin
Social and Economic Conditions	Population (million)	6.02	9.7
	Local people exported (k)	1,200	1,000
	Imported migrants (k)	600	300
	Residents with urban *hukou* (%)	32.6	40.7
	Local GDP (billion) Per capita GDP (*yuan)*	110.8 18,296	168.05 17,325
Social and Economic Conditions	Per capita urban resident disposable income (*yuan*)	11,021	8,940
	Per capita rural net income (*yuan)*	4,154	3,623
	Ratio of 1st, 2nd and 3rd industries	9.3 : 44.4 : 46.3	16.4 : 38.3 : 45.3
	Registered unemployed persons (%)	3.9	3.8
Social Security	No. of enterprise pension participants (k)	589	950
	No. of unemployment insurance participants (k)	60	1807
	No. of urban safety net beneficiaries (k) Annual Expenditure (million) Rural beneficiaries (k)	110 100 157.8	259 183 n/a

Results and Discussion

Three Pillars of Mingongzhi – Regulative

Of the three pillars, the regulative pillar was the easiest to illustrate. These features become evident in the findings through the provincial and municipal regulations as set out in both locations. These regulations were set up to protect and limit the movement of *mingong*. The locations had differing labour force needs and this was reflected through the regulations concerning *mingong*. Each government recognised the existence of the two-class system and took measures to address the inequalities as it suited their particular labour force needs. Thus, the regulative pillar appeared in the policies established by each city government as it reacted to the central government policies outlined in Table 1.

For example, although the *houku* system of household registration had been curtailed as a national regulative system, both cities had some form of household registration. In Changsha the representative of the Bureau of Public Security stated that a 'temporary residency permit' served as an important tool to manage migrant workers. *Mingong* eligible for the permit were to be treated on an equal footing with local citizens but were not allowed to buy 'economy houses' nor enjoy urban safety net benefits. Those who wished to purchase housing and become a permanent local resident in Changsha faced the following requirements:

1. own a local house at least as large as 60 square meters; or
2. legal representatives of local businesses with at least 500,000 yuan worth of investment (every 20,000 yuan worth of tax contributed by the enterprise per annum can be exchanged for the permanent residency of one person who is either a close relative to the legal representative or an employee thereof); or
3. are employed in paid work and approved by labour authorities, and who have at least technical school degree(s) and at least one year of contributions to a local old-age insurance scheme.

In Haerbin, to qualify as an urban resident, the *mingong* had to meet one of the following two requirements:

1. purchase a house of at least 150,000 yuan in value; or
2. own a house and live in the city for at least 10 years.

The average house priced out at between 2400 to 2500 yuan per square meter in Changsha; thus, a house of 60 square meters would cost between 144,400 and 150,000 yuan. *Mingong* earn an average monthly wage of 500 to 600 yuan in Haerbin and 400 to 800 yuan in Changsha and thus would find it extremely difficult to meet the requirements.

Furthermore, in Changsha the government enacted a decree in 2005 that was directly aimed at solving the problems associated with *mingong* and encouraging them to stay there. Areas covered in the decree ranged from public employment service facilities; vocational training programs; uniform labour contract registration and management systems; uniform labour remuneration systems; workplace health and safety; old-age pensions; medical insurance; housing; and to education for the children of *mingong*. Although Haerbin did not enact a similar decree, Haerbin offered subsidies for the education of *mingong* children, but had no special social insurance program specifically aimed at *mingong*.

Under the regulative pillar Changsha demonstrated rules and regulations that encouraged the migration of *mingong* to fill the need for cheap labour. Haerbin enacted minimal rules and regulations seemingly to discourage migration due to a surplus of labour from significant levels of lay-offs from SOEs. Thus the first pillar of the institution of *mingongzhi*, the regulative pillar, was illustrated by the fact that both cities enacted rules and regulations or complied with central government rules and regulations regarding *mingong*.

Normative

In terms of the second pillar, normative, the findings illustrate that norms, values, and roles exist within both sample populations for *mingong*. The first was evident in the roles that *mingong* played through the jobs in which *mingong* were primarily employed in both cities. Table 3 outlines the industries that are the primary employers of *mingong* and Table 4 the positions they fill.

As can be seen in Table 3, *mingong* were primarily employed in the manufacturing, construction or wholesale/retail trades. The role *mingong* were given and accepted as a norm was to take, as indicated earlier, the three-D jobs or to be used as cheap labour. Yet, as shown in Table 5, the levels of vocational skills did not reflect the differences in positions that are evident in Table 4.

A second example was the social norm of non-interaction between *mingong* and urbanites. As an example, none of the *mingong* interviewed had married, and very few were involved intimately with, an urbanite.

Table 3. Industries that employed *Mingong* in Changsha and Haerbin

Industries	Changsha		Haerbin	
	Urban workers	Mingong	Urban workers	Mingong
Manufacturing	13%	30.8%	14.5%	7.7%
Construction	8%	16%	5.2%	53.4%
Transport, carriage, warehousing and post	4%	0	9.3%	0
Wholesales / retailing	1%	9.5%	14.4%	13.9%
Social services	15%	36.2%	1%	7.7%
Health, sports and social welfare services	6%	1.1%	2.1%	3.1%
Education, arts and media	6%	1%	1%	0
Government departments	2%	1.1%	18.6%	0
Others	45%	4.3%	33.9%	14.2%
Total	100%	100%	100%	100%

Table 4. *Mingong* job classifications in Changsha and Haerbin

Positions	Changsha		Haerbin	
	Urban workers N= 102	*Mingong N=101*	Urban workers N=99	*Mingong N=70*
Technicians	22%	21.7%	20.6%	7.6%
Operational staff (labourers)	10%	18.5%	27.8%	54.5%
Management	13%	13%	13.4%	3%
Commercial service staff	25%	25%	13.4%	18.2%
Others	30%	21.8%	24.8%	16.7%
Total	100%	100%	100%	100%

Table 5. *Mingong* vocational accreditation levels

Vocational skills		Changsha (%)		Haerbin (%)	
		Urban workers N=102	*Mingong N=101*	Urban workers N=99	*Mingong N=70*
With vocational skills		65.7%	65.3%	53.1%	53.6%
With accredited vocational skills		60%	50.6%	43.9%	46.4%
Accreditation levels	Primary	25.4%	37.5%	37.6%	28.6%
	Intermediate	55.6%	54.2%	42.8%	57.1%
	Advanced	19%	8.3%	7.2%	14.3%

Cultural-Cognitive

As stated earlier, *mingong* are negatively labelled and treated differently, and this view was also evident in our findings. The lack of social interaction clearly indicated a desire to maintain a separation between *mingong* and urbanites. Our findings verified the findings of Wong et al. (2007) in that *mingong* were discriminated against by the very nature of the jobs they were given (see Table 3). According to interview participants and survey findings, urbanites generally had better job positions (Table 4), had better social insurance coverage (Table 6), were usually covered by a labour contract, worked shorter hours (Table 7), and were better paid.

Table 6. Social insurance coverage

Social Insurance Schemes	Changsha		Haerbin	
	Urban workers N=102	*Mingong N=101*	Urban workers N=99	*Mingong N=70*
Old-age pension	59.8%	33.3%	91%	18.57%
Medical insurance	61.8%	24.5%	69.7%	10%
Unemployment insurance	33.3%	15.7%	46.1%	5.71%
Insurance of industrial injuries	n. a.	20.6%	n. a.	21.43%
Maternity insurance	7.8%	4.9%	1.1%	0%
Not covered by any of the above	29.4%	55.9%	0%	57.14%

Table 7. Labour contract coverage and hours worked

Labour Contract	Changsha		Haerbin	
	Urban workers N=102	*Mingong N=101*	Urban workers N=99	*Mingong N=70*
Without labour contract	46.5%	50.5%	43.7%	88.5%
Over 25 days worked per week	54.3%	66.7%	43.1%	82.6%
Over 10 hours worked per day	21.3%	45.3%	4.1%	64.7%
Overtime rates denied	43%	34%	31.5%	46.9%
Monthly wage below 1200 *yuan*	67.1%	81.7%	87.6%	65.71%

Survey findings showed significant differences between urbanites and *mingong* by social insurance coverage. In Haerbin, all urbanites had some form of social insurance coverage whereas slightly over 57% of *mingong* were not covered by any social insurance schemes (see Table 6). Further, when accidents did occur it was reported that compensation plans for *mingong* differed from those for urban employees. The example given by a representative from the Changsha Office of Occupational Safety and Health was that of an employee losing a finger. An urban employee would receive the legally mandated compensation; however, *mingong* might only receive two- or three-month wages. The Haerbin Office of Occupational Safety and Health official admitted that if a *mingong* employee was not on a labour contract it was entirely likely that the employer would not pay any compensation even if the accident resulted in death. According to the same official, 80% of the workers killed in accidents were *mingong* and, in the mining and construction industries, 95% of all job-related deaths were *mingong*.

Mingong also faced discrimination when enrolling their children in urban schools. In both cities *mingong* were forced to produce several documents. In Changsha they were asked to supply the following: documents proving the status of stable local employment of the children's parents or guardians; documents proving the legal basis of cohabitation of the parents for at least one year; certificates of labour contract and employer-funded social insurance; household register, ID card, employment certificate, permit of temporary residence, property ownership certificate (if applicable) or house lease registration certificate and the certificate of the children's schooling. In Haerbin only three certificates were required - temporary residency permit, enterprise employment certificate and certificate of school transfer. Also, in both locations charges and fees applied to all students but 'poor' parents were provided with a government sponsorship for their children and 'poor' parents were primarily *mingong*. Although the representative from the Changsha Education Bureau claimed that sponsorship fees were all that was required, officials from other departments commented that this was not the case. They were aware of cases where enrolment requests were declined on the ground that the school roll was already full but children were nevertheless accepted, provided additional fees were paid by the parents. According to survey results, 33.3% of the respondents in Changsha and 30% in Haerbin confirmed that schools did charge additional sponsorship fees and fees for school transfer. Thus, children of *mingong* were denied access to education unless additional money was paid.

When viewing all of the above aspects, *mingong* were indeed treated like second class citizens; given the worst jobs; underpaid; and worked long hours. Through this treatment and the prevalence of discriminating attitudes in both cities the third pillar, cultural-cognitive, is supported by the preceding findings. The findings therefore indicate that the three pillars of an institution exist for *mingongzhi* in both sample populations. What now needs to be discussed is whether or not the institution needs to be deinstitutionalised to speed the unification of the labour market in China.

A Need to Deinstitutionalise and Policy Implications

Through the findings of this research project it was found that *mingong* were discriminated against merely because of their place of permanent residency or *hukou* status. The findings show that *mingong* often had the same qualifications as urbanites but were relegated to lower positions. Due to their status, *mingong* were commonly subjected to poor working conditions, which lead to serious injury or death. To make the situation even worse, *mingong* were given little training and had little to no social insurance coverage. These and many of the other issues described above are unethical. Any institution needs to be eliminated that degrades a group of people, encourages mistreatment or promotes unethical behaviour.

Although China's national government has taken steps towards the elimination of the *hukou* system, it is still supported by provincial and municipal governments. Our findings show that there is a significant difference in the treatment of *mingong* based upon the labour force needs of a particular area. In Changsha, *mingong* survey participants rated the attitude of urbanites towards them significantly better than did the respondents in Haerbin (see Table 8). As a consequence, when *mingong* were asked if they wished to become residents of the city, 76.8% replied in the affirmative; whereas, in Haerbin the figure was 41.8%.

Table 8. Perceived urbanite attitude towards *mingong*

	Friendly	Equal	Neutral	Looked down upon	No contact
Haerbin	4.3%	49.3%	37.7%	5.8%	2.9%
Changsha	28%	60%	8%	0	4%

Changsha enacted regulations protecting the rights of *mingong*. In Haerbin there is a significant difference between the number of *mingong* under labour contracts, the hours they worked and the payment of overtime when compared to Haerbin urbanites. In Changsha, although significant difference still exists, *mingong* are closer in all categories and even better off in terms of overtime payment than Changsha urbanites. The differences continued through all the categories in our findings. The simple reason was that Haerbin did not need migrant workers; Changsha did.

A further complication was the lack of regulatory enforcement. Corruption and evasion of social insurance payments are serious problems in China (Nyland, Thomson, & Zhu, 2008; Pringle & Frost, 2003). Central government policies and regulations were ignored or overridden by local government and/or officials. Participants in the focus groups spoke of extra fees being charged for education, workplace injuries not being reported, injury compensation not being paid and no labour contracts being offered.

To combat this growing issue our findings draw out three key points that have policy implications:

1. The reform of the social security system;
2. Abolishment of the *hukou* system; and
3. Democratization of the trade unions.

A key factor that arose during interviews with *mingong* was the fact that money paid into social insurance policies was not transferable. Therefore, *mingong* preferred to go without coverage and receive cash in hand. Also, their contributions were perceived to be unfairly distributed. Only a small portion of their contribution went into their own fund and the majority of the contribution was pooled, which many believed was unfair and again prompted the desire for cash in hand. Add to this the findings of the evasion of compensation payments to employees by employers, and it becomes clear that a serious overhaul of the social security system is required.

Despite efforts by the central government to reform the *hukou* policy, it is still in existence. Relegation of the legislation and enforcement of policies to provincial and municipal levels has resulted in a fragmented labour market with different policies and practices in different locations, based on local needs. In the popular press there are still calls for further reform of the *hukou* system (Liu, 2008) and Chan and Buckingham (2008) state that there is a long way to go before a unified labour market will be achieved. Our findings verify that the practice is still evident at the government, workplace and societal levels. It is found in policy at both the government and business levels and in norms in the workplace and social environments.

Mingong have only a few channels through which to voice their concerns. Our findings indicate that many *mingong* just accept their fate or leave the job. In order to achieve a balance between employers and employees, labour unions must take a larger role. The current weak link between trade unions and *mingong* needs to be strengthened to make unions a viable agent for migrant workers. Basic labour rights, including the right of industrial action, need to be sanctioned by all levels of government. The right of all workers to a fair and safe workplace is a basic need that must have a voice at all levels of government.

In regard to HRM, our findings confirm that HRM tends to be *hukou*-based. In many firms a clear division of urban-rural employees was found. Urbanites were the core employees primarily in technical and managerial jobs. Mingong were mainly rented workers or temporary employees. As stated earlier, in many firms, some positions had a clear *hukou* requirement; thus, effectively limiting job mobility for rural migrants. Although firms in China are increasingly utilizing western HRM practices, these practices seemed to be primarily used for regular urban employees. For example, firms provided urbanites with higher levels of training but only basic training for rural employees. The findings also confirmed that different levels of social protection coverage existed between urban employees and *mingong*. Generally, urbanites received compulsory or better social insurance coverage and *mingong* experienced little to no coverage.

Although we show *mingongzhi* as an unethical institution, there are positive aspects of the institution of *mingongzhi*. The traditional planned system deprived the right of rural residents to move to the city; thus, *mingongzhi* represents a form of social progress. *Mingongzhi* also acts to mitigate some social tension. This is primarily seen in the freedom of movement for the rural population and through the income sent back to families still living in rural areas; thus, *mingongzhi* does have its positive influences on the rural economy. For the urban economy rural migration greatly reduced the labour costs of most firms. When rural migrants are young, urban firms utilize their labour at an extremely low price, but when rural migrants become old or are seriously injured, they have to return to the countryside. In other words, cities enjoy the low-price labour of rural migrants, but are able to avoid the responsibility for pension, medical expenditures and other social security needs. Rural migrants have contributed significantly to maintaining a prosperous Chinese urban economy. Also, their remittance to relatives still residing in rural areas also boosts the rural economy. These social and economic benefits add to the governments' (especially local governments') reluctance to deinstitutionalize *mingongzhi* without delay. This reluctance must be overcome.

CONCLUSION

This chapter is among the first to examine the rural-urban migration and rural migrant workers from an institutional perspective. The institution of *mingongzhi* was identified and examined systematically. The in-depth investigation of the institution and its practices provides deeper insights into a growing social institution and contributes to the further development of institutional theory.

As discussed in the chapter, the institution of *mingongzhi* has developed clear regulative, normative and cognitive aspects that define the way rural migrants are treated. Some sub-national differences do not mean *mingongzhi* has not been institutionalized. In fact, the institution is now in the process of deinstitutionalization under the pressure of the Hu-Wen New Deal. The process of deinstitutionalization can partially explain why there are some sub-national differences. Since *mingongzhi* is an unethical institution, it is therefore inappropriate to nationalize it prior to its deinstitutionalization.

The central government has not shown the will to overcome resistance from the lower levels of government. This is a serious problem as it means that urban governments and organizations, especially those importing or employing a large amount of *mingong*, have little incentive to protect the legal rights of *mingong* and dual management systems have therefore become prevalent. As shown, these governments respond to issues based on their own needs, rather than a just system for all. The features of the institution have demonstrated that it is unjust and unethical and has a profound influence on the Chinese urban labour environment, industrial relations and the HRM practices of organizations. The existence of *mingongzhi* is not consistent with the covenant (ICESCR) that the Chinese government ratified in 2001 to grant economic, social and cultural rights to all individuals. Furthermore, the continued existence of this institution fails to show the expected outcome of a series of government policies introduced since 2001 to move towards a unified labour market. *Mingongzhi* carries a stigma that destabilises that move. The deinstitutionalization of *mingongzhi* has thus become an urgent ethical and economic issue, given China's status as an important international production base of labour-intensive FDI and as a provider of inexpensive labour.

In 2009 the unfolding global financial crisis has induced the central government to put labour reforms on hold. The current context is not one in which reforms will likely advance. However when the current crisis is overcome it will be important to remember why it was that, at a time of unprecedented growth, it was not possible to dismantle the *hukou* system. Given the entrenched nature of the institution of *mingongzhi,* the central government will invariably need to find the will if it is to move forward. One must recognize that great strides have been made in the ability of people to pursue a living and to be treated in a fair and just manner but there is still a long journey ahead to a truly unified labour market in China.

REFERENCES

[1] Association for Sustainable & Responsible Investment in Asia (ASRIA) (2002). Labour standards in China, the business and investment challenge. www.asria.org/publications/lib//LabourSummary.pdf, accessed on 18 February 2008.

[2] CECOC - Congressional-Executive Commission on China (2005). China's household registration system: sustained reform needed to protect China's rural migrants. www.cecc.gov, accessed on 1 March 2008.

[3] Chan, A., Madsen, R., & Unger, J. (1992). *Chen Village under Mao and Deng.* Berkeley: University of California Press.

[4] Chan, K.W. and Buckingham, W. (2008). Is China abolishing the hukou system? *The China Quarterly*, 195: 582-606

[5] Chan, K.W., & Zhang, L. (1999). The hukou system and rural-urban migration in China: processes and changes. *The China Quarterly, 160*, 818-855.

[6] Cheng, T., & Selden, M. (1994). The origins and social consequences of China's Hukou system. *The China Quarterly, 139*, 644-668.

[7] COD-Compilations of documents on improving urban employment environment for migrant workers (*guanyu kaishan nongmin jinchen jiuye huanjing wenjian huibian*关于改善农民进城就业环境文件汇编), Ministry of Labour and Social Security, April 2005.

[8] Doeringer, P. B., & Piore, M. (1971). *Internal Labor Markets and Manpower Analysis,* Lexington, MA: D.C. Heath and Company.

[9] Fan, P. (2006). Developing Report of Chinese Farmers in 2005 (2005 nian zhongguo nongmin fazhan baogao). in X. Ru, X. Y. Lu, & P. L. Li., Analysis and Forecast of Chinese Social Development Beijing. Press of Social Science Literature.

[10] Guang, L. (2001). Reconstituting the rural-urban divide: peasant migration and the rise of 'orderly migration' in contemporary China. *Journal of Contemporary China, 10* (28), 471-493.

[11] Hu, W., & Zhang, Z. (2007). How much of the difference of the contribution and income of rural migrant workers? Chinese Scientific Papers Online, http://www.paper.edu.cn, accessed on 18 February 2007.

[12] Huang, P., & Pieke, F. N. (2003). *China migration country study, paper presented at the conference on Migration*. Development and Pro-Poor Policy Choices in Asia, Dhaka.

[13] ICESCR – International Covenant on Economic, Social and Cultural Rights, http://en.wikipedia.org/wiki/International_Covenant_on_Economic_Social_and_Cultural Rights, accessed on 17 November 2008.

[14] ILO - International Labour Office (2000). World Labour Report. Income Security and Social Protection in a Changing World. Geneva: ILO. http://www.unesco.org/most/migration/imrdx.pdf, accessed on 4 April 2008.

[15] Knight, J., & Song, L. (1999). Employment constraints and sub-optimality in Chinese enterprises. *Oxford Economic Papers*, *51* (2), 284-298.

[16] Li, B. (2005). Urban social change in transitional China: a perspective of social exclusion and vulnerability. *Journal of Contingencies and Crisis Management*, *13*(2): 54-65.

[17] Liang, Z. (2001). The age of migration in China. *Population and Development Review*, *27*(3): 499-524.

[18] Lu, X.Y. (2006). Paying attention to research and resolve the problems related to mingong (yao zhongshi he jiejue nongmingong wenti), in Research Office of State Council (Eds.), *Survey Report on the Problems of Rural Migrant Workers in China* (zhongguo nongmingong wenti yanjiu baogao). Beijing: China Yanshi Press.

[19] Meng, F.Y. (2002). On the path dependency of the evolvement of labour migration institutions in China (lun zhongguo laodongli liudong zhidu bianqian de lujing yilai). *Journal of Beijing Institute of Planned Labour Management Cadres*, 2, 10-13.

[20] Ngai, P. (2004). Women workers and precarious employment in Shenzhen Special Economic Zone, China. *Gender and Development*, *12*(2): 29-36.

[21] Nyland, C., Thomson, S. B., & Zhu, C. J. (2008) Regulatory Compliance: Paper Tigers in China. The paper presented at IACMR (International Association for Chinese Management Research) conference hosted by Zhongshan University, Guangzhou, China, June 19-22, 2008.

[22] Roberts, K. D. (2002). Rural migrants in urban China: Willing workers, invisible residents', in Debrah, Y. A. (Eds.), *Migrant workers in pacific Asia*. London: Frank Cass Publishers.

[23] ROSC - Research Office of State Council (2006). *Survey Report on the Problems of Rural Migrant Workers in China* (zhongguo nongmingong wenti yanjiu baogao). Beijing: China Yanshi Press.

[24] Scott, W. R. (2001). *Institutions and Organizations* (2nd Eds.). Thousand Oaks: Sage Publications.

[25] Scott, W. R. (2008). *Institutions and Organizations* (3rd Eds.). Thousand Oaks: Sage Publications.

[26] Solinger, D. J. (1999a). Citizenship issues in China's internal migration: comparisons with Germany and Japan. *Political Science Quarterly*, *114* (3): 455-478.

[27] Solinger, D. J. (1999b). *Contesting Citizenship in Urban China: Peasant Migrants, the State, and the Logic of the Market.* Berkeley: University of California Press.

[28] Stockman, N., & Ding, J. (1999). The floating population and the integration of the city community: a survey on Shanghai residents' attitudes towards migrants, in H. Mallee,

& F. Pieke, (Eds.), *Internal and International Migration: Chinese Perspectives.* Honolulu: University of Hawaii Press.

[29] Survey Team of Ministry of Labour and Social Security (2006). A Study on the current employment of rural migrant workers and the construction of labour market (dangqian nongmingong liudong jiuye yu laodongli shichang jianshe went yanjiu), in Research Office of State Council (Eds.), *Survey Report on the Problems of Rural Migrant Workers in China.* Beijing: China Yanshi Press.

[30] Pringle, T.E., & Frost, S.D. (2003). The absence of rigor and the failure of implementation: Occupational health and safety in China, *International Journal of Occupational and Environmental Health, 9*(4), 309-316.

[31] Thakur, R. (2002). China's reform of the domicile system (Hukou Zhidu). *China Report, 38*, 299-306.

[32] Wang, F., & Zuo, X. (1999). Inside China's cities: institutional barriers and opportunities for urban migrants', *The American Economic Review, 89* (2), 276-280.

[33] Wang, F. L. (2005). *Organizing through Division and Exclusion.* Stanford: Stanford University Press.

[34] Windrow, H., & Guha, A. (2005). The Hukou System, Migrant Workers, & State Power in the People's Republic of China. http://www.law.northwestern.edu/journals/jihr/v3/3/, accessed on 1 March 2008.

[35] Wong, D. F. K., & Li, C. Y. (2007). Rural migrant workers in urban China: living a marginalised life, *International Journal of Social Welfare, 16*(1), 32-40.

[36] Xiang, B. (2003). Migration and health in China: problems, obstacles and solutions. http://www.populationasia.org/Publications/RP/AMCRP17.pdf, accessed on 18 February 2008.

[37] Xu, F. (2000). *Women Migrant Workers in China's Economic Reform.* London: Macmillan.

[38] Zhan, S. (2005). Rural labour migration in China: challenges for policies. http://unesdoc.unesco.org/images/0014/001402/140242e.pdf, accessed on 18 February 2007.

[39] Zhang, H. X. (1999). Female migration and urban labour markets in Tianjin. *Development and Change 30*, 21-41.

[40] Zhu, L.J. (2003). The hukou system of the People's Republic of China: a critical appraisal under international standards of internal movement and residence. *Chinese Journal of International Law, 2*, 519-565.

In: Thirty Years of China's Economic Reform
Editors: Yue Wang and Prem Ramburuth
ISBN: 978-1-60876-908-7
© 2010 Nova Science Publishers, Inc.

Chapter 3

GOVERNANCE THROUGH GOVERNMENTS: SINGAPORE'S TRANSFER OF PUBLIC SECTOR MANAGEMENT 'SOFTWARE' TO CHINA THROUGH JOINT VENTURES

Peter Sheldon*[*]*, David Morgan and Bernard Gan
School of Organisation and Management,
University of New South Wales, Sydney, NSW, Australia

ABSTRACT

This chapter discusses, from Chinese perspectives, three public sector joint ventures (JVs) between Singaporean and Chinese government and other public sector bodies. These developed during the 1990s within the context of China's national government devolving economic decision-making to provincial and municipal authorities. In encouraging JVs with Singaporean government entities, China's national authorities sought to secure the inward transfer and embedding of advanced management and technical expertise together with the desired Singaporean forms of 'western' norms of accountability and administrative conduct – or 'software'. Examination of the three projects – industrial parks at Suzhou and Wuxi, and a port development at Dalian – identifies contrasting experiences and outcomes resulting from the interplay of issues of economic, social and political control. Our comparative analysis suggests the importance of the *type* of public sector JV, its scale, and particular dimensions of local institutional context. Knowledge transfer faced fewer political and institutional impediments where it focused predominantly on technical and managerial systems, was defined as more commercially oriented, and took place within – rather than apart from – existing Chinese infrastructure and administrative structures. In particular, tensions with local Chinese authorities emerge over prioritising administrative 'software' transfer at arm's length from those authorities. These results point to the importance of institutional distance in the context of conflicting indications from the literatures on JVs and knowledge transfer.

---

* Email: p.sheldon@unsw.edu.au.

Keywords: China development, International Joint Ventures, knowledge transfer, public sector.

Introduction

When China's government opened the nation's economy to global capitalism, it chose to encourage massive inflows of foreign direct investment (FDI). FDI was to be a primary means for modernising China's economy, creating an export-oriented economy, generating rapid economic growth and creating employment sustainable under a market regime. This plan – largely realised – also envisioned that foreign-based multinational enterprises (MNEs), the sources of this FDI, would transmit advanced technologies and techniques to China, originally through joint ventures (JVs) with local organisations. Accordingly, most JVs have been in manufacturing.

Since 1991, China has encouraged FDI through wholly foreign-owned subsidiaries, and relaxed regulations for FDI, in the breadth of JVs. Through both ownership forms, local managers and workforces have absorbed relevant business, organisational and technical knowledge, as well as attitudes and behaviours essential for transforming China from a centralised, command economy to one enmeshed in competitive global capitalism. MNEs increasingly flocked to a newly opened Chinese economy, attracted by low production costs and exposure to huge local product markets. More recently, these foreign-invested enterprises (FIEs) have shifted productive focus from cost minimisation to higher quality products, more complex processes and a greater investment in localised research and development (Lau and Bruton 2008).

China's government has provided a range of incentives to attract FDI, including designated economic zones and purpose-built industrial parks. This emulates a global pattern of governments seeking to attract research and development (R&D) and innovation. After 1990, an invigorated FDI policy centred on special economic zones, particularly in Shanghai, neighbouring Jiangsu, and Guangdong Province adjacent to Hong Kong. While Guangdong accounted for most early FDI, the Yangtze River Delta provinces of Shanghai, Zhejiang and Jiangsu now account for 40 per cent of the national total. Jiangsu, the location of two JV industrial parks examined here – in Suzhou and Wuxi – had become the largest destination by 2006, with some 19 per cent (Lau and Bruton 2008: 32, 34). FDI inflow has since extended throughout China, including to the north coast province of Liaoning, the site of the Dalian development – our third case.

In this process, Beijing delegated much of the regulation and promotion of economic activity to provincial and local governments, while maintaining tight control over national politics (Liu 2008; Pereira 2003). Thus, special economic zones and industrial parks answer to local government bodies, which often also own and control them. These initiatives are therefore sources of local development, employment creation and prosperity as well as municipal revenues and autonomy.

The national government was soon aware of its diminished influence over how local governments used this delegated power. Beijing faced two sets of questions in its goal of propelling China to a more elevated role in the international division of labour. First, how to overcome the effects of decades of central planning, anti-capitalist rhetoric and associated political priorities that inhibited local officials from developing attitudes and behaviours needed for effective and efficient engagement with FDI? Would a bureaucratic culture imbued with personal risk avoidance and personalised exercise of authority impede FDI's positive spillover effects? Second, how to modernise (or 'westernise') the knowledge, skills, values, attitudes and behaviours of the country's vast number of provincial and municipal government officials – but at arm's length. How could Beijing generate these changes while maintaining its delegation of power and associated economic dynamism? Beijing has recognised that its answers involve identifying, locating and inculcating essential *tacit*, as well as explicit, knowledge and skills.

A further consideration has been the broader implications for Chinese politics and society of important sectors of state and economy embracing capitalist development. Would this excessively undermine longstanding socio-economic obligations that employers and government owed employees and wider society? Was there instead a variety of capitalism more attractive than recently abandoned Chinese paths and the most aggressive manifestations of western capitalism? Further, for Beijing, in any alternative path, the Communist Party had to retain monopoly over political power.

Beijing's responses, as in its strategy for private sector knowledge transfer through private FDI, was selective and measured, a pattern which echoed the preferences of earlier eras. Chinese authorities, rather than encourage open-ended, organic experimentation, chose the 'rapid adoption of techniques developed elsewhere' (Baark 2007: 349). This road to innovation poses fewer threats to social stability and political control, and promises a more institutionally harmonious development process.

This chapter explores an important contemporary variant of this knowledge transfer strategy: FDI through government-to-government JVs, this time between Singapore's government and/or its state-owned corporations and China's. These sets of arrangements, promoted by both governments, began in the early 1990s and included industrial parks as well as other JV entities. The most important and celebrated has been the China-Singapore Suzhou Industrial Park (SIP). Others followed the pioneering lines of these three projects, particularly SIP, including recent JV agreements for Dalian Changxing Island Harbour Industrial Zone, the Guangxi-Singapore Industrial Park in south China, and plans for a JV between Singapore and Jiangsu Province in Nantong (Sembcorp 2008; *Yangtze Evening Daily* 2008; IMC 2007).

While SIP has attracted substantial scholarly attention (Inkpen and Pien 2006; Pereira 2003, 2007; Wong and Goldblum 2000; Yeoh et al. 2005), most studies focus on Singaporean perspectives. Our focus is from Chinese perspectives and we extend discussion beyond SIP to two other projects – at Wuxi and Dalian – largely overlooked by the scholarly literature. This allows for comparative evaluation of these JV innovations.

The study responds to calls for more research on how China itself experiences the effects of FDI and how this plays out in different localities and realities. It contributes to understanding how new business systems are emerging as China adjusts to social and institutional demands for economic prominence (Lau and Bruton 2008; Redding and Witt 2006; Redding 2002). As an emerging system, China exhibits both contextual path dependence of socio-cultural and political institutions, as well as an institutional emergence underpinning development and growth. The role of FDI has been conspicuously successful. Moreover, developments at the local level, notably among part-private/part-local government hybrid companies, have injected a new vigour into Chinese economic development (Redding and Witt 2006: 107, 110).

The cases investigated here provide contrasting experiences of a wider emergent business system. Development of the contrasting features that this chapter discusses has come through their identification and confirmation as explanatory constructs (see Eisenhardt, 1991), from the literature and from inspecting our information. We have used diverse research sources and methods. The good secondary literature on SIP provides the basis for comparative work; authorities at the Suzhou and Wuxi parks provide updated information. Moreover, one of our team was a senior manager on the Dalian project, representing the Singaporean partner, PSA Corporation Ltd. The insights of a participant observer are particularly useful for understanding a project for which very little academic literature exists and research access is difficult. Extensive review of frequent media discussions in both countries, particularly of SIP, makes for more timely research. As the JVs' media releases and the Chinese official media tend towards the celebratory, we found that the secondary literature helps with decoding. So, too, have research visits conducted as part of linked research projects. These have included interviews with government and company officials, past and present.

The next section introduces the aims of governments from both countries. We then briefly examine the progress of each of these initiatives before developing our conclusions. As SIP is the most important, we deal with it in most detail.

The Objectives of the Singaporean and Chinese Governments

The origins of this JV program lie in the two national governments' complementary economic development strategies from the 1980s. Since the 1960s, Singapore's highly successful development strategy was centred on extensive and intensive government involvement in producing a pro-business environment very supportive of FDI. It combined high levels of technical proficiency, comprehensive longer-term planning, strategic adaptability and efficient, reliable and honest public administration.

Yet, as Singapore's government encouraged higher value-added and higher wage manufacturing after 1980, MNEs increasingly bypassed the island-state in favour of cheaper FDI alternatives in neighbouring countries. In responding, the government shaped a regionalisation strategy of expanding outward FDI – through state-owned profit-seeking corporations and the private sector –into neighbouring trading partners, including China (Pereira 2003).

However, many MNEs, bypassing Singapore for its lower-cost neighbours, were concerned at the poor quality physical, social and administrative infrastructure they encountered. They also faced greater cultural disparities and, in particular, much greater 'institutional distance' features than those found in Singapore. Xu and Shenkar (2002: 608) define institutional distance as 'the extent of similarity or dissimilarity between the regulatory, cognitive and normative institutions of two countries'. This presented Singapore's public sector with strategic opportunities to draw on its strengths in establishing and running industrial parks. Accordingly, the government developed a 'Regional Industrial Parks' project within its regionalisation strategy (Yeoh et al.: 2005). The plan was to create a number of Singapore run, Singapore-style industrial parks abroad, including in China.

The Singapore government's primary initial motivation was, 'to generate an income from the outflow of manufacturing to the neighbouring region through "servicing" the needs of multinational corporations that were intent on relocating' (Pereira 2007: 290). Former Prime Minister (later Senior and then Mentor Minister) Lee Kuan Yew took a particularly active, public role in promoting these initiatives. He saw them as vital opportunities for China-focused learning among Singaporean business and government leaders, and as opening spaces in China for Singaporean business. Lee particularly stressed that the most valuable knowledge transfer or sharing – in both directions – was tacit knowledge. We treat tacit knowledge as a socio-cultural capacity, drawing on unexpressed, uncodified 'know-how', 'a distinctly personal concept' as Nonaka puts it (1994: 24), as well as a broader non-verbalised orientation to norms and practices in organisational contexts. Under Lee's influence, Singapore's government itself took the leadership role in investing in, and managing, the Singaporean SIP consortium. For the other public sector JVs, these roles went to Government-linked corporations (GLCs), controlled through direct or indirect equity ownership. These included corporations such as Sembawang Corporation (Sembcorp) in Wuxi, Jurong Town Corporation (JTC) and, for Dalian, the Port of Singapore Authority (PSA) Corporation (Wong and Goldblum 2000; Inkpen and Pien 2006).

Chinese government goals for these JVs included the usual aspirations for local economic development, employment creation, rising prosperity and technological and business knowledge transfer. Concerned to counteract the 'race to the bottom' among competitors for FDI, Beijing also wanted a race to the top. This demonstrated an understanding that MNEs base their localisation choices not only on cost minimisation and proximity but also, at times, on 'created assets' (Yeoh et al. 2005: 481) or 'secondary factors of production' (Pereira 2003: 10-11). These include the quality of the physical infrastructure, the local labour force, and public administration. As Yeoh et al. (2005: 48) argue, the literature suggests that as firms' 'core competencies become increasingly knowledge-intensive', so their FDI location strategy tends to prioritise 'created assets'. As effective provision of these assets determines a state's credibility among MNEs, host governments take a greater role in ensuring their attractiveness. Yet, FIEs in many of China's special economic zones and industrial parks have long complained of poor quality urban utilities, substandard factory buildings and even roads (Periera, 2003: 59, 64).

A central, unique goal is the transfer and absorption of Singaporean public sector knowledge (and wisdom) – technical, governance, and administrative – and their subsequent wider diffusion beyond the original sites of innovation. These are therefore public sector 'learning alliances' (Inkpen and Pien 2006). Finally, Beijing has also seen an opportunity for some controlled social experimentation (Pereira 2003; Yeoh et al. 2005). We evaluate our three cases against these criteria.

With strong support from Deng Xiaoping, these concerns fused in Beijing's strategy to learn from Singapore's experience of rapid economic and social development. The Singaporeans had created a highly educated and skilled, high-wage workforce and a high standard of living. Crucially, its socio-political system succeeded in achieving rapid development while restricting political dissent and instability. In short, it is a model generating processes and outcomes attractive to China's government, notably as a framework maintaining Communist Party political control as development takes place.

For Beijing, Singapore had several advantages: a large ethnic Chinese majority; Mandarin and English language skills; and that it was small and displayed no strategic threat.

Government-to-government ('G2G') learning from Singapore avoided potential embarrassment or loss of face that might have bedevilled arrangements with a different nation-state. It opened greater opportunities for the tacit knowledge transfer and sharing that both governments sought. As one Chinese SIP official commented to Pereira (2003: 41), 'Westerners find it relatively easy to accept Singapore compared with China. And we find it easier to accept Singaporeans than Westerners.'

Further, Lee had assertively sought to (re-)embrace 'Asian' values, in part to consolidate his claims for a specifically Singaporean model of state-guided economic policy, where prosperity coexists with strong limits on democracy and some individual rights. Again, this model of authoritarian capitalism with oriental characteristics was appealing to Beijing. It was also useful for these JVs' political and organisational legitimacy and their chances of survival and success. Overall, these JV projects represented a convergence of the interests and strategies of not only the two governments, but also MNEs attracted by Singaporean quality amid China's low costs (Wong and Goldblum 2000) and burgeoning markets.

Beijing's assessment of patterns of institutional distance (Xu and Shenkar 2002) between the two countries encouraged its expectations of stimuli for Chinese individual and organisational learning, particularly through forms of 'institutional isomorphism' - that is, organisational adaptation towards successful exemplars. These public sector JVs would serve as learning laboratories for local officials working within Singaporean organisational environments, but in China. Commercial and non-commercial success would encourage diffusion of learning – formal and informal – among China's public administrators. In turn, this process would re-shape the institutions managing and regulating China's industrial parks towards the Singaporean model. This institutional adaptation would largely be 'mimetic', as Chinese officials adopted strategies and behaviours of a highly successful (and close-by) market competitor.

There was also a 'coercive' element to this adaptation. These JV projects involved formal agreements, Chinese laws and local regulations that – together with patterns of local political power – encouraged adherence to new routines. Indeed, much of the challenge in implementing the projects involved developing behaviours that fitted with and supported JV organisational structures and formal institutional relationships.

What factors were likely to improve the chances of success for these experiments and encourage such isomorphism? Bjoerkman and Lu's (2001) study of JVs in China suggests, in regard to HRM practices, that several factors raise the likelihood of a JV's practices resembling those of the foreign partner rather than local ones, particularly where the foreign partner intended such knowledge transfer. The factors include: the foreign partner being majority owner within the JV (and the greater the better) and its high levels of non-capital resources contributions; the choice of a greenfield site rather than immersion in, or takeover of, existing operations; and size of the expatriate workforce contributed (again, the more the better). Given that the Singapore government invested directly and heavily through attaching its prestige to these projects, we do not consider non-capital investment here. As well, for each JV, the Singaporean partners sent over their own managers and professionals in large numbers, but somewhat proportional to relative project size. However, we focus primarily on crucial dimensions of the projects themselves including majority ownership and greenfield status.

China-Singapore Suzhou Industrial Park (SIP)

Introduction

At the end of 1998, Suzhou Municipality's 1.07 million urban residents were part of its permanent population of 5.75 million. By 2008, the figures were about 2.0 million and over 6.0 million respectively (Suzhou Municipality website n.d.). The two governments' initial JV discussions from 1992 led to three agreements in February 1994 establishing SIP, followed by the start of its physical establishment a few months later. Since then, SIP has become the largest, most expensive and important Singapore JV industrial park, and one of China's most famous and successful industrial parks.

The choice of Suzhou as the location came ahead of other contenders, including the more-industrialised Wuxi. A subsequent choice was to prefer a greenfield site on rural land to the east of Suzhou, explicitly rejecting an invitation to locate SIP in the Suzhou New District (SND), a large industrial estate that Suzhou's city administration had recently developed – and wholly-owned – on the city's west. All these choices and events – from planning to early development – directly and heavily involved the very highest levels of Singapore's government, from Lee Kuan Yew down, and of China's, including Deng Xiaoping's son, Deng Pufang and officials who were to rise to the very top, like future President, Jian Zeming and future Premier, Zhu Rongji. This engagement signalled the project's official prestige and priority to potential FIEs and officials in both JV countries (Memorandum 1999; Pereira 2003: 42-47, 73).

The choice of location indicated what both national governments wished SIP to be – and be seen as – a separate, and Singaporean initiative. It was to be physically, politically and culturally removed from local Chinese influences. In terms of the JV research literature (Bjoerkman and Lu 2001), this choice offered the SIP JV its best chance of maximising the desired influence of the foreign JV partner (Singapore's government) – rather than local institutional influences – on SIP's managerial structure and culture. At the same time, the choice to exclude Suzhou's local government authorities from most direct benefits from SIP's location and operations was to create problems for the JV later.

Other early choices indicated the intended exclusiveness of SIP, its dedication to quality and its JV purpose as a 'learning laboratory' for China's public sector. One was to exclude Chinese-owned companies from taking up residence in SIP. Another one was to steer SIP's marketing to attract FDI for advanced-level production from prestigious firms domiciled in Europe, North America, north-east Asia and Singapore. This was to avoid attracting smaller, cost-minimising, lower quality FIEs from Taiwan and Hong Kong then dominating FDI in SND and southern China. However, with SIP's administrative character well-established and a new SIP administration in place, since 2001 it has encouraged large scale FDI from the latter two sources. More recently too, SIP has also welcomed local Chinese companies (Pereira 2003: 45, 48, 54, 156).

Also, from conception SIP was to serve as a vehicle for Singapore to transfer, in Lee's words, Singapore's policy and administrative 'software', its governance 'operating system' (Pereira 2003: 47). SIP and Suzhou city officials were to gain from intensive formal learning and through extensive partnering with Singaporean counterparts, embracing their values and absorbing their technical knowledge and skills. In this manner local officials would be better prepared – technically and morally – and could then disseminate this software further across China's public sector through similar patterns of formal and informal learning. Thus, SIP was to provide a learning laboratory for Chinese officials from near and far (Inkpen and Pien 2006).

For its part, Beijing was also keen to trial – under Singapore government leadership and in a controlled environment – three aspects of social policy. The first two derived from Singapore's own model: a contributory employee welfare pension scheme that provided retirement income; and a large-scale, public housing construction scheme that would make housing available for rent or eventual private ownership. The third, a greatly relaxed work/residence permit system for China's internal migrants to SIP, was a suggestion from the Singaporean partner (Inkpen and Pien 2006; Pereira 2003).

Organisation, Planning and Overall Results

At the start, the Singapore consortium – with its government as largest contributor – was a 65 per cent shareholder, another important factor in maximising the potential for Singaporean knowledge transfer. China's consortium, composed of governments – national, provincial and local – and state-owned enterprises, held 35 per cent. Singapore's government financed SIP's land purchase and development, construction of its infrastructure and development of SIP's administration (Pereira 2007).

Planning and development, strategy formulation and administrative control have proceeded under a high level, bi-national partnership. Overall coordination of SIP has rested with the Joint Steering Committee, jointly chaired by China's Vice Premier and Singapore's Deputy Prime Minister. Under this body is the Joint Working Committee (JWC), chaired by the Mayor of Suzhou and the Chairman of the Singapore Economic Development Board.

In operating SIP, the JV partners established two bodies that report to the JWC and the Joint Steering Committee. The first, the China-Singapore Suzhou Industrial Park Development Company (CSSD), has had responsibility for project planning and the development of the park's land and physical infrastructure as well as its marketing abroad. The knowledge transferred represents highly contemporary public sector directions typical of advanced countries, including 'land-use planning and development control, environmental regulation, planning and management of industrial estates, new towns and public utilities management, and human resource management' (Inkpen and Pien 2006: 786).

SIP's largely high-end FIEs value the park's high quality infrastructure ahead of cost minimisation. This is important as SIP's founders never designed it to compete with rival parks on price. In terms of China's own infrastructure expectations, the greenfield location, away from SND, allowed for purpose-built water supply and sewerage services, steam and gas plants and toxic waste treatment, all to Singaporean specifications. Master planning of land and factory development is also of the highest, user-oriented standards. Particularly popular has been the development for lease, by the local subsidiary of Singapore's JTC, of ready-built factories of varying dimensions on a 'plug and play' basis. This allows MNEs to minimise their sunk costs while sampling the benefits of SIP or of locating FDI in China (Pereira 2003: 60-63). CSSD has been an important vehicle for the transfer of technical knowledge.

The main avenue for the full gamut of public sector 'software transfer' has been SIP Administrative Committee (SIPAC), SIP's local government authority. SIPAC administers five townships and the 186 square kilometres around SIP proper (Inkpen and Pien 2006: 791). Intending and actual FIEs appreciate SIP's 'Singapore way' administrative ambience, rather than China's traditionally personalised networks and opaque and unpredictable administrative processes. This minimises the risks facing MNEs and thus the need for establishing JVs as local 'insurance'. As an administrative 'one-stop shop', SIPAC's main operational roles are to ensure that clients receive a 'Singaporean' industrial park experience. Among SIPAC's responsibilities in support of its tenants' business activity has been labour recruitment through SIP's labour market management body, the Human Resources Development Co. Ltd (SIPHRD).

The Singapore side supported its financial involvement with substantial early transfers of Singaporean staff – temporary and shorter-term – from the highest levels down. This is another significant factor predicting successful knowledge transfer. Early synergies also developed, as planned, through the high numbers of officials China sent to Singapore for specialised training (Inkpen and Pien 2006; Wong and Goldblum 2000; Yeoh et al 2005). During SIP's early years, very senior Singaporeans headed both CSSD and SIPAC. Importantly, both organisations departed from Chinese practices by open advertisement of their middle and lower levels from across both countries, with selection by meritocratic criteria. SIPAC also encouraged SIP's FIEs to use similar recruitment practices as part of an overall transfer of westernised personnel practices (Pereira 2003).

The planning of SIP envisaged three distinct phases – starting with an 8 square kilometre Phase One – and culminating in a 70 square kilometre park that was to be an integrated, high quality hub for industrial, commercial, administrative, residential and recreational activities. Unusually, it has involved constructing purpose-built residential areas to house park employees. This has a commercial real estate aspect, utilising Singaporean expertise, that serves as a further attraction for FDI and managerial and skilled labour, involves knowledge transfer, and plays a role in public policy experimentation (SIPAC 2001-2008; Inkpen and Pien 2006; Pereira 2003 and 2007).

As planned, SIP only accepted FDI for more complex products and production technologies, thus establishing an image as innovative. During Phase One, FDI was overwhelmingly wholly-owned and concentrated in the electronics-related sector, elevating manufacturing in China in the international division of labour. Unsurprisingly, heavier establishment costs for higher quality infrastructure made SIP more expensive than local competitors. Pereira (2003) and Yeoh et al (2005) found that, for senior FIE managers in SIP, direct costs related to leasing land and buildings is a low-level issue. Rather, for existing and prospective FIEs, SIP provides a combination of low labour costs and very high standards of physical amenity and public administration. These have, as planned, been crucial to its longer term success.

As Pereira (2007) points out, SIP has been the most successful FDI destination in highly-developed Jiangsu Province. Yeoh et al (2005: 493) found FIE managers there 'exceptionally upbeat, with almost all the respondents intending to scale up their operations.' By mid 2008, SIP had some 3,300 FIEs – among which were subsidiaries of 77 Fortune 500 companies. Several had annual sales revenue above $US1 billion. According to SIPAC too, 80 per cent of companies operating in SIP for more than two years were profitable. In 2007, SIP's workforce was over 500,000 and its GDP of RMB 84 billion was 15 per cent of the Suzhou

Municipality total. Since starting, SIP activities had contributed more than RMB 70 billion in taxation (Pereira 2007: 296; SIPAC 16 January 2008; SIPAC website in English and Chinese versions, 2009; Song 2008).

Chronic shortages of professionals, managers and skilled production labour have been one of the few problems since the late 1990s that FIE senior managers reported to Yeoh et al (2005). Electronics-related firms, SIP's main industry group and its largest employers are most affected. Li and Sheldon (2008) found employer labour poaching and employee turnover among skilled operatives particularly worrisome for FIEs as they accentuate skilled shortages and raise labour costs.

Qualitative results have also been impressive. First, FIEs in SIP – whether existing or newly arrived – display increasing technological and technical sophistication. One indicator has been many MNEs' readiness to bring their R&D facilities and SIP has further developed its infrastructure and other facilities to attract them. Most recently, SIP management has dramatically elevated the park's technological status and role by developing four new 'demonstration zones' – meaning that they lead rather than follow innovation elsewhere. One is an ecological demonstration zone focused on reaching high level environmental sustainability targets across workplaces, schools and housing. Another is a technological demonstration zone to further attract world-class high-tech and R&D initiatives. A third zone is for commercial and international trade logistics operations, and the fourth for major MNEs dedicated to services outsourcing, a relatively new initiative in China compared to say, India. The intention is to rapidly and massively increase the number and size of high-end tertiary sector or services FIEs in SIP, as well as aspire to be a hub of regional headquarters for large MNEs (SIPAC 4 and16 January 2008).

In addition, Pereira (2003), Yeoh et al (2005) and Inkpen and Pien (2006) all found solid evidence of successful transfer of technical knowledge and administrative software. FIE managers hail the speed, transparency, predictability and helpfulness of CSSD and SIPAC processes. They like the absence of corruption, emphasis on quality and dedication to problem solving at individual and organisational levels. Finally, as planned, SIP has become a learning laboratory and site for experimentation for China's public sector, providing diverse mechanisms for software transfer to other park administrations and China's wider bureaucracy. Given the aims set it, SIP has been enormously successful.

Along the way, SIP management has confronted challenges and conflicts. Financial problems from the East Asian crisis delayed development of subsequent phases. In mid-1999, Singapore's government announced it would sell down its stake to 35 per cent and, in January 2001, it transferred lead management of SIP to its Chinese partners headed by Suzhou's city administration. SIP now came under a senior local official who also oversaw Suzhou New District. However, knowledge transfer was embedded in SIP's operations, Singaporean officials remain involved – albeit to a much lesser degree – and the new administration maintains the Singaporean style and feel.

Researchers have different explanations for these ownership changes. For some, the changes result from a combination of organisational and political tensions flowing from perceptions of breaches of commercial trust. Misunderstandings and feelings of betrayal from the Singaporean side created friction between the partners right up the level of Lee Kuan Yew (Yeoh et al 2005) - the main problem being that Suzhou's city government, a crucial but financially marginalised part of the Chinese consortium, was using knowledge and MNE contacts gained through SIP to advance its own SND at SIP's expense. Offering similar sorts of services but at substantially reduced prices, SND attracted away potential SIP tenants. SIP's occupancy and employment levels fell short of targets, its revenue stream from leasing property lagged expectations, and the controlling JV continued to run at a loss. In fact, most of the losses accrued to the Singapore government. However, once majority ownership and control passed to the Chinese side, most problems appeared to soon fade, and within a couple of years, SIP registered its first profit (Inkpen and Pien 2006; Yeoh et al 2005).

Within a similar narrative of underhand behaviour, Pereira (2003, 2007) prefers to stress the interaction of financial, political and organisational factors. Given the Asian crisis, SIP's unprofitability encouraged similar Singaporean responses in its other regional parks. He also suggests that Singapore's government prioritised the political and the longer term – particularly inter-governmental relations with Beijing – over its more immediate commercial interests in SIP. The move to minority status reduces misunderstandings with local Chinese officials and, paradoxically – given China's decentralised strategic economic administration – potentially with the central government. Further, the Singaporean side, for all its commitment and goodwill to the project, underestimated aspects of 'institutional distance' between it and Suzhou's local administrators, generating perceptions of it as arrogant and uncooperative. As questions of 'face' lost or not given emerged, aspects of cultural distance between cultural 'false friends' reinforced local administrators' perceptions that promoting the city's wholly-owned SND ahead of SIP advanced their own best interests and those of Suzhou city (Periera 2003: 134-39). Thus, the original choices of majority Singaporean ownership and greenfield locations facilitated rapid and fulsome software transfer. However, the (inevitable) institutional distance created severe tensions within the JV. Resolution came through changing ownership and control which, in turn, reduced institutional distance but only after the Singaporean model was well established.

Wuxi Singapore Industrial Park (WSIP)

Introduction

Located 50 kilometres west of Suzhou and 130 from Shanghai, Wuxi city covers almost 5,000 square kilometres, including two county cities and several districts. In 2006, its population of 5.8 million included over 2.5 million urban residents. Its labour force, of just over 3 million, included 365,400 technical personnel (Wuxi China 2007: 6, 8, 22, 32, 88).

Announced in 1992 and formalized through agreement in late 1993, Wuxi Singapore Industrial Park (WSIP) formally opened in June 1996. Like SIP, it has focused on hi-tech industries. WSIP began as a JV between Chinese and Singaporean consortia in which the Wuxi Municipal Government and a major Singapore GLC, Sembcorp, were the dominant parties. Once again, the Singaporean side was the majority JV partner, and by a substantial margin, an important predictor for successful knowledge transfer (Pereira 2003; Sembcorp 2002).

Singapore's government at that time directly held 53.1 per cent of Sembcorp and Temasek Holdings – itself, a major government holding company – held the rest (Sembcorp 2007). Like many GLCs, the Singaporean government had established Sembcorp in the 1960s to provide vital state services and production - in this case, dockyard and marine services. By the early 1990s, Sembcorp had significantly restructured, diversifying and developing expertise in engineering, utilities and large-scale infrastructure projects (Zutshi and Gibbons 1998; Yeoh, How and Leong 2005).

In contrast to SIP, whose JV partners chose to locate away from the existing SND, the WSIP JV partners agreed to establish their park in the Wuxi New District (WND). Like SND, WND had opened a couple of years earlier under local government ownership and control. This choice was to have important consequences in Wuxi as did the SIP decision in Suzhou; in Wuxi, the local economy and local government gained much larger direct shares of WSIP-generated economic activity, for example, through local taxes. Through its location within WND, WSIP contributed directly and substantially to WND's own development and commercial success. As well, WSIP was able to generate technological and commercial spillover effects in the context of less politicized and conflictual JV relations. Yet, according to the JV literature, this choice of location and entry promised a reduced likelihood for effective software transfer than at SIP, because these factors weakened the likely Singaporean influence on WSIP practices. Tacit knowledge transfer and, in particular, social experimentation apparently had a lower priority in WSIP than in SIP and expectations were for more limited transfer in terms of breadth and depth.

Planning, Organization and Overall Results

The plan for WSIP was to develop a service-oriented, hi-tech industrial estate that would provide its client companies with operational inputs – such as communications and utilities infrastructure – well as administrative services. It was to unfold over three phases and, ultimately, include approximately 1000 hectares of business facilities. This made it substantially smaller than SIP (Yeung 2000, 828; SembCorp Industries 2002). As at SIP, later stages suffered delays in the wake of the Asian financial crisis.

WSIP has furnished Chinese provincial and municipal governments with a range of opportunities. There is the planned opportunity for knowledge transfer in design, operation and management of industrial parks, a developmental priority for Wuxi's local government. The JV itself has offered marketing opportunities in the form, once again, of high-level, central government support from both countries, providing a strong tool for recruiting FIEs. As has been the case, the Singaporean reputation for excellence in infrastructure development is evident. In WSIP too, the Singaporean side took responsibility for infrastructure development of utilities, communications, factories and commercial premises and housing. This met another primary policy objective for Wuxi's local government: development of a broader base of economic activity, and its social effects.

The Park's management structure and culture encouraged the park's commercial success. As at SIP, organizational design divided the park's development and marketing from its planning, sales, control and administrative functions. Development and marketing were the responsibility of WSDC. Governance and administration of the park came through the Wuxi-Singapore Industrial Park Development Company (WSIPDC). Although formally derived from the Singaporean consortium, senior park management has strongly focused its activities on the operational requirements of the park and, in particular, on attracting and servicing FIEs. In doing this, it was more successful than SIP in addressing the concerns and objectives of its local partner, the Wuxi Municipal Government.

This points to another factor in WSIP's commercial success: governance. In contrast to SIP's early administrative strategy, WSIPDC has closely involved the WND partner in decision-making on key issues that affected Wuxi local government and its interests. Further, in contrast to many other industrial park JVs, in practice WSIPDC has involved only the two main partners – Sembcorp and WND – who both possess authority to make committed and independent decisions directed to WSIP's operational performance. This minimises the need for negotiations *within* each consortium and provides a better context for inter-JV partner sensitivity and trust. Together, these factors have facilitated individual and organizational learning as well as behaviours that reduce rather than exacerbate institutional distance – particularly normative distance – between the Singaporean and Chinese sides.

WSIP was already very commercially effective prior to the Asian financial crisis. Within three years, with more than 35 FIEs in the park, its occupancy rate was 70 per cent (Yeung 2000: 828; Lau and Bruton 2008: 32, Fig 1). Less than a decade later, there were 75 FIEs in WSIP with contracted capital of over $US2 billion and paid-up capital of $US1.6 billion, much of it from leading MNEs. More than 30 enterprises had each committed over $US10 million in investment. WSIP directly accounted for more than 40,000 jobs and exports of more than $US4 billion, almost one-fifth of Wuxi city region's total exports (Yeung 2000: 828; Wuxi China 2007: 46).

The Park's sponsors, partners and clients deemed its early development to be successful, in quality and quantity. Alongside its commercial achievements, WSIP became the first industrial park in China to achieve ISO9001 quality certification (Chan 2006) and, for three successive years, Corporate Location UK rated it – among 25 in the Asia-Pacific region – as the Best Technology Industrial Park in terms of investment conditions (WSIP 2009). Not surprisingly, a senior WSIP executive identified the 'Singapore label' as a key strength of the park's 'brand' (cited in Yeung 2000: 828).

There were important symbolic returns for the WND too. WSIP contributed significantly to the top ranking that WND achieved among China's 54 high-tech zones (Wuxi 2007: 86). Apart from the commercial marketing kudos involved, this was important political capital for the local government and its officials. Visits from senior political leaders also kept WSIP's public prominence alive and raised the profile of Wuxi City and its officials.

Nonetheless, here too the effects of the Asian financial crisis appear to have spurred the Singaporean partner to pass majority ownership and control to the local partner. In Wuxi, this shift came later – through a May 2002 agreement – perhaps because WSIP had not suffered those JV problems which had commercially and politically compromised the SIP experiment. The Singaporean stake fell from 54.8 percent to 38.5 per cent, WND took majority ownership, it released a further 183.6 hectares of prepared land to the park and transferred 25 per cent of the equity in the Wuxi Garden City Mall Hotel Co. to add to the 70 per cent the Singaporean partner group already owned.

SembCorp Industries Group Chief Operations Officer, Ms Low Sin Leng, explained the need for these shifts as due to increasing competition amongst parks in China. She noted:

> The transfer of the majority shareholding and the management of the Wuxi-Singapore Industrial Park to the Wuxi Municipal Government would result in better alignment of interests and improved operating efficiency of the park .... The partners' common goal is the long-term growth and success of the Wuxi-Singapore Industrial Park (quoted in SembCorp Industries 2002).

The 'alignment of interests' resonates with the discourse at SIP indicating pressures from the local government for greater control and share of JV financial benefits. The emphasis on long-term success also suggests the Singaporeans' priority of maintaining good government-to-government relations in China and maintaining privileged access for Singaporean companies in Wuxi's dynamic economy. If in SIP the Singaporean government placed politics ahead of commerce, in the case of WSIP the Singaporean party appears to have prioritized longer-term commercial relationships over immediate financial returns.

Management of Phase 1 (1994-2002) thus came under the Singaporean partner in close cooperation with local government. This facilitated deployment and transfer of Singaporean knowledge and management skills to local managers and professionals within WSIP and, in particular, to those working for SWIPDC. The transfer of equity and management responsibility marked the move to Phase 2 (2002-2006). The focus, for Wuxi municipal government – now WSIP's major shareholder and controlling party – shifted to consolidating this local expertise and diffusing it across Wuxi's other technology parks. Phase 3 commenced in 2007, some four years behind schedule. It continued the emphasis on servicing tenants, but accelerated development of logistic, property, commercial and civil real estate (WSIP 2009).

Wuxi New District provided a framework for WSIP and for the relationship between Singaporean and local JV partners. In turn, the JV's success ensured continuing national government support for the region in building expertise in park development and management. By 2006, WSIP was a major contributor to WND, over-fulfilling major economic targets. Indeed economic activity in WND in 2006 exceeded that of Wuxi city as a whole a decade earlier (Wuxi China 2007: 86). The provision of infrastructure and expanded local taxation receipts afforded the local government greater political benefits and greater legitimacy.

In WSIP, Singaporean JV participation was thus more perceptive in recognizing literal demands of *political* economy. In the five years after the transfer of formal ownership in 2002, WSIP's contribution to local prosperity helped Wuxi government tax income more than double. Similar improvements in education, income and housing stock (Wuxi 2007: 58-72) raised the political standing of the local government. This pattern of expansion also provides – as Lee imagined – significantly expanded longer-term, bi-lateral business opportunities. For example, in 2005, the Wuxi local government established a Representative Office in Singapore providing access for Wuxi-based firms to timely market information and international business contacts. Of seven Wuxi overseas-listed enterprises in 2006, four were listed in Singapore (of a total of 87 Singapore-listed Chinese firms) (Chan 2006). Bilateral relations also open access to capital, services and networks for Wuxi firms. In turn, Singaporean firms receive facilitated access to Wuxi: in 2005, total investment in more than 50 projects reached almost half a billion US dollars (Chan 2006).

However, despite its Singapore-inspired, high quality infrastructure and administration, the WSIP project appears not to have generated the same depth or breadth of administrative 'software transfer' as in SIP. Technical and technocratic administrative knowledge transfer appears to have been successful. Some evidence indicates that the experiment falls short of SIP in the transfer and absorption of more profound and tacit learning, including those attitudes necessary for a more meritocratic and 'clean' administrative culture. In line with expectations from the JV literature more generally (Björkman and Lu 2001), WSIP's rules, routines and, perhaps mostly importantly, its administrative norms appear closer to local

Chinese ones than those in Singapore (Periera 2003: 91). Between the JV consortia, both normative and cognitive distance are lower than was true in SIP and the commercial orientation of partners succeeded in 'translating' some of the less challenging Singaporean 'software' into local forms. The original decision to locate the park within the WND, and the close, active engagement with Wuxi local government combined in a mimetic isomorphism of WSIP that was closer to other (and adjacent) industrial parks, which had no Singaporean influence. These mechanisms succeeded in reducing institutional distance between WSIP management and the local partner, but at the cost of reducing the degree of Singaporean tacit knowledge transfer compared to SIP.

Dalian Container Terminal Co. Ltd (DCT)

Introduction

Dalian in Northeast China, one hour's flight east of Beijing, has an administrative area with over 6 million people and an urban population of 2.6 million. Its strategic location and deep harbour have helped make it a valuable, major transhipment port, handling inter-modal cargo, and international trade, to and from China's industrial North-east and its population of some 200 million. Dalian's early experience in heavy industry – particularly ship-building and rail stock – brought physical infrastructure. In the 1970s, Dalian developed as an oil refining centre and it is now China's largest petroleum port. Dalian also grew through attracting manufacturing FIEs to the Dalian Development Zone. Additional economic zones have broadened the city's economic base, most recently to include the IT industry. By 2006, the port had become the seventh largest in China in terms of tonnage shipped, and the fifteen largest in the world (AAPA 2006).

Planning, Organization and Overall Results

In 1996, PSA Corporation Ltd, a major Singaporean GLC and global leader in container port operations, formed a port operations JV – Dalian Container Terminal Co. Ltd (DCT) – with the local Port Authority of Dalian. The latter was then owned by Dalian's municipal government, while PSA Corporation is wholly owned by Temasek. From the beginning, the local partner (PDA) has been the majority owner, with 51 per cent, while a Singapore consortium – of which PSA holds 71 per cent – has held the rest (*Asia Times* 19 April 1996).

Like SIP and WSIP, DCT formed part of Singapore's regionalisation strategy. However, whereas the earlier projects focused on manufacturing FIEs supported by high quality logistics, the Dalian project specialised much more narrowly on transportation and logistics. For PSA, DCT was its flagship project in China and a test case for its own overseas expansion plans (*Business Times* 19 April 1996). As in SIP and WSIP, success has been very crucial to diverse stakeholders, including the Singapore and Chinese governments.

The DCT JV was, at its founding, the third largest area of FDI in Dalian. A 'market-seeking' FDI initiative, the establishment of DCT as a transhipment hub for Northeast China aimed at attracting regional markets for transhipment volume overseas. Since then, it has received frequent positive publicity as well as high levels of approval from the Chinese government for a number of reasons. First, PSA Corporation has an excellent international reputation for successfully running its own 'home' transhipment operations, one of the world's busiest, most efficient, and technologically-advanced ports. With China's explosive emergence as a global trading power, Chinese coastal ports have been expanding rapidly. Through DCT, PSA has been a highly valued source of specialised knowledge-transfer for Chinese container port management and technology.

The PSA's knowledge transfer in DCT was in three important areas: organisation structure; technology transfer; and other managerial software. We discuss each of these in turn. Alongside its strong commercial orientation, the main purpose of the JV's organisation structure has been knowledge transfer; to capitalise on the port managing experience of the PSA's appointees. The Chinese partner is the majority JV shareholder and both PSA and Dalian Port Authority nominees sit on the JV board. Nevertheless, in its early years, the five key DCT managers – General Manager, Chief Accountant, Terminal Manager, Engineering Manager and IT Manager – were PSA appointees, while their deputies were all Chinese partner appointees. Chinese officials now hold all the main roles with a few Singaporeans as deputies (*South China Morning Post* 13 June 1996; Pillai 2005).

The focus of knowledge transfer for DCT has been much more specialised, explicit and technical than at SIP or even WSIP. Development of DCT has not involved building new towns, urban facilities, utilities or housing, nor in providing administrative services for a large number of FIEs located *in situ*. In terms of physical infrastructure, the Singapore partner was confined to providing a staged expansion of berths, wharf facilities and associated machinery at an existing, outdated port facility. That is, it provided a large, technologically sophisticated enterprise and workplace. This has shaped expectations and processes of knowledge transfer.

At the heart of PSA's technological capabilities and knowledge transfer are two major pieces of PSA proprietary technology – Portnet and CITOS – which integrate operations for optimal efficiency. Portnet, a one-stop IT system, connects DCT online with Chinese Customs authorities, shipping lines, warehouse operators and freight forwarders. CITOS I is PSA's first generation, automated container terminal management system. Through CITOS, control room operators can manage and direct operations. Examples are tracking the location and movements of each container and providing instructions to all port equipment electronically, online. These systems enable: ship stowage planners to electronically plan discharging and loading before the container vessels arrive; berth planners to allocate the appropriate berth and levels of container handling equipment to individual vessels ahead of time; yard stowage planners to plan the sequence of stacking at the container yard; and finally, gate operators to control traffic movement (*Straits Times* 22 September 2000).

Third, PSA transferred Singaporean labour management relations – based on notions of harmony through consultation and collaboration – albeit modified for local conditions. In practice, this has meant management working closely with the DCT union chairman. During the years when one co-author was a DCT manager, the union chairman was also the Communist Party's representative within DCT. Management confers on the union chairman a wide variety of roles, to ensure his participation across areas pertaining to workers' welfare and wellbeing. For example, the official presides over DCT's safety committees and investigates safety-related cases including near-misses. As well as that, DCT uses PSA's shift-based, container or 'box' rate incentive schemes to motivate employees to exceed output targets and maintain safety standards.

DCT was commercially successful within a short time. In 1999, it announced a record container throughput of 628,471 container units, a year-on-year growth of 32 per cent (Pillai 2005: 41; *Shipping Times* 29 December 1999). That year, it also received multiple awards, including the 'Best Emerging Container Terminal' at the Lloyd's List Maritime Asia Awards (Lloyd's List 18 November 1999); 'Best Container (High Efficient Operations)' from the *China Shipping Gazette* at the China Freight Industry Awards and 'Best Container Terminal in Mainland China' by *Cargo News Asia* (PSA 1999). It continues to be an important transhipment hub with a designed annual throughput capacity of 1.15 million units (Cullinane, Wang and Cullinane 2004: 46; SinoCast *Chinese Business Daily News*, 21 May 2008). Building on DCT's successes, PSA has expanded into port-management JVs in other Chinese ports including, since 2004, as a 25 per cent partner in a new JV port facility adjacent to DCT (Lloyd's List 23 October 2000; Lloyd's List 27 October 2000; Dalian Port Container Terminal website 2009).

At a qualitative level, the JV appears to have matched Chinese expectations by delivering the expected knowledge transfer, although this was of a much more limited and technical kind and less related to core public sector activities. These more restricted ambitions made it easier to collaborate and removed some of the potential institutional distance most evident in SIP. There were five main reasons for this. From the start, PSA allowed its Chinese partners to be majority shareholders in recognition that this would align local vested interests – organisational revenues, credit and face – with the JV's success.

Second, DCT's management centred more on purely technical and operational issues. Given the very limited public administration remit for DCT relative to SIP and WSIP, this reduced the risk that institutional distance – in an active sense – would generate a sense of cultural distance. Third, PSA appointees never took for granted the apparent cultural closeness with their Chinese 'shadowing' staff counterparts but were careful to emphasise respect, status and other Chinese protocols even towards Chinese managers who were formally their subordinates. This reduced the risk ambiguities that might have fostered misunderstanding and mistrust. Fourth, the gradual transfer of Portnet and CITOS as container volumes grew allowed time for local shipping communities, DCT staff and government agencies to adjust. Finally, the relationship between management and the union chairman has encouraged maintenance of harmonious industrial relations.

CONCLUSION

We find that transfer of business, organisational and technical knowledge and administrative 'software' has encouraged the commercial successes of the three public sector, profit-seeking JVs, all of which are now under majority Chinese ownership and control. In regard to Chinese objectives, the initial Singaporean-dominated JV management bodies embedded the desired Singaporean elements relative to each project. While the SIP and WSIP ownership changeovers came earlier than envisaged, their outcomes matched DCT. For the three projects therefore, JV knowledge transfer within the public sector has facilitated similar outcomes to those in the private sector. Unsurprisingly, these JVs have successfully met the expectations of the Chinese side/s.

Nevertheless, these achievements have not come without stresses, particularly where a prime goal has been transfer of tacit knowledge regarding public administration. In retrospect, this is not surprising given the findings of the intersecting literatures on JVs, China and knowledge transfer. Moreover, as Inkpen and Pien (2006: 785) conclude from the SIP experience, these types of public sector JVs are unique, 'involving multiple partner levels, cross-border knowledge transfer, knowledge transfer mechanisms, cross-cultural issues, and both cooperative and competitive partner behaviour.'

The story of this chapter suggests the following conclusions. First, narrower and less complex JV consortia make for easier JV operations. The central feature of the cases, over more than a dozen years of operations, is the nature or *type* of JV project (see Table 1). Large, complex projects, as in SIP, encounter greater difficulties than more limited, commercially oriented projects, as in WSIP, or projects for technical transfer, as in the case of DCT. Where a project is, by design, a national 'laboratory', and intended to focus commercial expertise and governance software at the national level, the burden in partner relations is large. Second, having multiple JV partners increases the number of stakeholders and the diffusion of vested interests. The risks of interest misalignment, for both *intra*- and *inter*- partner relations, were far higher for SIP. Misalignment occurred between China's national and local governments, as well as in Singaporean assumptions of national political efficacy. More limited commercial and technical projects, with a regional and local focus, and concentrated intra-partner authority – as for WSIP and DCT – made it easier to achieve cooperative inter-partner relations. Third, knowledge transfer in technical knowledge and techniques, as well as in more explicit business, organisational and administrative knowledge, displays lower transmission thresholds than 'software' embedded in governance and administrative norms and attitudes. These conclusions point to a more fundamental concern.

There may be irreconcilable difficulties for the more ambitious forms of cross-border public sector knowledge transfer of the type discussed here. These difficulties stem from apparent contradictions in managing the tensions between institutional distance (Wu and Shenkar 2002) – as well as the sense of cultural distance it can apparently provoke – and factors that Bjoerkman and Lu (2001) identify as significant predictors of in-bound transfer of managerial practices through JVs.

For Beijing, an important goal for SIP, in particular, and to a lesser extent for WSIP, was to expose local officials to the wide normative distance between themselves and those inherent in the Singaporean model, so as to effect change through learning. This remains an aim for the very recent JVs. Nevertheless, the literature suggests that this distance also creates greater difficulties for knowledge transfer, particularly as Chinese representatives from local government have their career development linked to the local institutional environment.

Which elements of JV design and operation overcome these challenges and allow knowledge transfer across wide institutional distances? One obvious lesson from these JVs is to remove incentives and opportunities for the local partner to exploit the foreign JV partner, as occurred in SIP's early years. As Inkpen and Pien (2006: 805) note, the literature suggests that, 'competitive behaviour for private gains will occur if there are asymmetric collaborative incentives'. On the other hand, those very elements that appear to have encouraged this exploitative behaviour – such as a greenfield site and (large) majority Singaporean ownership in SIP – are critical for inbound knowledge transfer, as shown in Björkman and Lu's (2001) research. In contrast, WSIP was not a greenfield site but nor, apparently, has it achieved the ambitious goals of transfer of values and norms expected for SIP. For Dalian, neither greenfield nor majority Singaporean-owned, expectations in this regard were much lower.

If choices of organisational ownership structure and location strategy suggest contradictory indications, does the answer lie in cross-cultural awareness and trust beyond institutional patterns? Lau and Bruton (2008: 36) summarise the literature on knowledge transfer in JVs thus: 'trust between partners aids in the development of knowledge … and cultural understanding facilitates learning'. In SIP, however, Singaporean-style meritocratic control over SIPAC's recruitment processes, as planned, introduced a new cohort of public officials *unconnected* to the local JV partner. This remained a sign of mistrust for local government and its politics. At the same time, it represented an essential, and perhaps the 'most tacit', aspect of the Singaporean model, and was thus necessary for the fullest transfer. It was this *necessary* lack of trust towards its own local officials that lay behind Beijing's commitment to SIP as a social laboratory for Chinese public administration and policy.

Table 1. China-Singapore Government to Government Case-Study Dimensions

	Project Case		
Dimension	SIP	WSIP	DCT
Project			
Type	'laboratory'/development	Commercial/development	technical/commercial
Focus	national/local	regional/local	local
Location	greenfield, away from SND	established local at WND	established local port; regional business
Scope	commercial, infrastructure & extensive governance/ administrative	commercial; medium-level infrastructure; limited governance	knowledge/ technical transfer; limited infrastructure
Intended Knowledge Transfer	Public policy/ administrative; commercial	Commercial; public administration	Technical; commercial
Ownership Pattern *Start-up (PRC/SG)*	one third/two-thirds	one third/two-thirds	majority owner 51/49
Partner relations			
Intra-partner	multiple	Concentrated	concentrated
Inter-partner	diffused	co-operative	co-operative
Project Outcome (at)	**2007-8**	**2006-7**	**2006-7**
Ownership (PRC cf SG)	majority two-thirds 7 years	majority > two-thirds 9 years	majority - initial
Commercial features	initial higher cost, high quality, slow then accelerated growth; 3,300 FIEs	strong initial and on-going growth; 'reputational' effects; local govt trade office Sg; local firms listing in Sg	strong technical transfer; increased traffic; trans-shipment growth
Transfer (content)	expertise; quality public administration; demonstration zones	expertise; quality; technology parks	expertise; technical quality; national extension
Tacit transfer (extent)	strong/successful; transparency, speed, quality etc	limited in scope; lower normative distance	limited to technical, and limited labour mgt system
Infrastructure (extent)	strong contribution; very broad	strong contribution; broad	facility contribution; phased in berth & wharf equipment
Revenue (local)	strong contribution	strong contribution	limited contribution

REFERENCES

[1] AAPA (2006). American Association of Port Authorities World's Port Rankings 2006, www.aapa-orts.org/Industry/content.cfm?ItemNumber=900&navItemNumber=551, Accessed 14th January 2009.

[2] *Asia Times* (19 April 2006). Singapore Calls on Dalian. Factiva Database, Accessed 14th January 2009.

[3] Baark, E. (2007). Knowledge and innovation in China: Historical legacies and emerging institutions. *Asia Pacific Business Review, 13* (3), 337-356.

[4] Björkman, I., & Lu, Y. (2001). Institutionalization and bargaining power explanations of HRM practices in international joint ventures--the case of Chinese--Western joint ventures. *Organization Studies*, *22* (3): 491-512.

[5] *Business Times* (19 April 2006), PSA in Berth Deals with China, Factiva Database downloaded on 14th January 2009.

[6] Cullinane, K., Wang, T.F., & Cullinane, S. (2004). Container terminal development in mainland China and its impact on the competitiveness of the port of Hong Kong', *Transport Reviews*, *24* (1), 33-56.

[7] Eisenhardt, K.M. (1991). Better stories and better constructs: The case for rigor and comparative logic. *Academy of Management Review, 16*, 620-627.

[8] Lau, C.M., & Bruton, G.D. (2008). FDI in China: What we know and what we need to study next. *Academy of Management Perspectives*, *22* (4): 30-44.

[9] Inkpen, A.C., & Pien, W. (2006). An examination of collaboration and knowledge transfer: China-Singapore Suzhou Industrial Park. *Journal of Management Studies*, *43* (4), 779-811.

[10] Li, Y., & Sheldon, P. (2008), 'Employers' experiences of shortages of skilled workers in Suzhou Industrial Park, China', Refereed Stream, *Third Conference of the International Association for Chinese Management Research (IACMR)*, Guangzhou, China, 19-22 June.

[11] Liu, L. (2008). Local government and big business in the People's Republic of China – Case study evidence from Shandong province. *Asia Pacific Business Review, 14* (4), 473-489.

[12] Lloyd's List (19 November 1999). Maritime Award – Top Honour for IMC Chief, Factiva Database, accessed 14th January 2009.

[13] Lloyd's List (23 October 2000). PSA Corp Builds on Its Great Wall of Success in China, Factiva Database, accessed 14th January 2009.

[14] Lloyd's List (27 October 2000). PSA itself to China in the long Term, Factiva Database downloaded on 14th January 2009.

[15] 'Memorandum of Understanding by the Chinese and Singapore Teams on Suzhou Industrial Park's Development' (1999), unpub., Singapore, 28 June.

[16] Nonaka, I. (1994). A Dynamic Theory of Organizational Knowledge Creation. *Organizational Science*, *5* (1), 14-37.

[17] Pereira, A.A. (2003). *State Collaboration and Development Strategies in China: The Case of the China-Singapore Suzhou Industrial Park, 1992-2002*. Curzon: Routledge.

[18] Pereira, A.A. (2007). Transnational state entrepreneurship? Assessing Singapore's Suzhou Industrial Park project. *Asia Pacific Viewpoint*, *48* (3), 287-298.

[19] Pillai, J.S. (2005). Service exports from a small city-state: The case of port authority of Singapore, *Discussion Papers on Policy and Governance, Asia Pacific School of Economics and Government, Australian National University*, 1-53.

[20] PSA (1999). *Annual Report of PSA*. Singapore: PSA.

[21] Redding, G. (2002). The capitalist business system of China and its rationale. *Asia Pacific Journal of Management, 19,* 221-249.

[22] Redding, G., & Witt, M.A. (2006). The 'tray of loose sand': A thick description of the state-owned enterprise sector of China seen as a business system. *Asian Business and Management, 5,* 87-112.

[23] Sembcorp (2008). Sembcorp signs master agreement for new integrated industrial township project in Guangxi, China. *Industrial Park News/Media Release*. 22 October. http://www.sembcorp.com/sembcorp/news_parks_detail.aspx?NewsID=716, Accessed 11 January 2009.

[24] Shipping Times (29 December 1999). PSA's Dalian Terminal Aims to Attract More Feeder Cargo, Factiva Database, downloaded 14th January 2009.

[25] *SinoCast Chinese Business Daily News* (21 May 2008). Transhipment System Around Bohai Sea to Start Operations in June, Factiva Database downloaded on 14th January 2009.

[26] SIPAC (2001). Great Achievements Sum up Seven Years' Development. http://www.sipac.gov.cn/sipac_e/news/news_sip_01_0518.htm, accessed 7 September 2001.

[27] SIPAC Development (n.d.) *Development Review*, http://www.sipac.gov.cn/sipac_e/development.htm, accessed 7 September 2001 (now available on www.sipac.gove.cn).

[28] SIPAC (2008), SIP Sets Goals for Next Round of Development. *SIPAC Media Release*, 4 January, http://www.sipac.gov.cn/english/news/200801/t20080106_24833.htm, accessed 7 February 2009.

[29] SIPAC (2008). SIP to Become a "New Model" of Restructuring for China's Development Zones, *SIPAC Media Release*, 16 January. http://www.sipac.gov.cn/english/news/200801/t20080119_26492.htm Accessed 7 February 2009.

[30] SIPAC Profile (2009). http://www.sipac.gov.cn/english/sipprofile/200901/t20090116_36701.htm, Accessed 7 February 2009.

[31] Song, W. (2008). *China Daily*, 24 September (see also www.sipac.gov.cn).

[32] South China Morning Post (13 June 1996). Dalian Seeks Role As Leading Northeast Deep-Water Port, *Factiva Database*, Accessed 14th January 2009.

[33] Straits Times (22 September 2000). Dalian Ports Use PSA System. *Factiva Database,* accessed 14th January 2009.

[34] Wong, T.-C., & Goldblum, C. (2000). The China-Singapore Suzhou Industrial Park: A turnkey product of Singapore? *Geographical Review, 90* (1), 112-122.

[35] Xu, D., & Shenkar, O. (2002). Institutional Distance and the Multinational Enterprise. *Academy of Management Review*, *27* (4), 608-614.

[36] Yangtze Evening Daily (2008). China and Singapore in Second Hand-shake: To Duplicate "SIP" in Nantong. SIPAC, 2 December 2008,

http://www.sipac.gov.cn/english/news/200812/t20081203_34977.htm, accessed 7 February 2009.

[37] Yeoh, C., How, W., & Leong, A.I. (2005). Created enclaves for enterprise: An empirical study of Singapore's industrial parks in Indonesia, Vietnam and China. *Entrepreneurship and Regional Development*, *17* (6), 479-499.

In: Thirty Years of China's Economic Reform
Editors: Yue Wang and Prem Ramburuth
ISBN: 978-1-60876-908-7
© 2010 Nova Science Publishers, Inc.

Chapter 4

CONTEMPORARY ENTREPRENEURS IN SOUTH CHINA: A DISCUSSION OF THEIR INDIVIDUAL VALUES

Romie Littrell*[1] and Elisabeth P. Montgomery+[2]
[1]AUT Business School, Auckland University of Technology, Auckland, New Zealand
[2]Regional General Manager - Pacific Rim, InterLangua.com

ABSTRACT

In this study we compare the individual cultural values of samples of two types of entrepreneurs with a random sample of businesspeople in South China, i.e. Guangzhou and Shenzhen. Our findings indicate that the individual cultural values of the types of businesspeople from 2004 and 2005 samples are similar, and are different from results of studies conducted in the mid-1990s. Our results lead to the expectation that, when engaging with businesspeople in South China in the Guangdong Province coastal regions, we can expect, based upon the average characteristics of our samples and compared to other sectors of society, that they are on average less adherant to tradition, value self-direction and indicate an openness to innovation. But they still express typical values of conformity, benevolence and universalism, are achievement oriented, value security highly, and perhaps see the business sector as a path to enhancement of personal and family security.

Keywords: Chinese private enterprise, Chinese entrepreneurship, China, Individual Cultural Values, Schwartz Values Survey

---

* Email: romie.littrell@aut.ac.nz.

INTRODUCTION

In this study we investigate how individual cultural values of randomly selected businesspeople and entrepreneurs vary in South China. We contend that from a social anthropological viewpoint the success of private enterprise is rooted in China's traditional society. For centuries, China's businesses operated as family-based entities across the country. The Communist collectivization efforts against this tradition in the 1950s and 1960s were economically disruptive and finally disastrous, which led to society embracing the modern day Communist Party of China's (CPC) definition of new market socialism when it revised its economic policies in the 1980s. Recently the CPC model of Chinese capitalism is studied extensively around the world, noting elements containing Confucian values that coexist in the modern landscape of economic, social and cultural ecologies. We frame this discussion in the regional context of Guangdong Province due to its mix of traditional and modern Chinese business tendencies. Our approach is the analysis and discussion of values using the Schwartz Values Survey (SVS) to study businesses and entrepreneurs in Guangdong.

Huang (2008) points out that "…many Western economists think China has discovered its own road to prosperity, dependent largely on state financing and control. They are quite wrong". In fact, Huang's research covering the 1980s and 1990s indicates that improved property rights and private entrepreneurship provided the dominant stimulus for high growth and lower levels of poverty in China since 1979. What actually happened is that early local experiments with financial liberalization and private ownership in the 1980s generated an initial burst of rural entrepreneurialism. Those earlier gains, not the massive state-led infrastructure investments and urbanization drive of the 1990s, laid the true foundation for the Chinese miracle. In fact, the city-oriented programmes of the 1990s led to stagnation in new business development by Chinese.

We review the available studies of the individual value dimensions of Chinese businesspeople, particularly entrepreneurs, and compare the values of contemporary entrepreneurs from Shenzhen and a random sample of businesspeople form Guangzhou.

Defining "Entrepreneur" in Contemporary China

In Chinese, the entrepreneur, or "enterpriser", is referred to as either:

- 主辦人, *zhu ban ren*, head of a family business; or
- 企業家 *qi ye jia*, private enterprise manager.

In February 1977, to help alleviate widespread unemployment, individual private businesses were permitted by the state to operate in the repair, service, and handicraft businesses, but hiring labour was not allowed. Nonetheless, business success breeds growth, and growth requires additional hands; local businesses expanded employment with local officials' support or by their turning a blind eye. Businesses in areas with liberal local leaders

+ Email: ElisabethMontgomery@netscape.com.

(e.g. the coastal provinces) enjoyed policies favouring private business, while those in conservative areas suffered harsher treatment (White, 1998). The CCP neither encouraged nor prohibited non-state-sector businesses, which were generating significant revenue and taxes. Many entrepreneurs hired employees with no personal consequences.

Spires, Zhang, Qian & Pan (2004), Lin & Bian (1991), and Bian (1994) found that in China in the 1980s, in contrast, for example, to the USA, occupational attainment was secondary to "work-unit attainment" in the eyes of most urban Chinese. Urban youths focused their efforts on finding better work units because government policies created a situation in which "working conditions, wage standards, fringe benefits, and access to housing and community resources are related more to workplace characteristics than to occupation" (Bian, 1994: 73). During the 1980s and 1990s, government practices concerning labour in urban China led to the state sector offering fewer and fewer employment benefits. University graduates were no longer guaranteed state sector jobs at graduation, and blue-collar workers found themselves at risk of being fired or laid-off (Davis, 1999). Wank (1999) believed that by the late 1980s state policies and practices had given rise to a three-part typology of entrepreneurs:

1. The first group, "the speculators", was mainly people from uneducated backgrounds who conducted illicit trade in the underground economy prior to the beginning of reform in 1979. They were also the first in Wank's study to legally enter the private sector as reforms were initiated.
2. The second group, "workers", was those who moved from unskilled or semi-skilled occupations in state-run work units to running their own private firms. This group contained the largest number of younger entrepreneurs, most of whom left their jobs in the mid-1980s.
3. Third, "former functionaries", comprised the largest category. These entrepreneurs formerly worked in white-collar occupations in state sector jobs and were the last group to enter private sector self-employment in the 1980s. They ranged in age from 20s to 50s and were on average the best educated in his sample. Analyses of these three entrepreneurial cohorts indicate that the most successful were the "former functionaries", and that their ties to the party provided an advantage over their competitors (Wank 1999: 123-136).

The 1990s saw further relaxing of restrictions on business ownership in China, which led to three distinct entrepreneurial sources: first, from private entrepreneurs (often family based); second, villages and townships initiated or expanded the entrepreneurial activities of their small local workshop and production units; the third source consisted of state-owned enterprises informally establishing new firms and locally controlling internal resources and residual profits.

In her research on self-employment in Shanghai, Davis (1999: 38) also found enhanced political capital among those who chose self-employment in the 1990-1995 period. In her sample, the men who became self-employed between 1990 and 1995 were very much like the average Chinese male businessperson in the sample, in terms of education, age, and workplace seniority. However, they possessed advantages such as cadre experience and having fathers who were party members and not blue-collar workers.

Regulatory Definition of Entrepreneur

Chinese government regulations and practices regarding privately owned enterprises identify two basic types of local privately owned business. The first is generally called *getihu*, which literally means "individual household", referring to a very small family-owned business. According to the regulations, a *getihu* is allowed to hire only one or two helpers and several apprentices; the number of employees should not exceed seven. Another type of private business, *siyingqiye*, is a category that was legalized in 1984, a private enterprise defined as a profit-making economic entity that employs at least eight persons with its assets privately owned (Tsang, 1996). Private enterprises are much larger in size and more influential in the business sector than *getihu*.

Chen, Li & Matlay (2006) find that in the beginning of the Reform Era *getihu* were the main form of entrepreneurs that were tolerated. They were often semi-skilled factory workers laid off from SOEs, looking to survive. They were not deemed a threat or a benefit to society. Yet, as reforms took hold in the 1990s, entrepreneurship began to be taken over as the domain of better-educated and socially connected private businesspeople. In part, many *getihu* were not looking to grow their businesses and so were content to remain small, family-based, intergenerational, and prosperous enough to support the family. However, by the late 1990s SOE managers with access to venture finance were taking on large projects that began to impact the storefront *getihu* style of business.

Qi (1999) described the goals of private, high-tech incubator companies as making decisions of their own accord, developing a market orientation, encouraging an internal flow of information, organizing standard boards of directors, and distributing profits proportional to the companies' success. As a result of Deng's technology-based economic vision, these Chinese companies were able to take advantage of the country's many scientific institutions for recruiting talent and encouraging them to commercialize their activities and "enter the sea" (*xiahai*) by going into business. By the mid-1990s, there were approximately 1,000 research institutions in the country, with over 300,000 scientists and technical personnel (Qi, 1999). Legend, for example, is probably the most famous example of a Chinese incubator company (Sheff, 2002).

Private Chinese businesses and entrepreneurs, though intermittently encouraged by the Chinese Government and recognized for their economic efficiencies, and their potential for creating jobs and wealth, continued to exist in a transitional state. They did not hold power, nor were these business men and women allowed to become or maintain membership in the Communist Party. During that period there was a "lying low" approach concerning the ways in which they conducted their business activities. Additionally, in general, direct foreign investment enterprises were more interested in generating revenue than in social liberalization (Wang, 1998; Stiglitz, 2002). A concern amongst national and local governments in the late 1990s (Holt, 1997) was whether China's entrepreneurs posed a threat to those who had been indoctrinated, from birth, to oppose free market business practices and private enterprise. However, the pragmatic Chinese Communist Party recognized the effect on growth due to impetus from private businesses and enhanced support and development.

Incubators

In March 1986 Deng's advisors in the Ministry of Science and Technology presented a long-range strategy for the country's high-technology revolution, which Deng saw as the chief path for China's social and economic development (Qi, 1999). High-tech private businesses in government-sponsored business incubators were officially launched that month to nurture future decades of technological entrepreneurship. The acceptance by the Party of the value of entrepreneurs to the economy led to the first Chinese incubator being started in 1987 in Wuhan, Hubei Province, by the Ministry of Science and Technology (Yan, 2003). Until then China's economic focus had been on large state-owned enterprises and foreign direct investment companies to the neglect of small, private businesses (Chandrasekaran & Ryans, 1996). Business incubators were developed in the mid and late 1990s to foster a range of high-tech industries (Xu, 2001). However, it soon realized that the most vibrant part of the high-tech industry was privately-owned small firms, which can act as engines of economic development as well as wellsprings of creativity and innovation. By the end of 2003, China had over 500 incubators, providing a raft of services ranging from real estate, financing, marketing, human resource management, training, and networking to advising on government policy. We will be specifically discussing incubator entrepreneurs and other business people in South China.

From economic ecology we move to the business cultural ecology. There has been a large volume of publications concerning business practice in China, of varying quality.

Theoretical Framework: Cross-Cultural Values Theory

Our cross-cultural value dimensions are derived from Schwartz (1992, 1994a), firstly from three universal human needs: needs of individuals as biological organisms (organismic needs), requirements for coordinated social interaction, and group welfare and group survival needs. Values have been of important concern for social science researchers for decades (e.g., Vernon & Allport, 1931, Allport, 1961; Parsons, 1951; & Rokeach, 1973). More recently, cross-cultural researchers have come to view values as an important basis for understanding cultural syndromes (e.g., Hofstede, 1980, Bond, 1988; Schwartz, 1994; Triandis, 1995, and House et al., 2004). Cross-cultural studies of values have flourished since Hofstede's 1980 work, especially since the 1990s.

The term "values" has been used variously to refer to interests, pleasures, likes, preferences, duties, moral obligations, desires, wants, goals, needs, aversions and attractions, and many other kinds of reasons to choose particular sets of behaviour (Williams, 1979: 15). Values are generally defined as cognitive representations of abstract goals, e.g. benevolence, security, justice. Values motivate individuals' actions, and are related to needs, motives, and goals. Values differ from specific goals in that they are valid across most types of situations. Schwartz & Bardi (2001) define values as desirable, trans-situational goals that vary in their importance as guiding principles in people's lives.

- Values are beliefs with emotional content, occasionally incongruent with what is considered rationality in a culture;
- Values are motivating, specifying desirable goals which people strive to attain or situations they wish to avoid; hence, values guide the selection and evaluation of actions, policies, people, and events;
- Values serve as standards or criteria for success, and failure;
- Values transcend specific situations;
- Values are abstract goals; the abstract nature of values distinguishes them from concepts such as norms and attitudes, which can refer to specific actions, objects, or situations.
- Values are ordered by importance relative to one another, forming a consistently ordered system of priorities, often unique to an individual or group; this hierarchical feature of values also distinguishes them from norms and attitudes.

Values theories define values as desirable trans-situational goals, varying in importance, that serve as guiding principles in people's lives. The crucial content aspect that distinguishes between values is the type of motivational goal they express. In order to coordinate with others in the pursuit of the goals that are important to them, groups and individuals express these cognitive requirements linguistically as specific values about which they communicate. Licht &Siegel (2006) note the paucity of research concerning values and entrepreneurship within cultures, and propose Schwartz' theory as a useful tool to study them.

The preference element in cultural value orientations, values as ideals, promotes coherence among the various aspects of culture. Because prevailing cultural value orientations represent ideals, aspects of culture that are incompatible with them are likely to generate tension, and to elicit criticism and pressure to change these aspects of culture. In a society whose cultural value orientations emphasize collective responsibility, for example, a firm that fires long-term employees in the interests of profitability is likely to elicit widespread criticism and pressure to change policies. Of course, cultures are not fully coherent. In addition to a dominant culture, subgroups within societies can espouse conflicting value emphases. The dominant cultural orientation changes in response to shifting power relations among these subgroups.

But change is slow. Another important feature of cultural value orientations is that they are relatively stable (Hofstede, 2001; Schwartz, Bardi &Bianchi, 2000). Some researchers argue that elements of culture persist over hundreds of years (e.g., Kohn & Schooler, 1983; Putnam, 1993). Yet, cultural value orientations do change gradually. Societal adaptation to epidemics, technological advances, increasing wealth, contact with other cultures, and other exogenous factors leads to changes in cultural value emphases. Studying value emphases directly is an especially efficient way to characterize cultures.

Individual Value Dimensions

Schwartz presents a theory of what he proposes to be universal aspects in the content of human values (for a more detailed discussion, see Schwartz, 1992, 1994a, 2006). Ten types of values, held to some degree by individuals in all cultures, are defined as motivating goals. The theory also postulates a structure of more or less bi-polar relations amongst the value types, along with a continuous relationship between adjacent values around a circumplex. A values instrument, based on the theory and designed for cross-cultural research, is available. The initial samples for assessing the theory consisted of 97 samples in 44 countries. Schwartz' approach is based upon Rokeach's (1973) work on values, and also on other theories and research on value dimensions. Most of the supporting research is not specific to businesspeople or business organisations.

Schwartz' work on values began with the effort to resolve the issue of classifying value contents. Somewhat modifying earlier definitions of values, he defines values as *desirable trans-situational goals, varying in importance, that serve as guiding principles in the life of a person or other social entity*. Implicit in this definition of values as goals is that (1) they serve the interests of some social entity; (2) they can motivate action and give it direction and emotional intensity; (3) they function as standards for judging and justifying action; and (4) they are acquired both through socialization to dominant group values and through the unique learning experiences of individuals. The above characteristics of values do not point to the substantive content of values. However, implicit in the view of values as goals, and critical for theory development, is the idea that the crucial content aspect that distinguishes between values is the type of motivational goal they express.

Schwartz derived a typology of the different contents of values using the following reasoning.

1. In order to cope with reality in a social context, groups and individuals cognitively transform the necessities inherent in human existence and express them in the language of specific values about which they can then communicate.
2. Specifically, values represent, in the form of conscious goals, responses to three universal requirements with which all individuals and societies must cope: needs of individuals as biological organisms, requisites of coordinated social interaction, and requirements for the smooth functioning and survival of groups.

Ten Individual Values

Schwartz developed 10 motivationally distinct types of individual values, using his three universal requirements (detailed explanations are in Schwartz & Bilsky, 1987, 1990, and Schwartz, 1992). Each of the basic values can be characterized by describing its central motivational goal, quoted near verbatim from Schwartz' publications:

1. **Self-Direction**. Independent thought and action; choosing, creating, exploring.
2. **Stimulation**. Excitement, novelty, and challenge in life.
3. **Hedonism.** Pleasure and sensuous gratification for oneself.
4. **Achievement**. Personal success through demonstrating competence according to social standards.
5. **Power.** Social status and prestige, control or dominance over people and resources.
6. **Security**. Safety, harmony, and stability of society, of relationships, and of self.
7. **Conformity**. Restraint of actions, inclinations, and impulses likely to upset or harm others and violate social expectations or norms.

8. **Tradition**. Respect, commitment, and acceptance of the customs and ideas that traditional culture or religion provide the self. Tradition and conformity values are especially close motivationally because they share the goal of subordinating the self in favour of socially imposed expectations. They differ primarily in the objects to which one subordinates the self. Conformity entails subordination to persons with whom one is in frequent interaction - parents, teachers or bosses. Tradition entails subordination to more abstract objects - religious and cultural customs and ideas. As a corollary, conformity values exhort responsiveness to current, possibly changing expectations. Tradition values demand responsiveness to immutable expectations set down in the past. The theory retains the distinction between these two values based on empirical findings.
9. **Benevolence**. Preserving and enhancing the welfare of those with whom one is in frequent personal contact (the "in-group"). (Benevolence and conformity values both promote cooperative and supportive social relations. However, benevolence values provide an internalised motivational base for such behaviour. In contrast, conformity values promote cooperation in order to avoid negative outcomes for self.)
10. **Universalism**. Understanding, appreciation, tolerance, and protection for the welfare of all people and for nature. (This contrasts with the in-group focus of benevolence values.)

The comprehensiveness of any set of value orientations in covering the full range of motivational goals cannot be tested definitively; however, Schwartz presents evidence of the comprehensiveness of the ten basic values (1992, 1994a). We will now relate the values in Schwartz' theory to Chinese values from the academic literature.

CHINESE VALUES

All interaction in Chinese cultures involves .dynamic social relationships among a hierarchy of concepts: *lian* face (*lian*), *mian* face (*mianzi*), reciprocation of favours (*renqing*), and relationships (*guanxi*). One might also add the art of gift-giving to this list. *Guanxi* and *renqing* must be understood in relation to one another, as the reciprocal favours define the value of the network. For example, failure to meet *renqing* obligations causes loss of *lian* face. Face is a critical issue among Chinese and is important to self-esteem and business and social functioning. Hu (1944) and Hu & Grove (1991) investigated "face" and identified the two basic categories in Chinese culture: *lian* and *mianzi*. Hu (1944) defined *lian* as representing the confidence of society in the integrity of one's moral character, the loss of which makes it impossible for him or her to function properly within the community. A person's *lian* face can be preserved by faithful compliance with ritual and social norms. One gains *lian* by demonstrating moral character. *Mian* corresponds to a more "Western" conception of face, that is, prestige and reputation achieved through success in life, and frequently through ostentatious display of wealth (automobile brands, conspicuous consumption, wanton waste), or perhaps some other desirable trait (education or position in an organisation). Redding & Ng (1982) investigated the degree to which Hong Kong Chinese managers believe in the importance of preservation of face in daily business transactions and negotiations. All of their 102 respondents strongly asserted the importance of reciprocity of favours and obligations (*renqing*) in the giving and receiving of face, and the instrumentality of face-concerns as a method of achieving business goals.

Renqing (favours) has many implications in Chinese cultures (Hwang, 1987; Chu, 1991). The direct translation of the Chinese characters for *renqing* is "human feelings". The dictates of *renqing* are that the human element should not be removed from human affairs, and a sympathetic give-and-take compromise should govern the relationships of men. The Chinese form lifelong, rich, networks of mutual relations, usually involving reciprocal obligations with hierarchies similar to Confucian rules, but with the obligations and reciprocity running much deeper. The relative permanence of such social networks contributes to the importance and enforceability of the Chinese conception of reciprocity in the form of *renqing* and *bao*, that is, morality (*bao ying*) based upon obligatory reciprocity of favours. See Yum (1988) for a comparison of reciprocity in Western and Chinese societies. The *guanxi* relationships are useful and used. Hwang (1987) thoroughly analyses the implications of this long-term reciprocity.

Renqing is also often the basis of manipulation of adversaries in business negotiations. An obligation is created through a gesture that might cost little, and the debt is called due when the adversary can only repay it with a more valuable concession. This aspect of *renqing* is worth remembering when engaged in business negotiations.

Chinese values in addition to these values include:

Chiku Nailao. Graham & Lam (2003) identify the important value of "*chiku nailao*" (Endurance, Relentlessness, or Eating Bitterness and Enduring Labour). The authors indicate that the Chinese are popularly believed to have a strong work ethic, but they take this one step further, to extreme endurance. Where, for example, U.S. business people place high value on talent as a key to success, the Chinese see *chiku nailao* as much more important and honourable. The use of the words "eating bitterness" is rather misleading. In Chinese, if the phrase "hard-working" is taken apart, the words are literally translated as "chi" (to eat) and "ku" (bitterness). But when the two words are put together, they only mean hard-working - they really do not have much to do with specifically "eating bitterness" in contemporary vernacular. The meanings are:

吃苦耐劳 *chi1 ku3 nai4 lao2*, Be hardworking and able to endure hardships
吃苦 *chi1 ku3*, 1. Suffer for it, 2. bear hardships
耐劳 *nai4 lao2*, Hardy; can endure hardship

The dimension is not addressed in the Schwartz dimensions, except perhaps as a pole of the value *Hedonism – Chiku Nailao* dimension.

Cultivation of the Self as a Member of the Community

The primary concern is to become a good person through learning for the sake of one's self, but not a quest for individuality. "Self," in the Confucian sense, refers to a centre of relationships. It has a communal quality that cannot be conceived of as an isolated or isolable entity. Confucian self-cultivation is a deliberate communal act (Tu, 1985). "Indeed, it could be said that a self lacking any interaction with others is unimaginable" (Tu, 2004). This value does not appear as a separate dimension in the Schwartz theory, perhaps indicating a poor fit of the theoretical dimensions to China.

Importance of Family

The family is seen as an enriching and nourishing support system, a vehicle for the true valuing of the self. The self, in turn, must develop in its various roles as son or daughter, parent or sibling. This value does not appear as a separate dimension in the Schwartz theory, perhaps indicating a poor fit of the theoretical dimensions to China.

Extending Relationships beyond the Family

However, familial relationships can also degenerate into nepotism. If we are committed to our family to the exclusion of a larger structure of human relationships, such commitment may become a closed system and turn into negative nepotism. If this happens, we will associate meaningfully only with members of our own family, and not with others. Therefore, true realization of the self, which begins in the context of the family, requires that one also extend one's relationships beyond the familial structure, and so beyond nepotism, in order to be able to relate meaningfully to a larger community. This value can be related to Benevolence and perhaps to Universalism in Schwartz theory.

Correct Behaviour

Rituals learned from childhood facilitate verbal and non-verbal communication to the benefit of human relationships. This is why ritual is important in the oldest Confucian philosophical tradition. This value can be related to Tradition in Schwartz' theory, though Schwartz' definition of Tradition is rather narrow.

Importance of History

History is collective memory, a knowing from whence we come. To have a sense of history is to know and to care about the major values and ideas that have shaped the larger community of which we are a part. To have no history is like being without memory. History, be it short or long, becomes significant as we become capable of relating to it, as we come to see in it our own past and enter into personal dialogue with those generations who contributed to the culture that shapes us today. Confucius found such a vision represented in the *Spring and Autumn Annals*. This value can be related to Tradition in Schwartz' theory, though Schwartz' definition of Tradition is quite distant from the importance of history.

Participation in Society

Human beings should also be thought of as participants in society. One is expected to participate in the polity of which one is a part. One is also a political being who should be a responsive and responsible participant in the political community. This vision of political participation is articulated in the Book of History, or the Book of Documents.

Universalism

An area essential to learning to be human is symbolized by one of the most difficult books in the classical tradition, the Book of Changes (*I Ching*, or *Yi Jing*), providing a cosmic vision. Using modern terminology, the Book of Changes represents an ecological concern, both in an environmental and in a spiritual sense. A human being does not exist only in the anthropological world of other human beings. Beyond this human world is a larger universe. Therefore, one needs an ecologically sound cosmic vision. Many scholars have noted that a distinctive feature of Confucian thought is its emphasis on the commonality rather than on the differences between human beings. Commonality can be understood in terms of human sensitivity: the human need for communication, for self-expression and for self-development which does not infringe on the self-development of others.

Table 1. China's Recent Generations

	Age in 2004	Characteristics
Consolidation Era	50-60+	During the Consolidation Era (1950-1965), the Chinese Communist Party sought to replace Confucianism with Maoist and Marxist-Leninist ideology; the Party placed the State and the Communist Party above traditional individual and family concerns. Due to increasing numbers of university graduates, this group is strongly urged by the Government to retire at 55 for women and 60 for men to make room for those below to move up.
The Great Cultural Revolution	30 - 50	1966-1976 saw the Chinese Communist Party intensify its attacks on Confucianism and Western influence in their quest for ideological purity; the Cultural Revolution escalated the discrediting of traditional education, and ideological moderation was actively suppressed so as to try to create a classless society that valued equality, conformity, and self-sacrifice for collective interests; the early Cultural Revolution was a period of extreme poverty and societal upheaval; reinstatement of moderate Deng Xiaoping as vice premier in 1972 restored a measure of societal and economic order, Mao Zedong's death in 1976 signalled the end of this period.
Social Reform Era	30 and under	Deng Xiaoping's policies from 1978 to the present encouraged individual achievement, materialism, economic efficiency, and entrepreneurship; foreign direct investment policy led to Western capitalistic ideologies having more influence in Chinese business and education; rapid industrialization and modernization has resulted in unprecedented economic growth and prosperity (Tian 1998, Yao 2000). Confucianism is now back in official favour, however, Chinese youth who have grown up during the Social Reform Era have been described as individualistic, materialistic, hedonistic, and entrepreneurial (Rosen 1990).

Business and Confucianism

Confucius spoke of merchants as branches of a tree of which farmers were the roots, not particularly denigrating merchants. However, his even-handedness was perverted by his interpreters, and historically the mercantile class in China has been on the outer edge of status and power (Huang, 2004; Trescott, 2002; Peng, 1995).

Confucius characterized himself as a transmitter, not a creator or innovator of culture, "I am a man among men -- I am a cultural transmitter" (Tu, 2004). Confucius, as a culture transmitter, wished to pass on his set of values as best for China.

Individual values are influenced by the social and economic ecology of the individual. Egri & Ralston (2004) have identified relevant generation cohorts in China, each of which experienced different economic and social ecologies during their lifetimes (shown below). Age-related differences in values shaped by these differences were observed by Egri & Ralston.

For the samples collected in Shenzhen and Guangzhou - our contemporary businesspeople - 100% were 57 years or younger, 93% were 40 years or younger, and 67% were 30 years and under, exemplifying the modern Chinese manager heavily influenced by the Social Reform Era.

Values of Entrepreneurs

The values of private business owners and entrepreneurs are studied relatively frequently in the West. Research studies using a variety of frameworks have shown that national cultural values are related to workplace behaviours, attitudes and other organizational outcomes (e.g., Kluckhohn & Strodtbeck, 1961; Hall, 1976; Hofstede, 1980a; Ronen & Shenkar, 1985; Trompenaars, 1993; Schwartz, 1994a; and House, Hanges, Javidan, Dorfman, & Gupta, 2004).

Birley (1987) and McGrath, MacMillan, and Scheinberg (1992) demonstrated that societies vary in their ability to create and sustain entrepreneurial activity. McGrath, MacMillan, Yang, & Tsai (1992) and Thomas & Mueller (2000) proposed explanations that cultural value differences between nations are one of the primary determinants of a nation's level of economic and entrepreneurial development.

While entrepreneurship is one of the most studied topics in business, findings have been mixed regarding the work traits entrepreneurs exhibit (Deakins, 1999; Van Gelderen, 2000; Watson, Ponthieu, & Doster, 1995). Some have argued that the trait approach has failed in identifying entrepreneurs (Gartner, 1988), and that the entrepreneurial personality is nothing but a myth (Shaver, 1995). Part of the problem may be that there are different personality types of entrepreneurs (Miner, 1997, 2000) and different entrepreneurial subgroups, such as opportunistic vs. craftsmen entrepreneurs (Cooper, 1973), or opportunity vs. necessity entrepreneurs (Reynolds, Bygrave, Autio, Cox, & Hay, 2003), and the fact that entrepreneurs operate in different cultures. The culture we are investigating is Chinese, which has a traditional appreciation and application of Confucian values.

Hierarchical Order of Schwartz' Value Dimensions from Past Studies in China

Schwartz & Boehnke (2004) believe Confucian values tend to fall in the higher rankings of individual level values: Universalism, Benevolence, Conformity, Tradition, and Security. If this definition of Confucian values is valid and the values are held by our samples then we expect the means of these dimensions will be higher than the remaining five. Studies by Holt (1997) and Ralston et al. (1996, 1997) provide views of value priorities of Chinese businesspeople in the 1990s. Table 2 indicates the relative rankings. None of the studies provide information as to how the raw scores were or were not transformed, so z-scores within samples are compared.

The consistently low scores for Tradition in the China samples (Schwartz 1992, 1994a; Littrell, Gregory & Alon, 2006) raise questions as to whether Tradition as defined in the SVS is general, as considerations of the past are omitted from the defining items. The SVS Tradition dimension is ranked well below the mean and usually near the lowest ranked value in the samples in Table 2. Assuming Confucius' teachings to be noted, understood, and influential today, his writings and their interpretation regarding the aspects of history and tradition and their role in Confucian cultivation of the self indicate that the Past is treated in the following ways (Lai, 2008):

- To provide examples to illustrate points;
- To provide knowledge about customs, norms, and traditions;
- To alert individuals to the diversity of situations and the possibilities for action and responses;
- As source material to reflect upon in one's development of critical and reflective skills; and
- As providing paradigmatic models that exemplify particular virtues.

In other words, the Past provides information, not rules of behaviour. The items defining "Tradition" in the SVS are:

Tradition
RESPECT FOR TRADITION (preservation of time-honoured customs)
MODERATE (avoiding extremes of feeling & action)
HUMBLE (modest, self-effacing)
ACCEPTING MY PORTION IN LIFE (submitting to life's circumstances)
DEVOUT (holding to religious faith & belief)

These items could be considered to define an idea of Tradition as Fatalism and Powerlessness, not fitting well with Confucian teachings concerning Tradition and the Past. Gentry, Tansuhaj, Manzer & John (1988) would recognise aspects of Fatalism here, the belief that all events are predetermined by Fate and therefore unalterable by man, that man must simply take events as they come, instead of being able to plan, avoid, or master the environment. Varying levels of fate orientation would seem to be explained in large part by differences in religious background with the more devout being more Fatalistic.

VALUE DIMENSIONS AND ENTREPRENEURSHIP

In China, a considerable amount of work has been done using the Schwartz Values Survey (SVS). Holt (1997) investigated how culture affects entrepreneurial outcomes in Wuhan. Holt's sample of 237 interviews included executives of either Chinese state-owned enterprises (SOEs) or domestic joint venture companies, and Chinese entrepreneurs who were founders and active managers of private enterprises. Holt concluded that the Chinese entrepreneurs were clearly nonconformist in their views, although they were Confucian in their high regard for family security (a single item in the SVS, not a dimension). Accumulation of wealth in China is for the entrepreneur's family. The values of managers and entrepreneurs convinced Holt that despite fifty years of socialism, Confucianism was still a dominant philosophy of life. Ralston's scores from randomly selected businesspeople from different geographic regions than Holts' give a different view (see Figure 2), and in fact the results from the four samples are quite diverse. The range of means for the Entrepreneur sample is wider than for the random samples of businesspeople. Schwartz (2007) speculates that entrepreneurship values are compatible with Power, Security, and Achievement values, but they may be in opposition to the values at the other poles in the value circle: Universalism and, perhaps, Benevolence. In these studies Achievement and Security are highly ranked, but Power is low. Benevolence and Universalism are mid-range.

METHOD

A pilot test of the SVS survey was carried out in Shenzhen City with good results in terms of the ability of local businesspeople to complete it without difficulty. In 2004 and 2005 we collected data employing the SVS from businesspeople in Guangzhou City and Shenzhen City in Guangdong Province. We excluded street vendors and farm workers. The samples were urban businesspeople. The Guangzhou sample consisted of randomly selected business people. Students from Sun Yat-sen University were employed to hand deliver the survey instrument to a random convenience sample of businesspeople within the city, and to retrieve them; 222 valid surveys were obtained after data cleaning. Two samples were collected in Shenzhen city and adjacent districts, one from "traditional" or "ordinary" entrepreneurs who chose this business lifestyle and developed their business on their own with their families, and the other consisting of entrepreneurs who choose to receive training, skill development, and support from a State-sponsored entrepreneurship incubator. Surveys were hand delivered to a random convenience sample of business owners, and the completed surveys were anonymously deposited into a drop box at the incubators, were collected by college students from Shenzhen University, or were collected by the researcher. After data cleaning 333 valid surveys were obtained, 202 from ordinary entrepreneurs and 131 from incubator entrepreneurs.

Table 2. Relative Rankings of Values Studies in China: Holt (1997), Ralston et al. (1996, 1997)

Year Data Collected	Holt 1995		Holt 1995		Ralston et al 1993		Ralston et al 1993
Guangzhou-Entrepreneurs		Guangzhou-Managers		China Random		Guangzhou & Shanghai Random	
Mean z-Scores:							
1 Self-Direction	**1.7**	**1 Benevolence**	**1.6**	**1 Benevolence**	**1.3**	**1 Achievement**	**1.3**
2 Achievement	**1.3**	**2 Conformity**	**1.1**				
				2 Security	**1.1**	**2 Benevolence**	**0.8**
3 Stimulation	**0.9**	**3 Security**	**0.8**	**3 Achievement**	**0.9**	**3 Security**	**0.7**
4 Benevolence	**0.2**	**4 Self-Dir**	**0.4**	**4 Conformity**	**0.7**	**3Self-Direction**	**0.7**
		5 Achievement	**0.4**	**5 Universalism**	**0.4**	**5 Universalism**	**0.3**
5 Security	0.0			**6 Self-Direction**	**0.1**	**5 Conformity**	**0.3**
5 Universalism	-0.0	6 Tradition	-0.1				
7 Conformity	-0.6	7 Universalism	-0.3	Stimulation	-0.6	7 Stimulation	-0.3
7 Hedonism	-0.6	8 Power	-0.9			8 Hedonism	-0.6
				9 Hedonism	**-1.2**	9 Power	-0.7
9 Power	**-1.2**	**9 Stimulation**	**-1.3**	**9 Tradition**	**-1.2**		
10 Tradition	**-1.6**	**10 Hedonism**	**-1.7**	**10 Power**	**-1.5**	**10 Tradition**	**-2.4**

ANALYSIS AND RESULTS

Multivariate analyses of variance were employed to investigate significance of differences between means among the samples. Descriptive statistics, including the raw-score means and z-score means may be seen in Table 3. In the mid-2000s Security was the highest ranked value for all samples, and Achievement was highly ranked for all samples. Stimulation and Tradition were lowest ranked in all samples. We see in Table 3 that for the 2005 samples from Shenzhen and Guangzhou, the random sample of businesspeople from Guangzhou value Benevolence higher than the entrepreneurs.

Security, Achievement, Conformity, and Self-Direction are highly ranked motivational values for both entrepreneurs and a random sample of businesspeople, with Conformity being ranked higher than Self-Direction for the sets of Entrepreneurs compared to the random sample. This outcome could indicate that entrepreneurs in China have developed an adaptive response of valuing conformity due to the erratic nature of their status and acceptance by national and local government over the past two decades.

In Figure 1 we see that the results from SVS samples from the mid-1990s in Southern and Eastern China vary amongst themselves, and are different from samples from South China in the mid-2000s; the latter being similar to one another. A possible explanation is differing data collection methodology (Holt administered the SVS in personal interviews), and in methods of transforming raw scores; none of these articles specify how scores were transformed.

Table 3. Relative Rankings of Values Studies in China by z-Scores of Means

Raw-Score Means		**SZ-Ordinary Ent.**	**SZ-Incubator Ent.**	**GZ-Random**
Security	**Security**	**1.37**	**1.34**	**1.20**
Achievement	Achievement	0.90	0.97	0.94
Conformity	Conformity	0.85	0.73	***0.30***
Self-Direction	Self-Direction	0.60	0.67	***0.81***
Benevolence	Benevolence	0.57	0.55	***0.94***
Universalism	Universalism	0.28	0.26	0.14
Hedonism	Hedonism	-0.67	-0.72	-0.35
Power	Power	-0.93	-0.67	-0.87
Stimulation	**Stimulation**	**-1.28**	**-1.43**	**-1.21**
Tradition	**Tradition**	**-1.69**	**-1.70**	**-1.91**

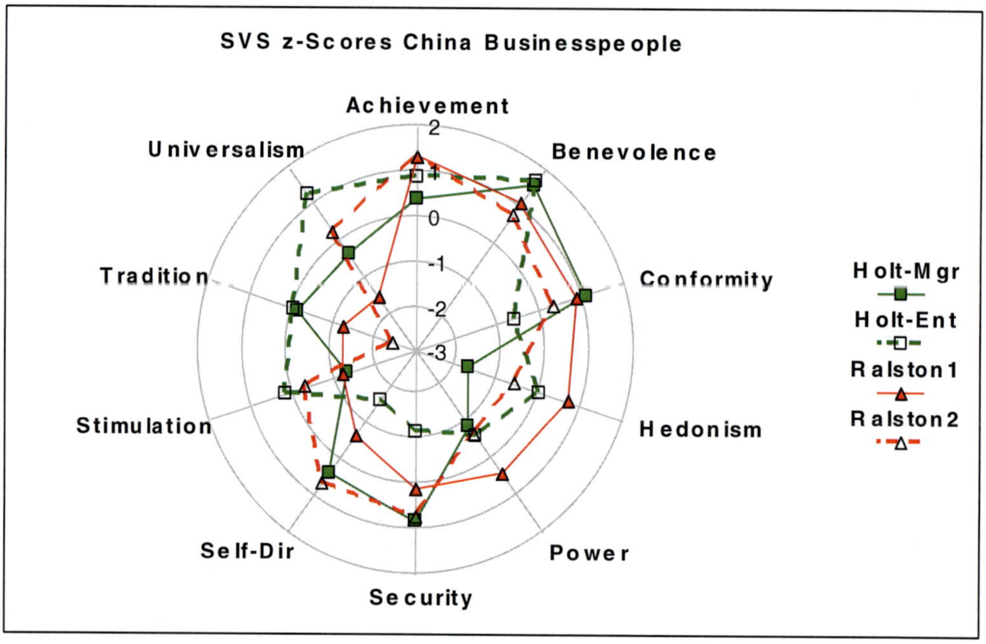

Figure 1. Continued on next page.

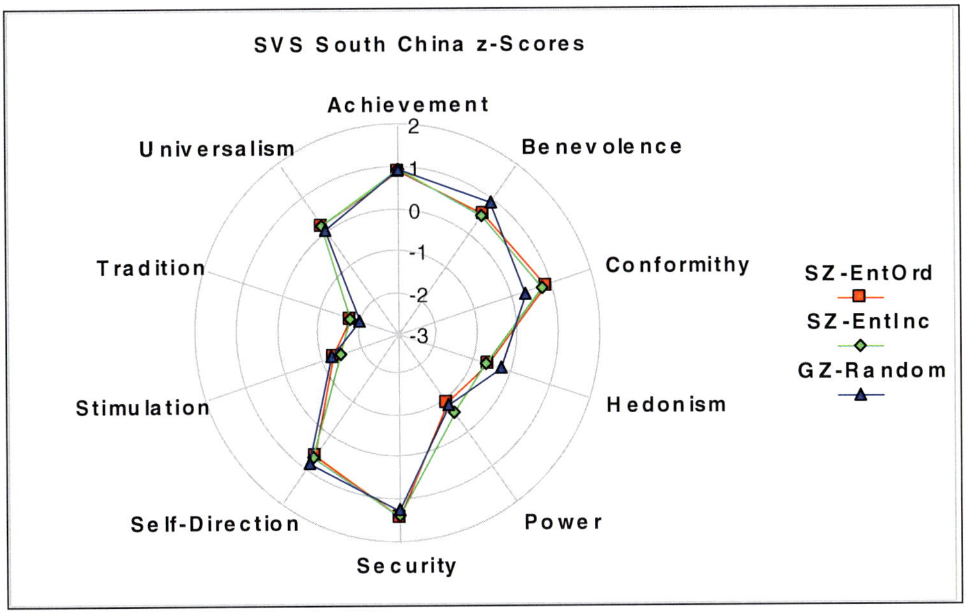

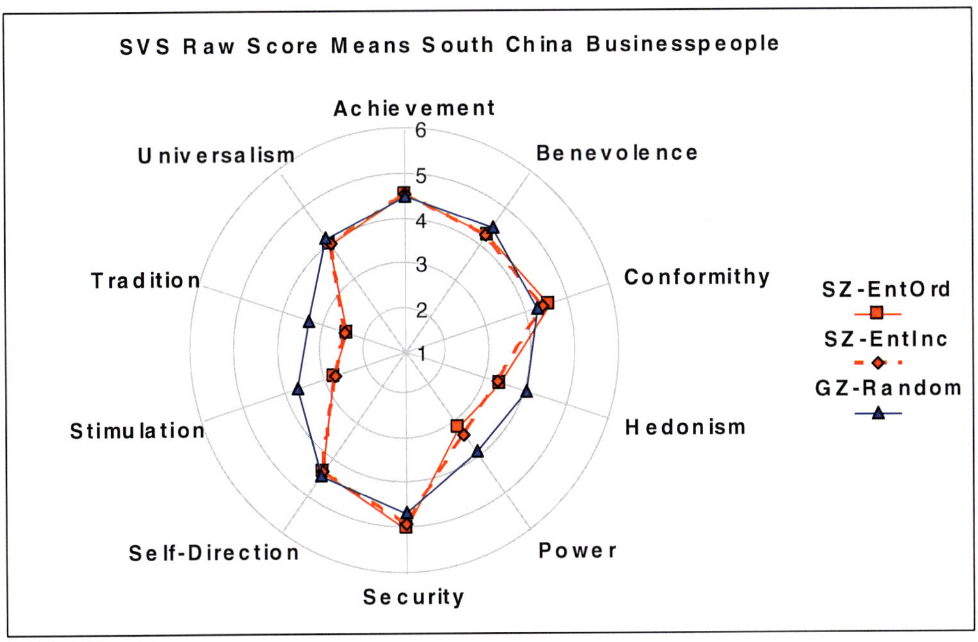

Figure 1. Comparison of SVS Scores for Businesspeople in China from All Studies

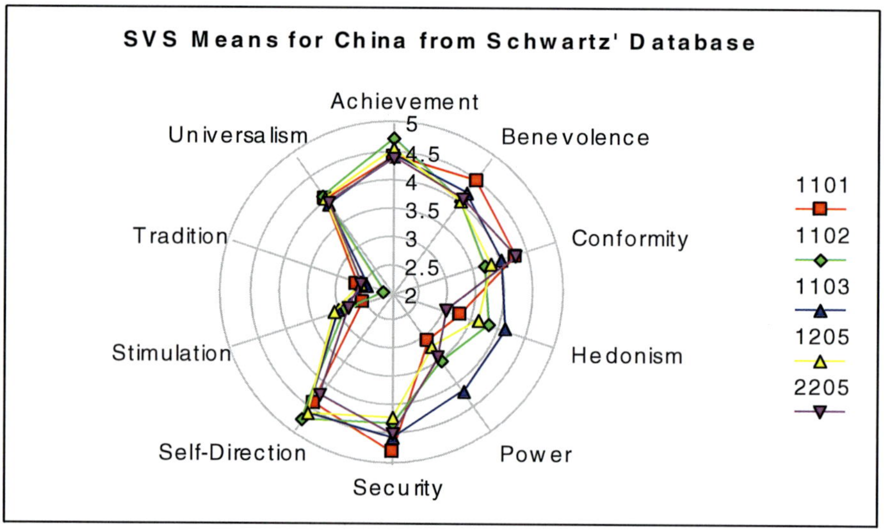

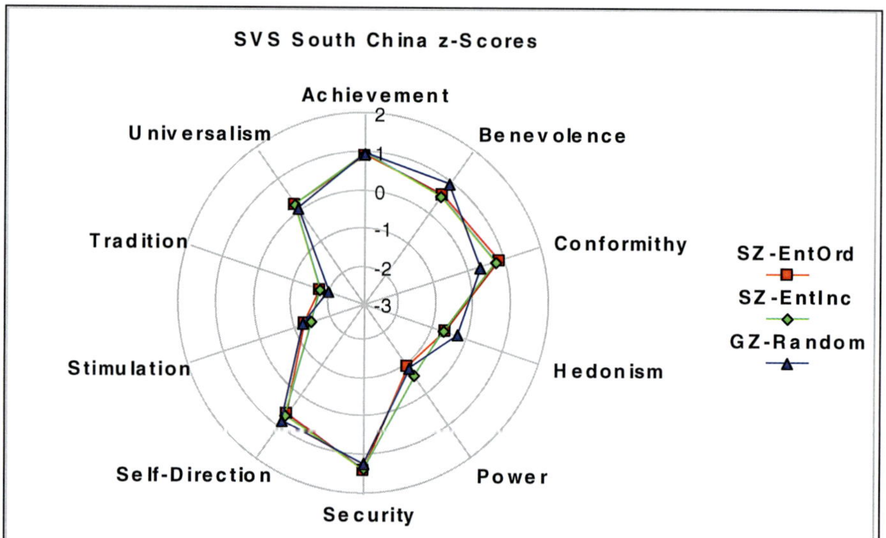

China Samples: 1101: Teachers, Shanghai, 1988; 1102: Teachers, Guangzhou, 1989; 1103: Teachers, Hebei, 1989; 1205: Students Shanghai, 1988; 2205: Students, Shanghai, 1995

Figure 2. Comparison of China Samples on SVS Value Dimensions

Results from the available sample data above do not provide consistent evidence that the individual cultural value dimensions of entrepreneurs in South China are different from those of a random sample of businesspeople in Guangzhou using the SVS as the comparative instrument. The question arises as to whether the values of businesspeople in China differ from the values of the samples of secondary teachers and tertiary students Schwartz (1992, 1994a) employed to develop his theoretical dimensions. Schwartz' publically available database provides several samples from China, depicted in the caption of Figure 2.

There were significant differences among the means of the samples on every dimension, $p<0.005$, with no discernable pattern amongst samples. General tendencies noted from

Schwartz' samples are that means are much lower for the Stimulation dimension and lower for the Hedonism, Benevolence and Universalism dimensions.

The comparisons in Figure 2 indicate similarities in rankings amongst Schwartz' samples and our South China samples, with the exception of the Hebei Province teacher sample (1103), with the Northern sample giving much higher rankings to Hedonism and Power. This outcome provides support for existence of differing Culture Areas in China and that the area studied is evolving from traditional Confucian values.

CULTURE AREAS

Littrell, Alon, & Chen (2006) found significant differences that were geographically related in ranks of preferred leader behaviours in samples from Guangzhou, Macau, Hangzhou, and Zhengzhou cities, indicating the influence of "culture areas". In anthropology a culture area is a contiguous geographic area comprising a number of societies that possess the same or similar traits or that share a dominant cultural orientation. The concept is that societal or ethnic entities are grouped on an ethnographic map and related to a geographical aspect of the environment. The concept defined by cultural area is supported in research and theory in sociology; national and societal cultures can differ, and regions within a society can differ, especially in large and complex societies (Robertson, 1993).

Today, and for at least 2000 years (Eberhard, 1965; Rickett, 1985, 1998), Chinese have identified cultural areas by distinct behavioural stereotypes in regions (e.g., North, South), provinces, counties, and cities (see Cartier, 2003 and Swanson, 1995). Kuan Tze (pinyin: Guanzi, also "Kuan Tse", 4th - 3rd Century BC) published treatises describing regional behaviour stereotypes in China. The stereotypes of North and South China are generally (Eberhard, 1965):

- The stereotypical northerner is loud, boisterous, more open, and with a quick temper, quick to anger. (Perhaps tending to use extreme anchor points on a Likert scale item.)
- The stereotypical southerner is clever, calculating, hardworking, and less open in displays of emotion. (Perhaps tending to use less extreme anchor points on a Likert scale item.)

As one source of culture areas, feudalism ties people to a location. It arose in China during the Western Zhou (1066 - 771 BC) or Eastern Zhou (770 – 256 BC) periods, and was to last more than 2,500 years until the chaos of the Opium Wars. This is compared with Europe, where feudalism lasted about one thousand years. The Chinese Communist Party reinstituted feudal rules with the *hu kou*, residence permit, which specifies where citizens must live and requires Party permission to change. Feudal rules support development of culture areas by isolating geographic regions, even to the extent of developing local mutually unintelligible language dialects.

Culture areas are seen to reflect clusters of behaviours that often reflected similar ecological adaptive strategies. Thus, culture areas could be defined by trait lists - those uniquely present, and those uniquely absent - hence, monolithic descriptions of the Chinese people will be in error. Even within the majority Han ethnic group there are many subtleties in their beliefs and practices that make it difficult to categorize this group as one homogenous group. Depending upon where a Chinese comes from, the spoken language, religion, and cultural practices can be different from other Chinese.

CROSS-REGIONAL DIFFERENCES

Ralston, Yu, Wang, Terpstra, & He (1996), in a study of regional differences in values in China, selected an ecological-materialist approach as a theoretical foundation for discussing regional differences, as it integrates both the evolution and the structure of a society. Ralston et al. found regional differences in China to be influenced by historic precedents, geographic location, economic development, educational level, and technological sophistication. Historic/geographic comparisons indicate that a clear dichotomy occurred historically due to the geographic differences between China's coastal and inland cities. As in many other countries, development began on the coast. China's coastal cities - Shanghai, Guangzhou, and Dalian - have been the international commercial and trading centers for many centuries. Thus, the historic/geographic comparisons identify a definite coastal-inland contrast. They state "… it is important for Western business people to understand the diverse values held across the various regions of China, because just as societal cultures can differ, regions within a society can vary, especially if that society is large and complex …".

Huo & Randall (1991) conducted an exploratory data analysis of the sub-cultural value differences among managers, all self-identified as being of Chinese culture but living in different geographic regions. Using survey responses to Hofstede's VSM, a comparison was made of the values among Chinese living in Taiwan, Beijing, Hong Kong, and Wuhan. Strong sub-cultural differences were revealed.

CONCLUSIONS

The conclusions that can be drawn are that in a nation such as China, with a continuing feudal tradition in the *hu kou*, a large geographic area and institutionalisation of the power of local government over national government, national generalisations are impossible. An understanding of China must be piecemeal; the study of China in the realm of the social sciences, including business, is only in the first stages of developing what the regions are and how they differ. Additionally, as the feudal controls of government are weakened, the character of regions may change based upon patterns of internal migration.

From our data we cannot conclude that individual cultural values held by entrepreneurs, a random sample of businesspeople, secondary school teachers, and tertiary students are significantly different within a region bounded by Shanghai, Wuhan, Guangzhou, and Shenzhen.

There is strong evidence indicating that geographically defined culture areas exist in China with different priorities as to individual values. Identifying these areas and then monitoring any change or homogenisation as the *hou ko* restrictions are relaxed could provide us with valuable indications of expectations of great regional differences in expression of values in business practices. From the past experience of the authors (both of whom have lived and worked in China for several years), when Chinese culture is initially encountered by a Westerner it appears to be an alien system; as one lives in China and gains knowledge, it becomes a collection of alien systems, different from one another.

For the samples collected in Guangdong Province in 2004 and 2005, Security is the highest ranked motivating value for businesspeople, followed by Conformity for entrepreneurs and Benevolence for other businesspeople. Low rankings were given to Power by all, and very low rankings to Stimulation and the SVS version of Tradition. Lenartowicz & Johnson (2003) propose that Achievement and Self-Direction should be positively related to entrepreneurship, whereas Security, the inverse of risk-taking, should be negatively related to it. For our 2004-2005 samples Achievement, Security, and Self-Direction were all highly ranked by entrepreneurs. In our reading of the literature on values of entrepreneurs, we frequently encountered a naive proposal by researchers that entrepreneurs are risk takers and did not value Security. This is incorrect. Entrepreneurs are risk evaluators and many undertake the path to remove the insecurity of working for others.

When engaging with businesspeople in South China in the Guangdong Province coastal regions, some expectations based upon the average characteristics of our samples are that we will tend to find that, compared to other sectors of society, they are on average:

- Less adherant to tradition and value self-direction, indicating openness to innovation;
- But still express typical values of conformity, benevolence, and universalism;
- Achievement oriented;
- Value security highly, perhaps seeing the business sector as a path to enhancement of personal and family security.

REFERENCES

[1] Allport, G.W. (1961). *Pattern and Growth in Personality*. New York: Holt, Rinehart & Winston.

[2] Bian, Y. (1994). *Work and Inequality in Urban China*. Albany, NY, USA: State University of New York Press.

[3] Birley, S. (1987). New ventures and employment growth. *Journal of Business Venturing*, *2*(2), 155-165.

[4] Bond, M.H. (1988). Finding universal dimensions of individual variation in multicultural studies of values: The Rokeach and Chinese value surveys. *Journal of Personality and Social Psychology*, *55*, 1009-1015.

[5] Cartier, C. (2003). Symbolic city/regions and gendered identity formation in South China. *Provincial China,* 8(1), 60-77.

[6] Chandrasekaran, A., & Ryans, J. (1996). The next Asian dragon? Economic reform and foreign direct investment in China. *Foreign Trade Review*, XXXI, *3*, 1–14.

[7] Chen, A. (2002). Capitalist development, entrepreneurial class, and democratization in China. *Political Science Quarterly*, *117* (3), 401-423.

[8] Chen, G., Li, J., & Matlay, H. (2006). Who are the Chinese private entrepreneurs? A study of entrepreneurial attributes and business governance. *Journal of Small Business and Enterprise Development, 13* (2), 148-159.

[9] Chinese Culture Connection (1987). Chinese values and the search for culture-free dimensions of culture. *Journal of Cross-Cultural Psychology, 18*(2), 143–164.

[10] Chu, C.N. (1991), *The Asian Mind Game-Unlocking the Hidden Agenda of the Asian Business Culture- a Westerner's Survival Manual.* New York, NY: Macmillan Publishing Company.

[11] Chua, B.L., Ho, K., & Le, Z. (2003). *Global entrepreneur monitor: Hong Kong and Shenzhen.* Hong Kong: Trade Industry Department and SME Development Fund.

[12] Cooper, A.C. (1973). Technical entrepreneurship: What do we know? *Research and Development in Management, 3*, 59-64.

[13] Cooper, A.C., & Gimeno Gascón, F.J. (1992). Entrepreneurs, processes of founding, and new firm performance. In D.L. Sexton, & J.D. Kasarda (Eds.), *The State of the Art of Entrepreneurship*, 301-340. Boston, MA: Kent Publishing Co.

[14] Davis, D.S. (1999). Self-employment in Shanghai: A research note. *China Quarterly, 157*, 22-43.

[15] Deakins, D. (1999). *Entrepreneurship and Small Firms*. London, UK: McGraw-Hill.

[16] Eberhard, W. (1965). Chinese regional stereotypes. *Asian Survey, 5*(12), 596–608.

[17] Egri, C., & Ralston, D. (2004). Generation cohorts and personal values: A comparison of China and the United States. *Organization Science, 15*(2), 210–220.

[18] Feather, N.T. (1995). Values, valences, and choice: The influence of values on the perceived attractiveness and choice of alternatives. *Journal of Personality and Social Psychology, 68*, 1135-1151.

[19] Fukuyama, F. (1999). *The Great Disruption: Human Nature and the Reconstitution of Social Order*. New York: The Free Press.

[20] Gartner, W.B. (1988). "Who is an entrepreneur?" is the wrong question. *American Journal of Small Business, 12*, 11-32.

[21] Gentry, J., Tansuhaj, P., Manzer, L., & John, J. (1988). Do geographic subcultures vary culturally? *Advances in Consumer Research, 15*(1), 411-417.

[22] Graham, J.L., & Lam, N.M. (2003). The Chinese negotiation. *Harvard Business Review, 81*(10), 82-91.

[23] Hall, E.T. (1976). *Beyond Culture*. Doubleday Garden City, NY: Anchor Press.

[24] Hofstede, G. (1980a). *Cultures Consequences: International Differences in Work-related Values*. Beverly Hills, CA: Sage.

[25] Hofstede, G. (2001). *Cultures Consequences: Comparing Values, Behaviors, Institutions, and Organizations Across Nations*. Thousand Oaks, CA: Sage.

[26] Holt, D. (1997). A comparative study of values among Chinese and U.S. entrepreneurs between contrasting cultures. *Journal of Business Venturing, 12*, 483-505.

[27] House, R.J., Hanges, P.J., Javidan, M., Dorfman, P.W., & Gupta, V. (Eds.) (2004). *Culture, Leadership, and Organizations: The GLOBE Study of 62 Societies*. Thousand Oaks, CA: Sage.

[28] Hu, H. (1944). The Chinese concept of Face. *American Anthropology, 46*, 45-64.

[29] Hu, W., & Grove, C.L. (1991). *Encountering the Chinese: A Guide for Americans*. Yarmouth, ME, USA: Intercultural Press.

[30] Huang, J. (2004). *The Dynamics of China's Rejuvenation*. London, UK: Palgrave Macmillan

[31] Huang, Y. (2008). Private ownership: The real source of China's economic miracle. *The McKinsey Quarterly*, December: http://www.mckinseyquarterly.com/Public_

Sector/Economic_Policy/Private_ownership_The_real_source_of_Chinas_economic_miracle_2279, accessed 24 Dec 2008.
[32] Huo, Y.P., & Randall, D.M. (1991). Exploring subcultural differences in Hofstede's value survey: The case of the Chinese. *Asia Pacific Journal of Management*, *8*, 159-173.
[33] Hwang, K.K. (1987). Face and favour: the Chinese power game. *American Journal of Sociology*, *92*(4), 944-74.
[34] Inglehart, R., & Carballo, M. (1997). Does Latin America exist? (And is there a Confucian Culture?): A global analysis of cross-cultural difference'. *Political Science and Politics*, March, 34-47.
[35] Inglehart, R. (1977). *The Silent Revolution*. Princeton, NJ: Princeton University Press.
[36] Inglehart, R. (1997). *Modernization and postmodernization*. Princeton, NJ: Princeton University Press.
[37] Inglehart, R., Basanez, M., & Moeno, A.M. (1998). *Human Values and Beliefs: A Cross-Cultural Sourcebook: Political, Religious, Sexual, and Economic*. Ann Arbor, MI, USA: University of Michigan Press.
[38] Kai, K.L. (2008). Learning from the Confucians: Learning from the past. *Journal of Chinese Philosophy*, *35*(1), 97-119.
[39] Kluckhohn, C. (1951). Values and value-orientations in the theory of action: An exploration in definition and classification'. In T. Parsonsand, & E. Shils (Eds.), *Toward a General Theory of Action*, 388-433. Cambridge, MA: Harvard University Press.
[40] Kluckhohn, F., & Strodtbeck, F.L. (1961). *Variations in Value Orientations*. Row, Peterson: Evanston, IL.
[41] Koh, H.C. (1996). Testing hypotheses of entrepreneurial characteristics. *Journal of Managerial Psychology*, *11*, 12-25.
[42] Kohn, M.L., & Schooler, C. (1983). *Work and Personality*. Norwood, NJ, USA: Ablex.
[43] Miner, J.B. (2000). Testing the psychological typology of entrepreneurship using business founders. *Journal of Applied Behavioral Science*, *36*(1), 43-69.
[44] Morris, C.W. (1956). *Varieties of human value*. Chicago: University of Chicago Press.
[45] Parsons, T. (1951). *The Social System*. Glencoe, IL, USA: Free Press.
[46] Peng, W.T. (1995). *The Origins of Chinese Kongsi*. Sengalor Darul Ehsan, Malaysia: Pelanduk Publications.
[47] Putnam, R.D. (1993). *Making Democracy Work: Civic Traditions in Modern Italy*. Princeton, NJ, USA: Princeton University Press.
[48] Qi, Y. (1999). *The Implementation of China's Science and Technology Policy*. Westport, CT, USA: Quorum Books.
[49] Ralston, D.A. Yu, K.C., Wang, X., Terpstra, R.H., & He, W. (1996). The cosmopolitan Chinese manager: Findings of a study on managerial values across six regions of China'. *Journal of International Management*, *2*, 79-109.
[50] Ralston, D.A., Gustafson, D.J., Cheung, F., & Terpstra, R.H. (1993). Differences in managerial values: A study of U.S., Hong Kong and PRC managers. *Journal of International Business Studies*, *24*, 249-275.
[51] Ralston, D.A., Holt, D.A., Terpstra, R.H., & Yu, K.C. (1997). The impact of national culture and economic ideology on managerial work values: A study of the United

States, Russia, Japan, and China. *Journal of International Business Studies*, *28*, 177-208.

[52] Ralston, D.A., Pounder, J., Lo, C.W.H., Wong, Y.Y., Egri, C.P., & Stauffer, J. (2006). Stability and Change in managerial work values: A longitudinal study of China, Hong Kong, and the U.S.A.. *Management and Organization Review*, *2*, 67-94.

[53] Redding, S.G., & Ng, M. (1983). The role of "Face" in the organisational perception of Chinese managers. *International Studies of Management and Organisations*, *3*, 92-123.

[54] Reynolds, P.D., Bygrave, W.D., Autio, E., Cox, L.W., & Hay, M. (2003). *Global Entrepreneurship Monitor (GEM): Executive Report*. Babson College, Babson Park, MA, London Business School, Ewing Marion Kaufman Foundation.

[55] Rickett, W.A. (1985). *Guanzi: Political, Economic, And Philosophical Essays From Early China: A Study And Translation*. Vol. I. Princeton, NJ, USA: Princeton Library of Asian Translations, Princeton University.

[56] Rickett, W.A. (1998). *Guanzi: Political, Economic, And Philosophical Essays From Early China: A Study And Translation*. Vol. II. Princeton, NJ, USA: Princeton Library of Asian Translations, Princeton.

[57] Rokeach, M. (1973). *The nature of human values*. New York, NY, USA: Free Press.

[58] Ronen, S., & Shenkar, O. (1985). Clustering countries on attitudinal dimensions: a review and synthesis. *Academy of Management Review*, *10*(3), 435–454.

[59] Schwartz, S.H., & Boehnke, K. (2004). Evaluating the structure of human values with confirmatory factor analysis. *Journal of Research in Personality*, *38*, 230-255.

[60] Schwartz, S.H. (1992). Universals in the content and structure of values: Theory and empirical tests in 20 countries. In M. Zanna (Ed.), *Advances in Experimental Social Psychology*, *25*, 1-65. New York: Academic Press.

[61] Schwartz, S.H. (1994a). Are there universal aspects in the content and structure of values?. *Journal of Social Issues*, *50*, 19-45.

[62] Schwartz, S.H. (1994b). Beyond individualism/collectivism: New cultural dimensions of values. In K. Uichol, H.C. Triandis, C.Kagitcibasi, S.C. Choi, & Y.Gene (Eds.), *Individualism and Collectivism: Theory, Method, and Applications*. Thousand Oaks, CA: Sage.

[63] Schwartz, S.H. (1999). Cultural value differences: Some implications for work. *Applied Psychology: An International Journal*, *48*, 23–47.

[64] Schwartz, S.H. (2004). Mapping and interpreting cultural differences around the world. In Vinken, H., Soeters, J., & Ester, P. (Eds.), *Comparing Cultures*, 43–73. Leiden, The Netherlands: Brill Academic Publishers.

[65] Schwartz, S.H. (2006). A theory of cultural value orientations: Explication and applications. *Comparative Sociology*, *5*(2/3), 137-182.

[66] Schwartz, S.H. (2007). Basic Human Values: An Overview. http://www.fmag.unict.it/Allegati/convegno%207-8-10-05/Schwartzpaper.pdf, accessed 30 December 2007.

[67] Schwartz, S.H., & Bardi, A. (2001). Value hierarchies across cultures: Taking a similarities perspective. *Journal of Cross-Cultural Psychology*, *32*, 268-290

[68] Schwartz, S.H., & Bilsky, W. (1987). Toward a psychological structure of human values. *Journal of Personality and Social Psychology*, *53*, 550-562.

[69] Schwartz, S.H., & Bilsky, W. (1990). Toward a theory of the universal content and structure of values: Extensions and cross-cultural replications. *Journal of Personality and Social Psychology, 58*, 878-891.

[70] Schwartz, S.H., Bardi, A., & Bianchi, G. (2000). Value adaptation to the imposition and collapse of communist regimes in East-Central Europe'. In J. Duckitt, & S. A. Renshon (Eds.), *Political Psychology: Cultural and Cross Cultural Foundations*, 217-237. Macmillan.

[71] Scott, W.A. (1965). *Values and organizations: A study of fraternities and sororities*. Chicago: Rand McNally.

[72] Sheff, D. (2002). *China Dawn: The Story of a Technology and Business Revolution.* New York, NY, USA: HarperCollins.

[73] Smith, M. B. (1969). *Social Psychology and Human Values*. Chicago, IL: Aldine.

[74] Spires, A.J., Zhang, F.Q. and Pan, Z.Z. (2004). Working Paper: Jumping into the Sea: Entry into Self-Employment during China's Reform Era. http://www.yale.edu/ccr/zhang2.doc+%22Abrami%22+%22Self+making+class%22and hl=enandct=clnkandcd=1, accessed 18 October 2006.

[75] Stiglitz, J. E. (2002). *Globalization and Its Discontents*. New York, NY, USA: W.W. Norton.

[76] Thomas, A.S., & Mueller, S.L. (2000). A case for comparative entrepreneurship: Assessing the relevance of culture. *Journal of International Business Studies, 31*(2), 287-301.

[77] Trescott, P. B. (2002). H. D. Fong and the Study of Chinese Economic Development. *History of Political Economy, 34*(4), 789-809.

[78] Triandis, H.C. (1995). *Individualism and Collectivism*. Boulder, CO: Westview Press.

[79] Trompenaars, F. (1993). *Riding the Waves of Culture: Understanding Diversity in Global Business*. Chicago: Irwin.

[80] Tsang, E.W.K. (1996). In Search of Legitimacy: The Private Entrepreneur in China. *Entrepreneurship, Theory and Practice, 21*(1), 21-30.

[81] Tu, W. (1985). *A Confucian Perspective on Learning to Be Human from Confucian Thought: Selfhood as Creative Transformation*, 51-66. Albany, NY, USA: SUNY Press.

[82] Tu, W. (2004). Core Values in Confucian Thought. Lecture to Department of Religion, Trinity University, USA. http://www.trinity.edu/rnadeau/FYS/Tu%20Wei-ming.htm, accessed 22 October 2006.

[83] Van Gelderen, M.W. (2000). Enterprising behavior of ordinary people. *European Journal of Work and Organisational Psychology, 9*, 81-8.

[84] Vernon, P.E., & Allport, G.W. (1931). A test for personal values. *Journal of Abnormal and Social Psychology*, 26, 233-248

[85] Wang, M. (1998). Diverging Cultural Values in Contemporary China. James A. Baker Institute for Public Policy, Rice University, Houston, TX. Available at http://www.ruf.rice.edu/~tnchina/commentary/wang0398, Accessed 18 December 2006.

[86] Wank, D.L. (1999). *Commodifying Communism: Business, Trust, and Politics in a Chinese City*. Cambridge, UK: Cambridge University Press.

[87] Watson, W., Ponthieu, L., & Doster, J. (1995). Business owner-managers' descriptions of entrepreneurship: A content analysis. *Journal of Constructivist Psychology, 8*, 33-51.

[88] Weber, M. (1958). *The Protestant Ethic and the Spirit of Capitalism.* (Translated by T. Parsons). New York, NY, USA: Scribner. (Originally published 1904-1905.)

[89] White, L.T, III. (1998). *Unstately Power: Local Causes of China's Intellectual, Legal, and Governmental Reforms.* Armonk, NY, USA: M. E. Sharpe, Inc.

[90] Williams, R. M., Jr. (1968). Values. In E. Sills (Ed.), *International Encyclopedia of the Social Sciences.* New York, NY, USA: Macmillan.

[91] Williams, R. M., Jr. (1979). Change and stability in values and value systems: A sociological perspective. In M. Rokeach (Ed.), *Understanding human values: Individual and societal.* New York: Free Press, 15-46.

[92] Xu, G. (2001). Preface. In J. Zhang (Ed.), *Chinese Science and Technology Incubators: Case Studies and Development Strategies*, 1–3 (Beijing, China: Scientific and Technical Documents Publishing House) (in Chinese).

[93] Yan, Z. (2003). The development history of science and technology incubators in China. In Y. Zhao et al. (Eds.), *A Report on the Development of Science and Technology Incubators in China*, 3–9. Xiamen, China: Xiamen University Press (in Chinese).

[94] Yum, J.O. (1988). Network theory in intercultural communication. In Y.Y. Kim, & W.B. Gudykunst (Eds.), *Theories in Intercultural Communication*, 239–258. International and Intercultural Communication Annual, vol. XII. Newbury Park: Sage.

PART II: ORGANISATIONAL CHANGES AND INNOVATIONS

In: Thirty Years of China's Economic Reform
Editors: Yue Wang and Prem Ramburuth

ISBN: 978-1-60876-908-7
© 2010 Nova Science Publishers, Inc.

Chapter 5

UNDERSTANDING BUSINESS GROUP GOVERNANCE IN CHINA

Akira Tanaka* [1] ***and Yue Wang***+[2]

[1]Faculty of Economics, Nagoya City University, Nagoya, Japan
[2]School of Strategy and Entrepreneurship, Australian School of Business, University of New South Wales, Sydney, Australia

ABSTRACT

Despite the rapid development of business groups in China and their ability to compete in the world market, little is known about their governance structures in comparison to their Asian counterparts. This paper examines one of the key features of business group governance, namely inter-firm relationship, in one of China's major automobile groups, Tianjin Automotive Group (TAG). Compared to the established practices of Japanese automobile groups, we found that TAG's inter-firm relationship is characterized by top-down hierarchical administration rather than a truly quasi-market, quasi-hierarchy network structure typically found in Japan. The paper shows that the emerging Chinese business groups are in essence administratively-driven rather than economically-driven industrial organizations, which explains why their governance structures are fundamentally different from the common features of business groups in Japan and the rest of the world.

Keywords: inter-firm relationship, business groups, automobile industry, China, Japan

INTRODUCTION

Business groups are becoming a major player in the world economy and have recently emerged as a distinctive theme in management research, partly because of the rapid

---

* E-mail: tanaka@econ.nagoya-cu.ac.jp.
+ Email: yue.w@unsw.edu.au.

internationalization of such groups from developing countries and partly because of their ability to compete with developed-country firms (Guillen, 2000; Cuervo-Cazurra, 2006). In Asia, business groups – including Japanese *Keiretsu*, Korean *Chaebol*, Indian trading houses and family-owned or controlled conglomerates in Southeast Asia – have proven to be an important form of industrial organization, playing a significant role in the economic development of Asian economies. Though diverse in their organizational structures, the business groups all feature a long history. But in the People's Republic of China, business groups are a relatively new phenomenon. The concept first appeared in China's official documents in 1986 (Ma and Lu, 2005), eight years after the country embarked on a market-oriented economic reform. Yet, with the support of central government, business groups (particularly the state-owned variety) grew rapidly. By 2003, China featured 189 large state-owned business groups (Ma and Lu, 2005). By 2005, 18 of them were large enough to be ranked near the top of *Fortune's* largest 500 global enterprises, including Sinopec, Haier and Lenovo (Xu *et al.*, 2006). Little is known, however, about the governance structure of business groups in China in relation to their counterparts in other Asian countries. This paper aims to provide managerially relevant empirical insights into one of the key features of business group governance, namely the management of inter-firm relationship, in the emerging Chinese business groups. Based on a case study of Tianjin Automobile Group (hereafter referred to as "TAG"), we evaluate the extent to which TAG's inter-firm system differs or resembles well-established Japanese practices.

The rest of the paper is organized as follows. Section 2 provides background on the development of business groups in China since the start of economic reform in 1979 and introduces the case of Tianjin Automobile Group (TAG). Section 3 reviews conceptualizations of business groups and identifies inter-firm relationship as the key to understanding business group governance. Section 4 provides a detailed case study of the governance of inter-firm relationship within TAG, with a comparison to the practices typically adopted by Japanese auto groups. Section 5 draws broader conclusions for our understanding of the emerging Chinese business groups.

RESEARCH BACKGROUND

This section provides some background information on business groups in China and the Tianjin Automobile Group (TAG), the case under investigation.

In China, business groups are called *qiye jituan* (enterprises groups) or *jituan gongsi* (group corporations). They only started to emerge as an important economic force in the late 1980s. Fifty-five large business groups were approved by the State Council in 1991. Most of these business groups were formed by grouping together some large, state-owned enterprises (SOEs), many of which were established between the 1950s and the 1970s under the old, planned-economy system to develop the nation's key industries such as resource, telecommunication and heavy machinery. Aiming to promote SOEs' efficiency and reduce the burden of state financing, the government used the state-owned business groups to facilitate the corporate restructuring and property rights reform for large SOEs (Yiu et al. 2005). Thus, China's business groups emerged as the direct result of a government initiative to fill the ownership voids (Ma et al. 2006) rather than as an entrepreneur response to market failures, as is commonly found elsewhere in the world (Khanna and Palepu 1999, Li et al. 2006).

But by the mid-1990s, the establishment of these large business groups did little more than consolidate the "triangle debts" of SOEs (i.e. transfer the inter-firm debts owed between formally dispersed SOEs into the newly established business group), with little improvement in their efficiency and competitiveness (Cheng 2000). The fundamental nature of the business-group governance remained very similar to the management and organization of a typical large SOE under the old planned-economy institutions. As a result, most of the business groups and their affiliated member companies continued losing money throughout the 1990s.

In order to turn the situation around, the government introduced further measures of reform in 1997 aimed at the establishment of modern enterprise systems (i.e. limited liability companies) in some selected SOEs by 2000. The government implemented a separation of ownership and control of many SOEs (including business groups) by removing itself from the operation and management of these companies. The move was reflected in the change of the Chinese terminology of SOEs from *Guoying* (state-operated) to *Guoyou* (state-owned) enterprises. For most business groups, multiple owners (other than the government) were allowed, although the state was still the majority shareholder of more than 50 percent of the business groups in 2004 (Mao and Wang 2005). Business groups were also encouraged to operate cross-sector, cross-region or even cross-border. Groups such as Lenovo, Haier and Sinopec have successfully established significant overseas operations through Greenfield projects and acquisitions. The diversification of business-group ownership, industries and geographic areas is significant. But the separation from the state is never complete (Meyer and Lu 2005) and the boundaries among ownership and governance are blurred (Tsui et al. 2004). Unlike other developing countries' business groups, which are often founded by entrepreneurs and characterized by unrelated diversification in response to market opportunities (Kock and Guillen 2001), the institutional arrangements between the state and the business groups have had the most important influence on the governance structures of business groups in China.

In the automobile industry, business groups started to appear with a mandate from the Chinese government in the early 1980s. Under the central government's 1982 policy to establish "seven consolidated automobile groups", Tianjin Automobile Industry Company (TAIC) and its affiliated parts factories were merged with other car manufacturers and parts suppliers controlled by different administrative bodies of the Tianjin municipal government. The merged unit was the prototype of the current Tianjin Automobile Group (TAG) and became an affiliated company of the Jing-Jin-Ji Automobile Consolidated Company.

The central government drove the "seven consolidated automobile groups" policy with the aim of subordinating local automobile manufacturers to the China National Automotive Industry Corporation (CNAIC). But local governments resisted the move, and the policy failed. As a result, the Jing-Jin-Ji Automobile Consolidated Company was broken up in 1985, and TAIC was placed under the administrative oversight of Tianjin municipal government. With local government support, TAIC commenced production of small car model *Xiali* in 1986. *Xiali* was for a long period of time ranked second by sales volume in the small car sector in China. At the height of its popularity it commanded a little more than 20 percent of the entire country's market share.

Following the 1994 "Car Industry Policy" which aimed to group more than 100 car manufacturers into eight to ten groups by 2000, TAIC was further granted independence from the Tianjin municipal administration in 1996 and renamed the "Tianjin Automobile Industry (Group) Corporation" (Tianjin Automobile Group as its shorthand).

CONCEPTUALIZATIONS OF BUSINESS GROUPS

Despite extensive studies on business groups, there remains a high degree of definitional ambiguity in the literature. This section provides a review of a variety of conceptualizations of business groups and identifies inter-firm relationship as the key to understand business group governance.

Early studies on industrial organizations stress unrelated diversification and common ownership as key elements of business groups. Leff (1978), for example, defines a business group (which he calls an 'economic group') as a group of companies that does business in different markets under common administrative or financial control. Similarly, Ghemawat and Khanna (1998) view business groups as an organizational form characterized by diversification across a wide range of businesses. Unrelated diversification, however, is not a common characteristic of a large number of Chinese business groups, which were created through government-led consolidation of some large SOEs in the same industry. Emphasizing the aspect of family ownership, Chang and Hong define business groups as "a collection of formally independent firms under single common administrative and financial control, which are owned and controlled by certain families" (2002: 266). However, although there is a general consensus that common control of some sort is a key characteristic of a business group, there is less accord with respect to family ownership as a defining feature (Cuervo-Cazurra 2006). Many firms under common ownership and control – such as Japanese *Keiretsu* and state-owned business groups in China – are not family owned but are often discussed as business groups (Keister 1998). Networks of family-controlled businesses do exist in China, but they are defined as networks, not business groups (Tsui et al. 2004). Business groups in developing countries are often characterized by constellations of loosely connected firms through entrepreneur coordination (Kock and Guillen 2001), but these characteristics also fail to capture the reality of these emerging Chinese state-owned business groups with their tight organizational structures.

To provide an all-encompassing definition of a business group, some authors choose to incorporate elements agreed upon by previous literature (e.g. common control of some sort) and leave out those with less agreement among scholars (particularly the family aspect). For example, Delios and Beamish (2004) define business groups simply as legally independent but organizationally affiliated companies. Similarly, Yiu, Bruton and Lu (2005) view business group as a collection of legally independent firms that are bound by economic and social ties, and Cuervo-Cazurra (2006) conceptualise business groups as a set of legally separate firms with stable relationships under common ownership and control. In this paper, we follow these broad definitions to capture a sense of the increasing number of large, state-owned business groups in China that are not entrepreneur founded, family controlled or engaged in unrelated diversification. Such broad definitions highlight the independent legal status of member firms, as well as the organizational connection of some kind among them, thus pointing to relationships between member companies as the key to understanding the nature of business group governance (Keister 2000, Ma et al. 2006).

As a collection of independent firms, the success or failure of a business group depends heavily on how their member companies are affiliated with each other through effective group organizations. Managing the inter-firm relationship within a business group embodies quasi-market and quasi-hierarchy features. These independent companies are often connected through cross-shareholding, reciprocal trading agreements and intra-group financing (Delios and Beamish 2004). In Japan, historical ties among affiliated companies in the pre-war family-controlled *Zaibatsu* played a crucial role in the formation of post-war *Keiretsu* (Miyashita and Russell 1994). In Korea, *Chaebols* are still dominated by founding family members, through direct and sole ownership, and by interlocking ownership or a holding company (Chen 2004). In overseas Chinese-controlled business groups in Southeast Asia, affiliated companies are often bound together by family or kinsmen ties in response to hostile local government policy towards ethnic Chinese minorities (Whitley 1992, Redding 1996, Yeung 1998). In China, business groups are a relatively new phenomenon and their governance structure of inter-firm relationship is less understood compared to their Asian counterparts. Because Japanese post-war industrial organization has had the most significant influence over the way Chinese business groups were established and managed (Mao and Wang 2005), below we provide a focused comparison of the inter-firm governance of Chinese and Japanese automobile groups.

THE CASE STUDY FINDINGS

Based on onsite interviews with senior executives and purchasing managers in TAG's Group Corporation (GC), we focused our investigation on some major practices in managing buyer-supplier relationship within the TAG, including payment settlement, pricing and intra-group dealing. These areas were chosen because there is well-established knowledge about how they are practiced in Japanese automobile groups. In this section, we report the field research results on the organization of TAG's inter-firm relationship with a direct comparison to the practices typically adopted in Japanese auto groups (particularly Toyota). Our case analysis revealed that unlike the automobile groups in Japan, the inter-firm relationship in TAG was governed by hierarchical coordination rather than a true network structure, consisting of a core assembler and quasi-independent associated supplier companies.

The first feature under investigation is payment settlement practices. Unlike in Japan, the settlement of the TAG's parts payment did not correspond to each purchasing transaction in parts. Instead, income from finished car sales was collected and distributed by the TAG Sales Company (which in reality was treated as a sales department) to the group's affiliated companies. Revenue from finished car sales at directly-managed stores and at dealerships was first sent to the Sales Company. On the last Wednesday of each month, a payment distribution meeting was held between the Sales Company's accounting center and companies at the core level of the TAG, and payments to each company were determined. Distribution was basically made to each of these core companies according to the cost of sold parts. Then, payment was made from these core companies to each subordinate supplier to cover their parts and components costs.

Although monthly settlement is also a common feature in Japan, it must be noted that in China payment does not necessarily correspond to the quantity of parts supplied. In the TAG, a lag between business results and the estimation of demand or the production plan would produce an increase of stocks of finished cars. If the costs of finished cars were not recovered, payment was not made for parts costs. The arrangement resulted in the so-called "triangle debts" which expand upstream as a chain reaction. This is a serious issue, as suppliers' dependence on group sales was extremely high in China.

The reason that the settlement of TAG's parts payment did not correspond to each purchasing transaction in parts was because the group's affiliated supplier companies were not treated as independent profit centres. The supplier companies were instead treated as internal departments or factories to bear the costs for the whole group. Any inter-firm purchasing/supplying exchanges were still considered "business within the group." In Japan, where suppliers were also often encouraged to share the costs with the assemblers, the assemblers cannot impose cost-reduction through hierarchical means. Car makers can only use a combination of market incentives and other relational mechanisms such as supplier associations to work with suppliers to reduce costs through continuous innovation of parts and components production, passing the savings on to the assemblers (Dore, 1987; Gerlach, 1987; Nishiguchi, 1994). The arrangement provides a win-win situation for both car assemblers and parts suppliers, an example of what relational contracting means in Japan (Williamson, 1985). In the case of the TAG, such features of relational contracting were completely absent prior to 1999, and the payment settlement practice reflected the administrative nature of relationship between GC (*de facto* headquarters of the TAG) and its subsidiaries, despite their nominal independent legal status.

Second, the GC held the right to set the parts price, although the GC and suppliers could negotiate for price changes at the end of every year. According to reports from parts suppliers, the demand for price cuts by the GC during these negotiations was so aggressive that they completely siphoned off the fruits of any improved efficiencies. In some cases, the prices set for the parts were lower than the production costs. This kind of price-setting practice would not be possible if the supplier companies were treated as independent firms. As a result, negotiations on parts costs with some suppliers could extend for prolonged periods during which time parts had been supplied in the absence of fixed prices.

In Japan, renewal negotiations on parts unit prices are usually held every six months. The reduction in the purchase price for parts is less than any reduction in suppliers' production costs gained from rationalization conducted by suppliers. This method encourages suppliers to invest in rationalization. If the price cut for purchasing is too large, suppliers will not have the capacity to invest in further rationalization. Inversely, if it is too small, they will have less incentive to invest in rationalization. Again, on pricing, we can see the TAG's inter-firm relationship was actually hierarchical, in contrast to the quasi-market, quasi-hierarchy feature of the Japanese practice.

Finally, in the TAG each affiliated company dealt almost 100 percent within the group, demonstrating an extremely high level of exclusiveness. In interviews with the Japanese managers in Tianjin, we often heard them observe that business relationships in China were based on the group to a greater extent than in Japan. This exclusiveness is partly due to the fact that most suppliers in the TAG were spin-offs from its predecessor TAIC's branch factories. The arrangement can also be attributed to Tianjin Municipal Government policies known as "The priority of dealing within the group" (*xian nei, hou wai*) and "The priority of dealing within the city" (*xian benshi, hou waibu*). It is noteworthy that TAG has been granted "independence" from local government since 1996, but in practice its GC and core-affiliated companies maintain extensive organisational and personal ties with the Tianjin municipal government and are heavily influenced by the local government's policies.

While intra-group business dealings were once a core feature of the Japanese vertical *Keiretsu* system, the exclusiveness of such dealings has weakened dramatically as the competition for buyers significantly intensified since the 1980s. Within the automobile industry, for example, the buyer-supplier relationship has shifted from more of a quasi-hierarchy system to one that is more quasi-market based (Sako et al., 2004). In the Toyota Group, as early as the mid-1980s, more than one third of its group-affiliated companies had already reduced their reliance on delivery within the group to less than 70 percent.

CONCLUSION

This paper is among the first to examine the governance of inter-firm relationship within the emerging Chinese business groups. Compared to the established practices in Japan, our case study of Tianjin Automobile Group (TAG) offers a rich understanding of the inner-running of the emerging Chinese business groups. Although TAG and Toyota Group share the basic features of an organic whole consisting of a parent company at the apex of a supporting cast of group-affiliated companies, there is a significant difference between them. In TAG the independence or autonomy of group-affiliated companies is much weaker than in Japanese automobile groups. This is explicitly shown in the three major practices in governing inter-firm relationship within the automobile groups, comprising the settlement of payments, pricing and intra-group dealing. This is due to the historic factor that TAG was established through the administratively-driven re-structuring of a large state-owned enterprise, into a business group with nominal constituent companies. Unlike most business groups in other developing countries, which are often entrepreneur founded, family owned, and engaged in unrelated diversification with a loosely coupled structure (Kock and Guillen 2001), the causes for the creation of the emerging business groups in China are different. The formation of business groups such as the TAG was part of the government's broad agenda to reform property rights in large state-owned enterprises. Although TAG formally has a holding company, General Corporation (GC), at the apex of the group, in practice GC was the headquarters within a large state-owned company called "business group". Thus, the group-affiliated supplier companies are treated as member-companies first, independent legal entities second. Their existence is to serve the group interest more so than their self-interest, which is completely different from the concept of the business group in Japan and the rest of the world. This paper thus shows that emerging Chinese business groups are in essence administratively-driven, rather than economically-driven industrial organizations, which explains why their governance structures are fundamentally different from the common features of business groups in Japan and the rest of the world.

REFERENCES

[1] Chang, S., & Hong, J. (2000). Economic performance in group-affiliated companies in Korean: Intra-group resource sharing and internal business transactions, *Academy of Management Journal*, *43* (3), 429-448.

[2] Chen, M. (2004). *Asian Management Systems*, Singapore: Thomson.

[3] Cheng, Q. T. (2000). *China's Large Enterprises at the Turn of Century (Shiji Zhi Jiao De Zhongguo Daxing Qiye)*, The Centre of Development Studies, State Council, Beijing.

[4] Cuervo-Cazurra, A. (2006). Business groups and their types, *Asia Pacific Journal of Management*, *23* (4), 419-437.

[5] Delios, A., & P. W. Beamish (2004). *International Business: An Asia Pacific Perspective*, Singapore: Prentice Hall.

[6] Dore, R. P. (1987). *Taking Japan Seriously*, Stanford University Press: Stanford.

[7] Gerlach, M. L. (1987). Business alliances and the strategy of the Japanese firm, *California Management Review*, *30* (1), 126-142.

[8] Ghemawat, P., & Khanna, T. (1998). The nature of diversified business groups: A research design and two case studies, *Journal of Industrial Economics*, *46*, 35-61.

[9] Guillen, M. F. (2000). Business groups in emerging economies: A resource-based view, *Academy of Management Journal*, *43* (3), 362-380.

[10] Khanna, T., & Palepu, K. (1999). Policy shocks, market intermediaries, and corporate strategy: The evolution of business groups in Chile and India, *Journal of Economics and Management Strategy*, *8*, 271-310.

[11] Keister, L. A. (1998). Engineering growth: Business group structure and firm performance in China's transition economy, *American Journal of Sociology*, *104*, 404-440.

[12] Keister, L. A. (2000). *Chinese Business Groups: The Structure and Impact of Interfirm Relations during Economic Development*, Oxford, NY: Oxford University Press.

[13] Kock, C. J., & Guillen, M. F. (2001). Strategy and structure in developing countries: Business groups as an evolutionary response to opportunities for unrelated diversification, *Industrial and Corporate Change*, *10* (1), 77-113.

[14] Leff, N. (1978). Industrial organization and entrepreneurship in the developing countries: The economic groups, *Economic Development and Culture Change*, *78*, 661-674.

[15] Li, M., Ramaswamy, K., & Petitt, B. S. P. (2006). Business groups and market failures: A focus on vertical and horizontal strategies, *Asia Pacific Journal of Management*, *23* (4), 439-452.

[16] Ma, X., & Lu, J. W. (2005). The critical role of business groups in China, *Ivey Business Journal*, May/June: 1-12.

[17] Ma, X., Yao, X., & Xi, Y. (2006). Business group affiliation and firm performance in a transition economy: a focus on ownership voids, *Asia Pacific Journal of Management*, *23* (4), 467-483.

[18] Mao, Y. S., & Wang, J. C. (2005). *The top 50 enterprises in Guangdong: Growth and Restructuring (Guangdong Qiye Wushi Qiang: Chenzhang Yu Chonggou)*, Beijing: Qinghua University Press.

[19] Miyashita, K., & Russell, D. W. (1994). Keiretsu*: Inside the Hidden Japanese Conglomerates*. New York: McGraw-Hill.

[20] Nishiguchi, T. (1994). *Strategic Industrial Sourcing: The Japanese Advantage*, New York: Oxford University Press.

[21] Redding, S. G. (1996). Weak organizations and strong linkages: managerial ideology and Chinese family business networks, in G. G. Hamilton (ed.), *Asian Business Networks*, 27-42, Berlin: Walter de Gruyter & Co..

[22] Sako, M., Lamming, R., & Helper, S. R. (2004). Supplier relations in the UK car industry: good news, bad news, *European Journal of Purchasing and Supply Management, 13*, 237-248.

[23] Tsui, A. S. (2004). Contributing to global management knowledge: A case for high quality indigenous research, *Asia Pacific Journal of Management*, 21, 491-513.

[24] Whitley, R. (1992). *Business systems in East Asia: firms, markets, and societies*, London: Sage.

[25] Williamson, O. E. (1985). *The Economic Institutions of Capitalism*, New York: Free Press.

[26] Xu, D., Pan, Y., Wu, C., & Yim, B. (2006). Performance of domestic and foreign-invested enterprises in China, *Journal of World Business*, *41*, 261-274.

[27] Yeung, H. W-C. (1998). *Transnational Corporations and Business Networks: Hong Kong firms in the ASEAN region*, London: Routledge.

[28] Yiu, D., Bruton, G. D., & Lu, Y. (2005). Understanding business group performance in an emerging economy: Acquiring resources and capabilities in order to prosper, *Journal of Management Studies*, *42*, 183-206.

In: Thirty Years of China's Economic Reform
Editors: Yue Wang and Prem Ramburuth
ISBN: 978-1-60876-908-7
© 2010 Nova Science Publishers, Inc.

Chapter 6

WORKER MOTIVATION DURING CHANGING PERIODS: THE ROLE OF PSYCHOLOGICAL CAPITAL IN CHINA'S ECONOMIC REFORM

Putai Jin*
The University of New South Wales, Sydney, Australia

ABSTRACT

The aims of this chapter are (a) to examine the economic progress of China using historical comparisons, (b) to analyze the psychological capital of China's workforces, and (c) to highlight emerging issues associated with Chinese human resource management for sustainable development. The four-stage cycle "Turbulent times – Concessions, constraints, and reforms of the new regime – Recovery of social productive forces – Prosperity of economy and associated aspects" (TCRP) can be identified in Chinese history, such as the golden age of the West Han and Tang Dynasties. It is argued that, whereas the catalytic functioning of a series of policy changes initiated by the current Chinese government should be acknowledged, the relatively emancipated Chinese social productive forces in various types of enterprises need to be regarded as one of the crucial factors in recent remarkable economic growth in China. During this rapidly changing period, Chinese workers' positive motivational states, such as hope, resiliency and realistic optimism, provide invaluable psychological capital for coping with work stress and attaining high performance. Although China is faced with a number of problems associated with the global economic crisis, the positive psychological capital of Chinese workers will play a constructive role in the reforming and opening-up processes.

Keywords: the four-stage cycle, Chinese workers' motivation, positive psychological capital, hope, resiliency, realistic optimism.

* E-mail: p.jin@unsw.edu.au.

INTRODUCTION

The world has witnessed rapid, steady economic growth in mainland China over the last three decades. In the current financial crisis, some politicians and economists hope that China's continuous development may to a certain degree contribute to the recovery of the global/local economy in the not too distant future. What has happened in China's economy in the last thirty years is impressive. Top officials in mainland China attribute this economic achievement to the specific policies of recent economic reforms and to the implementation of those policies. While such claims may be partially substantiated at face value, we need to further analyze this phenomenon from historical, cultural, and social psychological perspectives.

It is reasonable to acknowledge the catalytic impact of a series of initiatives on economic growth by the Chinese government, such as guided economic reforms, fiscal policy changes, market-oriented strategies, and invitation of investment from foreign, Taiwanese, and Hong Kong entrepreneurs. However, the relatively emancipated Chinese social productive forces should be regarded as the crucial factor in the recent remarkable economic growth occurring in China. The aims of this chapter are (a) to examine China's economic progress by using historical comparisons, (b) to analyze the psychological capital of China's workforces, and (c) to highlight emerging issues associated with Chinese human resources management for sustainable development.

HISTORICAL COMPARISONS: A FOUR-STAGE CYCLE

A trend analysis of Chinese history in terms of the interactions between the regime and workforce can be informative. Historically, after a severely disturbing and politically chaotic period, the newly established regime (Han Dynasty, Tang Dynasty, etc.) tended to loosen its bureaucratic control as a gesture of compromise between the government and the ruled; subsequently, the gradual rehabilitation of the social productive forces occurred (Bai, 1982). A four-stage cycle "Turbulent times – Concessions, constraints, and reforms of the new regime – Recovery of social productive forces – Prosperity of economy and associated aspects" (TCRP) can be identified in the golden age of West Han Dynasty (206 B.C. – 48 B.C.) and Tang Dynasty (618 – 907). At the early stage (about 100 years or so) of both regimes, the nation was well-known for its economic boom and cultural affluence coupled with a series of governmental concessions and political-economic reforms. In both cases, the dynamics of social productive forces should be regarded as the main factor for social, economic, and cultural progress, whereas the top-down political/economic reforms and association policies acted as a catalyst in those high-impact processes.

The events in China during recent decades have shown a similar pattern. During the destructive period (1966-1976) of the Cultural Revolution in China, almost all industries were not functioning normally; workers' wages were virtually frozen; peasants were not allowed to work outside the people's commune and not even permitted to stay long-term in the cities; universities and colleges were shut down; essential resources were diverted for internal fighting among politically-motivated groups and wings; workers' morale was very low; most of the secondary school leavers were unemployed and sent to the countryside or to uncultivated remote areas for so-called "re-education"; many intellectuals with higher degrees were removed from their posts to ideological remoulding camps, farms or other profession-irrelevant places to do manual work; numerous individuals were confined or even executed without any civilized procedures, just because of their would-be defiant belief systems, unfavourable family background, or deviant cultural identities; and the influences from western democratic countries were reduced to a minimal level. It is not surprising that after ten years of such upheavals China's economy was almost ruined, even though the regime had managed to produce massively destructive nuclear weapons and intercontinental missiles at any cost.

The Cultural Revolution stopped soon after the death of Mao Zedong in September 1976. After several power struggles within the Chinese central ruling authorities, the Chinese policy makers realized and advocated that it was urgent "to bring order out of chaos" (i.e., *bo luan fan zheng*) in 1978. The Chinese regime decided to adopt a relatively pragmatic approach that was slightly and gradually deviated from Mao's hard line. Facing the severe situation that "over one thousand tasks remain to be undertaken" (i.e., *bai fei dai jü*) and being uncertain about its own supreme status in the future, the Chinese central ruling body started the processes of concessions, constraints, and reforms thereafter. The complex, winding but no-return processes since 1979 can be roughly divided into three stages, each having a few phases (see Table 1).

In line with the economic transition from the state-planned administration to the market-oriented mode, including public ownership reform and private business establishment, China has obtained impressive economic and international trading growth since 1979. Today China is the third largest (and soon probably the second largest) economy in the world. While the state-owned enterprises still control key aspects of the economy, such as banking, petroleum, steel, electricity, telecommunications and the nuclear industry, the contribution of China's private sector to its GDP has been above 65% since 2006. The reforming and opening-up processes are characterized by the interaction between the Chinese central and local ruling bodies, social productive forces, external input and globalization.

A question of interest is: what is the psychological reaction of the ordinary Chinese workforce to the dramatic changes in economic, social and technological environments? According to Bandura (1997), frequent changes, transfers, high turnover resulting from short-term contracts and job losses tend to increase employees' feelings of uncertainly and perceived stress. Under such conditions, workers may perceive that the vast, rapid and ongoing changes imposed upon them are overtaxing their own physical and mental resources and thus heighten their arousal levels. Moreover, if those concerns are not addressed properly, the negative psychologically aroused states can lead to employees' lowered organizational commitment, decreased job satisfaction, increased anxiety, and ineffective work performance (Ambrose & Kulik, 1999). Workers in China, whether employed by down-sizing state-owned enterprises or recruited by newly emerging private enterprises, are experiencing unprecedented transformations. How do they cope with the associated work stress and anxiety? The following section will analyze the psychological capital possessed by the ordinary Chinese workforce.

Table 1. Economic reforms in China (1979 – present)

Stage I: The Unfrozen Period (1979-1982)	Granting state-owned enterprises more autonomy Introducing the Industry Economic Responsibility System Allowing small private or self-employed businesses to operate Setting up Special Economic Zones with favourable policies and flexible measures on foreign economic activities Practicing the Household Contract Responsibility System in rural areas, which links farmers' incomes to their own contributions
Stage II: The Forming Period (1983-1992)	Introducing a new taxation system for state-owned enterprises to replace the all-profits-handed-to-state system Reviving the domestic economy and upholding the opening-up policy Creating conditions for breaking up the planned economic system Encouraging competition in a market-driven environment Experimenting with various contract responsibility systems and leasing operations Expanding village-township enterprises Allowing rural workforces to be contracted workers in factories and construction sites
Stage III: The Changing Period (1993-present)	Transforming the "socialist" planned economy into the "socialist" market economy system Adjusting China's economic growth mode from the labour-intensive type to a quality-oriented intensive type Introducing a modern enterprise management system Allowing the former British colony Hong Kong to maintain its highly capitalist economy under the "one nation, two systems" policy, after its returning to China in 1997 Confirming the private-sector economy as an important part of the "socialist" market economy in 1999 Joining the World Trade Organization in 2001 to facilitate Chinese commodities entering the world market Establishing a state-owned property management system in 2002 Announcing a "scientific strategy of development" for balanced and sustainable growth in 2003 Abolishing agricultural taxes from 2006 to reduce the financial burden on farmers Implementing the "Property Rights Law" to protect private properties and benefits in 2007 Hosting the Olympic Games in Beijing in 2008, with national efforts and relatively transparent administrations Starting direct air and sea transport and postal services between the Chinese mainland and Taiwan in December 2008 Negotiating further economic collaboration with the Taiwanese regime in 2009
Stage III: The Changing Period (1993-present)	Expanding the domestic market to stimulate the slowed economy Pursuing a variety of plans and measures to retrain millions of unemployed migrant workers returning to their villages Participating in international forums to deal with the global financial crisis

Chinese Workers' Motivation and Psychological Capital

Empirical Studies on Work Motivation at the Early Stage of China's Economic Reforms

Independent empirical studies on Chinese workers' motivation and enterprise reforms started in the early 1980s (e.g., Chamerlain, 1987; Chiu, 1986; Chen, An, & Jin, 1985; Chen & Jin, 1984; Hofstede, 1984; Jin, 1984; O'Toole, 1981; Shenkar & Ronen, 1987; Shirk, 1981; Xu, 1986). For instance, in their pioneering investigation on managerial practice, workers' motivation and productivity in a Haiyan Shirt Factory (a well-known test case in China for reforms toward market-oriented business administration and merit-based incentive systems), Chen and Jin (1984) evaluated the feasibility of those measures for enterprise autonomy and recommended using balanced participatory decision-making procedures to involve and benefit all workers for sustainable growth.

Research has demonstrated that there is a significant correlation between motivations to work and organizational performance (e.g., Friedlander, 1966). Xu (1986) urged Chinese researchers in the areas of Industrial/Organizational Psychology to focus on work motivation, organizational restructuring and development, managerial performance, and management-worker relations. Various forms of incentive systems based on goal-setting theory, expectancy theory and attribution theory were used in factories in an attempt to raise Chinese workers' motivation (Jin, 1984, 1992, 1993; Wang, 1991). In a series of controlled field experiments in Chinese knitwear, boiler-making, automobile engine and electric meter industries conducted by Jin (1993), voluntarily formed work teams were set up in comparison with management-assigned control groups. It was found that voluntarily formed work teams had higher work motivation and better performance than did workgroups with assigned members. According to Jin (1993), the motivation in Chinese work teams was influenced by group participatory decision-making, group cohesiveness and task interdependence. In general, it appears that Chinese workers value not only self-efficacy but also group-efficacy (Chen & Jin, 1991; Jin, 1993; O'Toole, 1981; Shenkar & Ronen, 1987; Shirk, 1981).

Chinese Cultural Architecture and its Impact on Workplace Behaviour

Although the central ruling body has, in the past, launched numerous political campaigns (particularly the anti-human-nature Cultural Revolution), social cohesion was destroyed at the surface level and even injected distrust into various aspects of interpersonal relations. The deep roots of fundamental Chinese cultural values, which have enabled Chinese civilization to develop and sustain itself, are unshakable. For instance, as observed by a number of researchers (e.g., Chen & Jin, 1991; Jin, 1993; Shirk, 1981), Chinese workers believe Confucius' teaching "is harmony that is prized" (*he wei gui*), even when tensions among the rank and file on many occasions were deliberately created by the political authorities in the workplace, who were fond of the "divide and rule" strategy (Chen & Jin, 1991; Jin, 1992, 1993). This "harmony as priority" social psychological principle was subconsciously upheld by ordinary workers even when Confucian ideology was officially denounced in the darkest days of the Cultural Revolution. At the deeper level of an organization or work unit (*danwei*), Chinese employees on the whole are subconsciously attached to, or keen, in a working environment that fosters long-term interpersonal relationships, psychological comfort and general well-being.

As pointed out by a number of researchers (e.g., Ang, 2000; Jackson & Bak, 1998; Wright, Berrel, & Gloet, 2008), the basis of China's cultural architecture consists of the orientation of collectivism, established group norms, benign relationships (*guanxi*), mutually reinforced dignity (*mianzi*), humility and self-restraint, avoiding public reproachment for poor performance, practical ways to maintain balance or harmony, and obtaining purposeful positive outcomes. More recently, researchers interested in organizational behaviour in China have taken Chinese cultural values and belief systems into consideration and generated multifaceted studies, such as conflict avoidance (Tjosvold & Sun, 2002), Chinese work values (Song & Gale, 2007), feedback-seeking behaviour (Lam, Huang, & Snape, 2007), affective commitment effects of performance-oriented human resources subsystems (Gong, Law,

Chang, & Xin, 2009), public service motivation and job satisfaction (Liu, Tang, & Zhu, 2008), and creating a supportive workplace environment to reduce emotional stress (Sun & Pan, 2008).

Psychological Capital of Chinese Workers

As highlighted by Humphreys (2007), although the recent processes of globalization have been blurring the cultural and trading boundary between China and the western world, there are still vast differences in their political-economic systems and personal social values. The collectivist nature leads to culturally-bound group dynamics that are characterized by perceived harmony and conformity. In group processes, Chinese workers tend to exhibit strong organizational commitment, accept the leaders' vision that is associated with seniority, and express the desire to foster and maintain congruent relationships between leaders and followers (Chen & Jin, 1991; Earley, 1989; Humphreys, 2007; Jin, 1984, 1992, 1993).

As mentioned earlier, the immense and dynamic Chinese workforce plays an active role in the global economy and should be regarded as the vital factor in the equation of China's reform. According to Luthans, Avolio, Walumbwa and Li (2005), the Chinese workforce possesses three main features: human capital (i.e., *what you know*), social capital (i.e., *who you know*), and psychological capital (i.e., *who you are*). While the aspects of human capital (O'Leary, Lindholm, Whitford, & Freeman, 2002) and social capital (Adler & Kwon, 2002) have been widely examined, the construct of psychological capital has been relatively neglected and thus deserves more attention (Luthans, Luthans, & Luthans, 2004). The positive organizational behaviour approach is part of the new school of positive psychology proposed by Seligman and Csikszentmihalyi (2000), which emphasizes human potentialities and strengths for thriving and progressing at individual, group, organizational, and cultural levels.

The psychological capital can be trait-like or state-like. According to Luthans and associates (2005), the positive psychological states are significantly associated with desirable performance in enterprises.

They conducted a survey with a sample of over four hundred Chinese workers in two private and one stated-owned representative factories to investigate Chinese employees' psychological states and their performance as indicated by superiors' ratings and merit-based salary data. It was found that (a) the Chinese workers' positive psychological states were characterized by the factors of hope, optimism and resiliency, which formed a global psychological capital construct, and (b) the combined efficacy of positive psychological states acted as a significant determinant of the Chinese workers' rated performance.

The state of hope is a motivational drive which enables individuals to mobilize goal-oriented energy and seek pathways via active planning to meet desired goals (Luthans & Jensen, 2002; Peterson & Luthans, 2003; Snyder, 2000). The state of optimism indicates a general mood tendency or attitudinal inclination to realistically interpret work environmental factors and work processes as challenges and opportunities for further improvement and success (Luthans & Youseff, 2004; Peterson, 2000; Scheier & Carver, 1985; Tiger, 1971). The state of resiliency, a concept borrowed from physics, refers to the capacity of an individual's buoyancy in a fast-changing work environment to recover from disturbance, deal with adversity and adapt to transformations. China's economy has reached a stage where it cannot simply rely on its cheap intensive labour and abundant natural resources for sustainable and relatively high-speed growth. The future growth will also be dependent on the continuous upgrading of technology and the effective development of human resources. China encounters a number of difficult conditions, such as the uncertainty of the global market, less developed domestic demands, immature entrepreneurship, irregularity of business practices, inexperienced management and personnel, inefficiency of various levels of governmental bureaucracies, resistance resulting from a history of rigid planned economic policies and ideology, inadequacy of social security and welfare systems, and uncontrollability of huge mobile workforces from inlands and rural areas. Chinese workers' positive motivational states (e.g., hope, realistic optimism, and resiliency) provide invaluable psychological capital to act as a buffer zone for coping with work stress and to continuously attain desired progress that has been impressive.

LONG MARCH AHEAD: MULITFACETED FEATURES OF HUMAN RESOURCES MANAGEMENT IN CHINA

In order to thrive on challenges, China needs not only to attract foreign direct investment and to introduce modern technology, but also to implement reforms on its political-economic systems and manage its huge human resources (Xie, 2005; Zhu, Thomson, & De Cieri, 2008). Using system perspectives, the following sections will focus on the multifaceted features of human resource management and the associated aspects of crucial system reform in China.

Workers in Enterprises with Different Types of Ownership

Before 1978, there were only three types of business ownership; namely, the mainstream state-owned enterprises, a certain proportion of collectively owned enterprises, and self-employed businesses (usually in non-significant service sectors). In rural areas, the village-township enterprises were usually in the form of collective ownership. During its thirty years of economic reform, China has developed various additional types of enterprise ownership, such as private-owned businesses and foreign-invested enterprises (FIEs) which include JVs (both equity and contractual joint ventures) and WFOEs (wholly foreign owned enterprises) (Wang, Bruning, & Peng, 2007). Organizational behaviour research in China must take variety in work ecology into account.

Workers in State-Owned Enterprises

The state-owned enterprises have undertaken comprehensive restructuring or downsizing processes. Independent evaluations (e.g., Hassard, Morris, Sheehan, & Xiao, 2006; Ralston, Terpstra-Tong, Terpstra, Wang, & Egri, 2006) show that the state-owned enterprises, after thirty years of reform, including the tough implementations of the enterprise bankruptcy law and organizational restructuring changes, are more competitive domestically and globally than before. The state-owned enterprises have substantially transformed into a configuration, or are turning to a direction, desired by the Chinese government. Although the "Eat on the Big" (*daguofan*) system (i.e., a "mess together" distribution system based on extreme and indiscriminate egalitarianism) has been altered, workers in the state-owned enterprises, relative to those working in the private-owned enterprises, still have a certain degree of job security and other benefits. However, they are afraid that one day the enterprises, by definition owned by the state, may fall into private hands due to the process of privatization or the implementation of a shareholder system. They may, therefore, lose their tenure and current benefits provided by the state-owned enterprises (Mak, Wong, & Lee, 2002).

Workers in Private-Owned Enterprises

In the same period, private enterprises started almost from scratch to form what is today a significant component of China's economy. It is informative to examine the differences in motivational aspects between workers in the state-owned enterprises and employees in the non-state-owned enterprises. Empirical research (e.g., Qin & Tan, 2006) shows that workers in the private-owned enterprises had significantly lower scores in comfort and security than their counterparts in the state-owned enterprises. In contrast, workers in the private-owned enterprises reported significantly higher scores in competence and growth in comparison with those working in the state-owned enterprises. In a study on organization citizenship behavior in mainland China, it was found that workers in the state-owned enterprises, compared with employees in the non-state owned enterprises, expressed more interest in social welfare participation and showed less concern about taking initiatives, protecting enterprise properties and saving company resources (Farh, Zhong, & Organ, 2004). Private-owned enterprises, on the other hand, have strong motivation to take innovative approaches and are indeed flexible in implementing research and development. In general they lack both sufficient financial support and skillful human resources, and are vulnerable to the downturn of the global market and to bureaucratic interference from local governments. The recently proclaimed Property Rights Law may, to a certain degree, ease both private firm employers' and employees' fears of any sudden and undesirable changes in current reforming and opening-up policies.

Workers in Village-Township Enterprises

Both collectively-owned and family-owned village-township enterprises, with business autonomy in capital-raising, operational, managerial and marketing levels, have expanded rapidly since the later 1970s reforms. In the processes of China's rural industrialization, the kinship networks are conducive to kin solidarity and kin trust, thus having significantly positive effects on the development, as well as protection, of private/collective entrepreneurship at its initial stages of marketing-oriented reform (Peng, 2004). Village-township enterprises today contribute significantly to China's value-added economy and absorb a considerable proportion of the young labour force in rural areas (Chow, 2004). On the one hand, being solely responsible for profits and losses, village-township enterprises are usually relatively small in size, and thus are fairly flexible and competitive. On the other hand, village-township enterprises are faced with a number of difficulties, such as a lack of local infrastructure (transportation, energy resources, material supply, etc.), a shortage of qualified technical staff and experienced managerial personnel, low levels of education/training in the workforce, an absence of long-term strategic management, inadequate measures for product upgrading, and limited financial resources for development or contingency support to deal with the global economic crisis. To a great extent, the prosperity of village-township enterprises is associated with favourable policies pursued by different levels of local government. In some areas, especially the east and south coastal regions (e.g., Jiangsu, Zhejiang, Fujian and Guangdong Provinces), local authorities and officials have rendered timely aid, including technical support and credit assistance, to village-township enterprises. Some of the returned migrant workers (who previously moved from their homes in the countryside or inland to work in urban enterprises), with acquired skills and savings, may also be helpful in reenergizing village-township enterprises.

Workers in Foreign-Owned Companies

Foreign companies were permitted to establish businesses with Chinese enterprises by "the Law of the PRC on Chinese-Foreign Equity Joint Ventures", approved at the Second Session of the Fifth National People's congress on 1 July 1979. Since then, Chinese-foreign joint-ventures and foreign-owned enterprises have been mushrooming in China, with currently more than 40 million Chinese employees. Research shows that (a) Chinese workers highly value collectivism, (b) local (i.e., Chinese) employees tend to pursue ongoing relationships with the companies, and (c) Chinese workers appreciate rewards and benefits provided by the firms (Ang, Dyne, & Begley, 2003; Jackson & Bak, 1998; Leung & Bond, 1984). Attempts have been made to integrate foreign management systems, combined with Chinese regulations and culture (e.g., Björkman & Lu, 1999). It should be noted that there are variations in terms of different foreign ownerships (Liu, Tjosvold, & Wong, 2004; Walsh & Zhu, 2007). Japanese joint-ventures emphasize permanent employment contracts with Chinese employees and tend to reach collective agreements through negotiations with enterprise unions; US-invested and European-owned companies prefer to establish fixed-term contracts with local employees and eschew collective bargaining. In spite of the relatively higher salaries offered by foreign-owned enterprises in comparison to domestic industries, the turn-over rate in foreign-owned companies is noticeably high. To retain skillful Chinese employees, a challenging task for human resource management in foreign-owned companies is to configure a strategic blueprint for their long-term operations in China, incorporate Chinese cultural architecture into enterprise policy making, and enhance interaction between foreign staff and local employees in their daily managerial practices (Hamilton, Knouse, & Hill, 2009; Yu & Egri, 2005).

Modern Enterprise Management Training, Research and Development

While China has ample labourers who are young and low-paid, the bottleneck of human resources is in the lack of skilful and vigorous managers with the new concept of modern enterprise operations. According to Hsiao (2008), many experts have estimated that China would need at least 1.5 million MBAs, or equivalent qualification holders, between the period of 1999 and 2009. The rapidly expanded programs for management training and education are still not able to meet the huge demands. Another barrier is the shortage of professionals for research and development. This problem becomes more prominent when China's economy growth relies not only on labour-intensive manufacturing but also on the development of technology-rich industries. In the three decades' reform, China has re-installed the higher education system, which was destroyed by the Cultural Revolution, and significantly increased the yearly tertiary education intake. Although those efforts have been effective, China still urgently needs millions of qualified and experienced human resources for management, professional service, research and development.

Since 1979, the western world has experienced an unprecedented increase in overseas students from mainland China. More than 1.3 million educated young Chinese have studied various disciplines in developed countries, and about 20% of them have already returned to mainland China, taking up senior positions in governmental administration, state-owned or private-owned enterprises, research institutes, and higher education sectors. In addition to forming a strong tie between China and developed countries, these young Chinese intellectuals contribute to the international trading, joint-ventures and innovative research collaborations. During the last ten years, more and more overseas Chinese students have decided to seek career development opportunities in China after the completion of their overseas study, either aiming to apply for executive/professional posts or setting up their own enterprises (Chen, Liu, Wang, Jin, P., & Low, 2007; Jin, Chen, & Low, 2007). With their advanced knowledge and work experience obtained in developed countries, plus their network already established internationally and domestically, they are equipped to join the vital changing forces that will push China toward further economic, technological, and political modernizations.

Rural Migrant Workers in Urban Areas, Women Workers, and Other Vulnerable and Disadvantaged Workers

Rural-Urban Migrant Workers

Since the economic reform of 1979, more and more rural job-seekers have moved from their villages to cities. Before the downturn of the global economy, the number of rural-urban migrant workers reached around 120 million in China (Li, Wang, Ye, Jiang, Lou, & Hesketh, 2007). This is the fastest and largest workforce transfer both in China's and the world's history. The main drive of this unprecedented "tide" is the discrepancy in the average income per capita between rural areas and cities, whereas the catalyst is the Chinese government's policy change that allows farmers to enter urban areas for employment as contract workers.

In general, the rural-urban migrant workers are between 20-40 years old; relative to other peasants in their villages of emigration, the majority of migrant workers have received certain basic education in literacy and numeracy. Therefore, in a sense they are not just rural surplus labourers but also the "elite" in China's rural areas. They work in construction sites, manufacturing factories, and many service sectors. To a significant extent, the competitiveness of products made in China is due to the utility of such massive, low-cost workforces in various industries. The earnings of migrant workers are added to their household farming income, thus reducing the gap in incomes between rural and urban areas.

Moreover, the experiences, skills, and savings gained by many of them are conducive to private and collective entrepreneurship in rural and remote areas.

However, migrant workers are faced with a number of barriers and difficulties. First, under the urban residence registration system (*Hukou* system), migrant workers are excluded from housing subsidies, social security and medical benefits that are available to officially registered residents in the cities where they work (Wong, Chang, & He, 2007). Such inequalities have forced a number of rural-urban migrant entrepreneurs to use license-renting from locals in order to run their business, in which local license holders, officers in the law enforcement bureaucracy, and local governmental authorities have a vested interest (He, 2005). In the workplace, migrant employees work longer hours, yet receive lower salaries than other employees within the urban citizenship (Li, 2005). Their frustration has been exacerbated not only by work stress and workplace discrimination, but also by the lack of their childrens' educational accessibility. Under the existing regimented governmental management of education, migrant workers' children have no access to public-funded schools. Since the Chinese culture regards children's education as the first priority in the family plan, their children's educational problems become "the fear of disturbance in the rear" (*hou gu zhi you*) for many migrant employees, and thus negatively affects their work motivation (Wong et. al, 2007; Wong, He, Leung, Lau, & Chang, 2008; Xiang & Ye, 2008; Yan, 2005; Yan & Bing, 2006; Zheng, 2003). In addition, it has been reported that the psychosocial acculturation of migrant workers was not satisfactory (Chi, Tian, & Wu, 2008). Despite being marginalized in their workplace and daily life in urban areas, migrant workers' resilience to the stress imposed on them has been remarkably strong to protect them from massive mental health problems (Wong & He, 2008). This is probably due to the following two factors: (a) migrant workers still anticipate better living conditions than their kin in the rural and remote areas, and (b) special social networks (via after-work informal gatherings, mobile phone communication, etc.) have evolved among them to provide job-seeking information and emotional support (Law & Peng, 2008; Wong & He, 2008).

During the current global economic crisis, the unprecedented large-scale workforce transfer from China's rural areas to cities has begun to turn the clock back, or at least come to a halt. In the beginning of 2009, millions of migrant workers returned to their rural homes for the Chinese New Year's family reunion ritual, but might not have job opportunities in the cities afterwards. The State Council has initiated projects to expand the demands of the domestic market in order to compensate for reduced exports. Local governments in different areas have taken various measures, such as programs for re-training and schemes for encouraging the unemployed to start their own business. Assisting the returned migrant workers in finding jobs remains a very challenging task.

Women Workers

In China's long feudal history, the subservience of women to men was advocated as a virtue. Under the current regime, inequalities are still serious. For instance, the gender ratio of enrolments at different educational levels shows that women are in a disadvantaged position relative to men: for every 100 females in primary schools, junior middle schools, high schools, and tertiary institutions, there are 110, 113, 138, and 144 males, respectively (Department of Development and Planning Ministry of Education PRC, 2000). Female workers are paid less than males; and women, in comparison with men, are more likely to be employed to fill semi-skilled positions in export-oriented, labour-intensive manufacturing industries (Shu, Zhu, & Zhang, 2007). Women are not only less likely to be hired and more vulnerable to being laid off than men, but are also required to retire five years earlier than men (Bowen, Wu, Hwang, & Scherer, 2007). In addition, many women have dual-role responsibilities: after work, they take on primary family duties at home. In the rapidly changing working and social environment, female workers experience high levels of stress.

Although the political slogan in China is "Women hold up half the sky", there are more males than females in powerful positions in various levels of organizations, ranging from the ruling party's central committee, parliament and governments, to business. For instance, in Chinese state-owned enterprises, despite the overall managerial motivation of Chinese women being as high as that of Chinese men, the latter still dominate most senior managerial positions (Chen, Yu, & Miner, 1997). This is probably due to the long-term influence of Confucian principles of governance that emphasized the subservience of women to men, incongruence between policy making and implementation, the social norm that men are in charge of public affairs whereas women look after private matters, and the negative stereotype of women in competence, organizational commitment, emotional stability, and work attitudes, that spread socially to every corner of the country (Bowen et al., 2007). The positive trends are that more women are educated and employed in enterprises and public services than before; in particular, young unmarried women swarming from villages to urban areas to become effective workforce members in China's manufacturing industries - though there is still a long way to go in correcting gender inequality (Bowen et al., 2007; Shu et al., 2007; Xin, 2008).

Other Vulnerable and Disadvantaged Workers

Since China's economic reform of 1979, the restructuring of state-owned enterprises has resulted in the breaking of "iron rice bowl" job security and massive unemployment (*Xiagang*, i.e., leaving their posts). Among those laid-off, the most vulnerable groups are workers close to their retirement age, workers with disabilities, and middle-aged employees who did not receive basic primary or secondary education during the Culture Revolution, because schools were either malfunctioning or shut down (Price & Fang, 2002). For instance, many middle-aged women in the labour-intensive industries were laid off, and had fewer opportunities to participate in reemployment programs than younger women (Sung-Chan & Yuen & Tsang, 2008). According to a cluster analysis of the data from a large-scale survey (N = 1950), conducted in seven Chinese cities (Beijing, Guangzhou, Chongqing, Shiyan, Yichang, Luoyang, and Yantai), apart from "the discouraged old", "the worried young" deserve similar attention (Price & Fang, 2002). Among the workforce, the worried young workers receive incomes even less than the discouraged old workers, express high levels of job stress, and show little confidence in their job-search skills and financial coping strategies in the emerging competitive labour market. Currently, only one officially backed trade union is allowed to function in mainland China. The trade union needs to exert more innovative efforts to be representative for all workers in the negotiation of critical issue such as pay rises, benefits, and occupational health and safety (e.g., Yu, 2008).

More recently, the situation has been exacerbated by two additional factors due to the global economic downturn. First, a large number of returned migrant workers have lost their job in the cities and desperately need to be re-employed elsewhere. Local governments have set up a supporting system to provide training courses and small business guidance. Second, many graduates experience great difficulty in getting jobs suitable to their qualifications. The

Department of Education and Bureau of Human Resources at different governmental levels are trying to convince enterprises to use the on-job training allowance scheme for recruiting inexperienced graduates. It appears that there are some promising signs. However, the long-term effects are yet to be demonstrated.

CONCLUSION

After the end of the disastrous Cultural Revolution, the government in mainland China adopted reforming and opening-up policies. The speedy and steady economic growth in mainland China during the recent three decades has been unprecedented. From a historical perspective, China's four-stage cycle, "Turbulent times – Concessions, constraints, and reforms of the new regime – Recovery of social productive forces – Prosperity of economy and associated aspects" (TCRP) can also be identified in the golden age of the West Han and Tang Dynasties. Whereas the catalytic functioning of a series of policy changes and initiatives made by the current Chinese government is widely acknowledged, the relatively emancipated Chinese social productive forces should be regarded as one of the crucial factors in recent remarkable economic growth in China. During this rapidly changing period, Chinese workers' positive motivational states, such as hope, resiliency, and realistic optimism, provide invaluable psychological capital to act as a buffer zone for coping with work stress, and to attain desired progress continuously. Although China faces a number of problems associated with the recent global economic crisis, Chinese workers' positive psychological capital will play a constructive role in various types of enterprises that are structured and operated in line with the reforming and opening-up measures.

REFERENCES

[1] Adler, P. S., & Kwon, S. (2002). Social capital: Prospects for a new concept. *Academy of Management Review*, *27*, 17–40.

[2] Ambrose, M. L., & Kulik, C. T. (1999). Old friends, new faces: Motivation research in the 1990s. *Journal of Management*, *25*, 231–292.

[3] Ang, S. (2000). The power of money: a cross-cultural analysis of business-related beliefs. *Journal of World Business*, *35*, 43-51.

[4] Ang, S., Van Dyne, L., & Begley, T. M. (2003). The employment relationships of foreign workers versus local employees: A field study of organizational justice, job satisfaction, performance, and OCB. *Journal of Organizational Behavior, 24*, 561-583.

[5] Bai, S. (1982). *An outline history of China.* Beijing: Foreign Languages Press.

[6] Bandura, A. (1997). *Self-efficacy: The Exercise of Control.* New York: Freeman.

[7] Björkman, I. & Lu, Y. (1999). The management of human resources in Chinese-Western joint ventures. *Journal of World Business, 34* (3), 306-324.

[8] Bowen, C., Wu, Y., Hwang, C., & Scherer, R. F. (2007). Holding up half of the sky? Attitudes toward women as managers in the People's Republic of China. *The International Journal of Human Resource Management, 18* (2), 268-283.

[9] Chamerlain, H. B. (1987). Party-management relations in Chinese industries: Some political dimensions of economic reform. *The China Quarterly*, 112, 631-661.

[10] Chen, C. C., Yu, K.C. Miner, J. B. (1997). Motivation to mange: A study of women in Chinese state-owned enterprises. *The Journal of Applied Behavioral Science, 33*, 2, 160-173.

[11] Chen, L., & Jin, P. (1984). Report on the reform of Haiyan Shirt Factory. *Journal of Hangzhou University (Social Sciences), 3*, 1-9.

[12] Chen, L., Liu, Y., Wang, L., Jin, P., & Low, R. (2007). Chinese Students' Experiences and Orientations in Australia: A Qualitative Analysis. *Journal of Wuhan University of Science and Engineering*, *20*, 4, 67-69.

[13] Chen, P., An, H., & Jin, P. (1985). *Labour management*. Hangzhou, China: Zhejiang Human Resource Management Academy.

[14] Chen, P., & Jin, P. (1991). Managing human resources in China. In J.M. Putti (Ed.), *Management: Asian context*, 198-221. New York and Singapore: McGraw-Hill.

[15] Chi, Z., Tian, X., & Wu, T. (2008). An investigation on the acculturation of migrant workers in labor-intensive enterprises in Suzhou. *Psychological Science (China), 31* (1), 210-213.

[16] Chiu, H. (1986). Analysis on the reform of the Chinese Communist Labor Employment System. *Studies on Chinese Communist Monthly*, *20*, 89-99.

[17] Chow, I. H. (2004). Human resource management in China's township and village enterprise: Change and development during the economic reform era. *Asia Pacific Journal of Human Resources, 42,* 318-335.

[18] Department of Development and Planning Ministry of Education PRC (2000). *Educational Statistics Yearbook of China*, 2 (19), 200. Beijing: Peoples Education Press.

[19] Earley, P. C. (1989). Social loafing and collectivism: A comparison of the United States and People's Republic of China. *Administrative Science Quarterly*, *34,* 565–580.

[20] Farh, L. L., Zhong, C. B., & Organ, D. W. (2004). Organizational citizenship behaviour in the People's Republic of China. *Organization Science, 15* (2), 241-253.

[21] Friedlander, F. (1966). Motivations to work and organizational performance. *Journal of Applied Psychology, 50* (2), 143-152.

[22] Gong, Y., Law, K. S., Chang, S., & Xin, K. R. (2009). Human resources management and firm performance: The differential role of managerial affective and continuance commitment. *Journal of Applied Psychology*, *94*, 263-275.

[23] Hamilton, J. B., Knouse, S. B., & Hill, V. (2009). Google in China: A manager-friendly heuristic model for resolving cross-cultural ethical conflicts. *Journal of Business Ethics*, *86*, 143-157.

[24] Hassard, J., Morris, J., Sheehan, J., Xiao, Y. (2006). Downsizing the danwei: Chinese state-enterprise reform and the surplus labour question. *International Journal of Human Resource Management*, *17* (8), 1441-1455.

[25] He, X. (2005). Why do they not comply with the law? Illegality and semi-legality among rural-urban migrant entrepreneurs in Beijing. *Law & Society Review, 39* (3), 527-562.

[26] Hofstede, G. (1984). *Cultures' consequences: International differences in work-related values.* Beverley Hills, CA: Sage.

[27] Hsiao, R. L. (2008). Review of business and management education in China: Transition, pedagogy, and training. *Academy of Management Learning & Education, 7* (2), 285-287.

[28] Humphreys, J. (2007). Adapting the congruent temperament model with culturally specific work motivation elements. *Cross Cultural Management, 14* (3), 202-216.

[29] Jackson, T., & Bak, M. (1998). Foreign companies and Chinese workers: Employee motivation in the People's Republic of China. *Journal of Organisational Change Management, 11* (4), 282-300.

[30] Jin, P. (1984). Establishing a contribution-card system. *Journal of Fujian Tribune, 9*, 40-47.

[31] Jin, P. (1992). Cultural influences and the dynamics of human resource management in China. *Asian Profile, 20,* 109-114.

[32] Jin, P. (1993). Work motivation and productivity in voluntarily formed work teams: A field study in China. *Organizational Behavior and Human Decision Processes, 54,* 133-155.

[33] Jin, P., Chen, L., & Low, R. (2007). Human resources for China's revitalization in the 21st Century: Analysis of Chinese students studying and living in Australia. *Hong Kong Teachers' Centre Journal, 6*, 131-136.

[34] Lam, W., Huang, Xu., & Snape, E. (2007). Feedback-seeking behaviour and leader-member exchange: Do supervisor-attributed motives matter? *Academy of Management Journal, 50* (2), 348-363.

[35] Law, P., & Peng, Y. (2008). Mobile networks: Migrant workers in southern China. In J. E. Katz *Handbook of mobile communication studies*, 55-64. Cambridge, MA: MIT Press.

[36] Leung, K., & Bond, M. H. (1984). The impact of cultural collectivism on reward allocation. *Journal of Personality and Social Psychology*, *47*, 793-804.

[37] Li, B. (2005). Urban social change in transitional China: A perspective of social exclusion and vulnerability. *Journal of Contingencies and Crisis Management, 13* (2), 54-65.

[38] Li, L., Wang, H., Ye, X., Jiang, M, Lou, Q., & Hesketh, T. (2007). The mental health status of Chinese rural-urban migrant workers: Comparison with permanent urban and rural dwellers. *Social Psychiatry and Psychiatric Epidemiology, 42*, 716-722.

[39] Liu, B., Tang, N., & Zhu, X. (2008). Public service motivation and job satisfaction in China: An investigation of generalisability and instrumentality. *International Journal of Manpower, 29* (8), 685-699.

[40] Liu, C., Tjosvold, D., & Wong, M. (2004). Effective Japanese leadership in China: Co-operative goals and applying abilities for mutual benefit. *International Journal of Human Resource Management, 15*, 730-749.

[41] Luthans, F., Avolio, B. J., Walumbwa, F. O., & Li, W. (2005). The psychological capital of Chinese workers: Exploring the relationship with performance. *Management and Organization Review, 1* (2), 249-271.

[42] Luthans, F., & Jensen, S. M. (2002). Hope: A new positive strength for human resource development .*Human Resource Development Review, 1,* 304–322.

[43] Luthans, F., Luthans, K. W., & Luthans, B. C. (2004). Positive psychological capital: Going beyond human and social capital. *Business Horizons*, *47*, 45–50.

[44] Luthans, F., & Youssef, C. M. (2004). Human, social, and now positive psychological capital management: Investing in people for competitive advantage. *Organizational Dynamics, 33*(2), 143–160.

[45] Mak, K., Wong, L., & Lee, G. (2002). The challenges of global capitalism: Unemployment and state workers' reactions and responses in post-reform China. *International Journal of Human Resource Management, 13* (3), 399-415.

[46] O'Leary, B. S., Lindholm, M. L., Whitford, R. A., & Freeman, S. E. (2002). Selecting the best and brightest: Leveraging human capital. *Human Resource Management, 41*, 325–340.

[47] O'Toole, J. (1981). The good managers of Sichuan. *Harvard Business Review, 81*, 28-40.

[48] Peng, Y. (2004). Kinship networks and entrepreneurs in China's transitional economy. *American Journal of Sociology, 109* (5), 1045-1074.

[49] Peterson, C. (2000). The future of optimism. *American Psychologist, 55*, 44–55.

[50] Peterson, S. J., & Luthans, F. (2003). The positive impact and development of hopeful leaders. *Leadership and Organizational Development Journal, 24*, 26–31.

[51] Price, R. H., & Fang, L. (2002). Unemployed Chinese workers: The survivors, the worried young and the discouraged old. The International *Journal of Human Resource Management, 13* (3), 416-430.

[52] Qin, Q., & Tan, X. (2006). A comparative study of workers' work values in state-owned and private enterprises. *Psychological Science (China), 29* (2), 440-442.

[53] Ralston, D. A., Terpstra-Tong, J., Terpstra, R. H., Wang, X., & Egri, C. (2006). Today's state-owned enterprises of China: Are they dying dinosaurs or dynamic dynamos? *Strategic Management Journal, 27* (9), 825-843.

[54] Scheier, M. F., & Carver, C. S. (1985.) Optimism, coping, and health: Assessment and implications of generalized outcome expectancies. *Health Psychology, 4*, 219–247.

[55] Seligman, M. and Csikszentmihalyi, M. (2000). Positive psychology. *American Psychologist, 55*, 5–14.

[56] Shenkar, O., & Ronen, S. (1987). Structure and importance of work goals among managers in the People's Republic of China. *Academy of Management Journal, 30*, 564-576.

[57] Shirk, S. L. (1981). Recent Chinese labor policies and the transformation of industrial organization in China. *The China Quarterly, 88*, 575-593.

[58] Shu, X., Zhu, Y., & Zhang, Z. (2007). Global economy and gender inequalities: The case of the urban Chinese labour market. *Social Science Quarterly, 88* (5), 1307-1332.

[59] Snyder, C. R. (2000). *Handbook of Hope*. San Diego: Academic Press.

[60] Song, S., & Gale, A. (2007). The work values of Chinese project managers. *Cross Cultural Management, 14* (3), 217-228.

[61] Sun, L.Y, & Pan, W. (2008). HR practices perceptions, emotional exhaustion, and work outcomes: A conservation-of-resources theory in the Chinese context. *Human Resource Development Quarterly, 19* (1), 55-72.

[62] Sung-Chan, P., & Yuen-Tsang, A. (2008). Our journey nurturing the voices of unemployed women in China through collaborative-action research. *Qualitative Social Work: Research and Practice, 7* (1), 61-80.

[63] Tiger, L. (1971). *Optimism: The biology of hope*. New York: Simon & Schuster.

[64] Tjosvold, D. & Sun, H. F. (2002). Understanding conflict avoidance: Relationship, motivations, actions, and consequences. The International *Journal of Conflict Management, 13* (2), 142-164.

[65] Walsh, J., & Zhu, Y. (2007). Local complexities and global uncertainties: A study of foreign ownership and human resource management in China. *International Journal of Human Resource Management, 18* (2), 249-267.

[66] Wang, X., Bruning, N. S., & Peng, S. (2007). Western high-performance HR practices in China: A comparison among public-owned, private and foreign-invested enterprises. *International Journal of Human Resource Management, 18* (4), 684-704.

[67] Wang, Z. (1991). Recent developments in industrial and organizational psychology in People's Republic of China. In C. L. Cooper & I. T. Robertson (Eds.), *International review of industrial and organizational psychology* (pp. 1-15), Oxford: John Wiley.

[68] Wong, D., Chang, Y. L., & He, X. S. (2007). Rural migrant workers in urban China: living a marginalized life. *International Journal of Social Welfare, 16*, 32-40.

[69] Wong, D., & He, X. S. (2008). The resilience of migrant workers in Shanghai China: The roles of migration stress and meaning of migration. *International Journal of Social Psychiatry, 54* (2), 131-143.

[70] Wong, D., He, X. S., Leung, G., Lau, Y., & Chang, Y. (2008). Mental health of migrant workers in China: Prevalence and correlates. *Social Psychiatry and Psychiatric Epidemiology. 43* (6), 483-489.

[71] Wright, P. C., Berrell. M., & Gloet, M. (2008). Cultural values, workplace behavior and productivity in China: A conceptual framework for practicing managers. *Management Decision, 46* (5), 797-812.

[72] Xiang, Y., & Ye, X. (2007). The relation of migrant workers' children's and parental rearing behavior. *Psychological Science (China), 30* (6), 1489-1492.

[73] Xie, J. (2005). Human resource development roles in the People's Republic of China: Investigation from seven provinces. *International Journal of Training and Development, 9* (1), 33-46.

[74] Xin, T. (2008). Women's labor activism in China. *Signs, 33* (3), 515-518.

[75] Xu, L. (1986). Development in organizational behavior study in China. *Acta Psychologica Sinica, 18* (4), 343-348.

[76] Yan, F. (2005). Education problems with urban migratory children in China. *Journal of Sociology and Social Welfare, 32* (3), 3-10.

[77] Yan, Z., & Bing, W. X. (2006). Community-based education for children of migrant peasant workers. In L. D. Adams & Kirova, A. (Eds.) *Global migration and education: Schools, children, and families,* 307-319. Hillsdale, NJ: Lawrence.

[78] Yu, B. B., & Egri, C. P. (2005). Human resource management practices and affective organizational commitment: A comparison of Chinese employees in a state-owned enterprise and a joint venture. *Asia Pacific Journal of Human Resources, 43,* 332-359.

[79] Yu, X. (2008). Impacts of corporate code of conduct on labor standards: A case study of Reebok's athletic footwear supplier factory in China. *Journal of Business Ethics, 81,* 513-529.

[80] Zheng, X. (2003). A preliminary research on migrant workers' parenting styles and their children's peer relation. *Psychological Science (China), 26* (4), 762-763.

[81] Zhu, C. J., Thomson, S. B., & De Cieri, H. (2008). A retrospective and prospective analysis of HRM research in Chinese firms, implications and directions for future study. *Human Resource Management, 47* (1), 133-157.

In: Thirty Years of China's Economic Reform
Editors: Yue Wang and Prem Ramburuth

ISBN: 978-1-60876-908-7
© 2010 Nova Science Publishers, Inc.

Chapter 7

UPPER ECHELONS IN THE PEOPLE'S REPUBLIC OF CHINA: EVIDENCE FROM THE 15 LARGEST COMPANIES

Snejina Michailova*
Department of Management and International Business,
The University of Auckland Business School, New Zealand

ABSTRACT

This chapter explores how executive elites' demographic attributes shape their companies' strategic behaviour. The chapter utilizes upper echelon theory to examine the demographic attributes of executive elites (Chief Executive Officers and/or Presidents) in the 15 largest companies across the manufacturing and services sectors in Mainland China. These companies are all state-owned enterprises, have long histories and all but one are engaged in cross-border business activities. I examine executive elites' age, functional track, career experience and formal education. I also suggest that executives' political affiliations are an attribute relevant in the Chinese context, although not considered by the original (Western) upper echelon theory. I find that the executives of the 15 largest Chinese companies are all above 50 years old, have a high level of formal education, and are strongly affiliated with the Communist Party. Most of them were internally promoted to the top. This study indicates that large Chinese firms' strategic innovative behavior (in terms of international expansion) can partly be attributed to their executives' demographic characteristics.

Keywords: China, large companies, executive elites, upper echelon theory, firm internationalization.

* E-mail: s.michailova@auckland.ac.nz.

INTRODUCTION

The importance of the People's Republic of China (PRC) to the global economy has been widely recognized and emphasized by academics, executives and policymakers alike. Thirty years of economic reform has propelled the country to the center of the world's economy and in recent years has attracted increasing research attention and coverage. While there are a variety of views and perspectives on PRC's impressive development and reforms, the role corporate elites play in shaping Chinese firms' strategic behaviour has not been studied in detail. It is, therefore, meaningful to examine who PRC's executive elites are. Compared with the existing extensive research on management and managers in the West, little has been devoted to corporate elites in the PRC. Despite the growing interest and amount of conducted research, we still lack systematic knowledge about important specific features of managing in the context of this fascinating country.

Managers are often theoretically treated as instruments through which organizations pursue their interests, thus assuming individual managers' attributes to be irrelevant to organizational behaviour (Barber & Palmer, 2001: 87). Studies developed in the framework of upper echelon theory (UET) (Hambrick & Mason, 1984), on the other hand, argue that organizations are reflections of their top managers' background and experience. UET suggests that there is a close association between corporate elites' demographic characteristics and the elites' cognitive bases and values, which, in turn, determine their strategy preferences and dispositions. The cognitive structures of top managers, which are a function of their demographic characteristics, shape to a great extent how executives gather and filter information from their environment and how they make decisions on the basis of the interpretation of this information.

While UET is a theory developed by US researchers and while most of the UET-based studies are conducted in Western organizational settings, I take Mainland China as the context of this study. My purpose is to understand how demographic characteristics might have had an impact on large Chinese firms' strategic behaviour. I examine four demographic characteristics of corporate elites (i.e. CEOs and company Presidents) from the 15 largest Chinese companies – age, functional background, tenure in the organization, and formal education – and how they are likely to influence these firms' internationalization. Due to the exploratory nature of the study and difficulties in collecting demographic data, I have limited the sample to 15 companies and realize that this limits the generalizability of my analysis and findings. There are three dimensions in Hambrick and Mason's (1984) theory on which I was not able to collect data: the CEOs' socioeconomic background, their financial positions and their group characteristics. At the same time, I suggest that the CEO's political affiliation, while not proposed in the original UET, is of great importance in the Chinese context.

THEORY

Addressing the question "Why do organizations act as they do?", Hambrick and Mason (1984: 193) pointed out that organizational outcomes are reflections of the values and cognitive bases of powerful actors in the organization. These authors argued that "organizational outcomes can be partially predicted from managerial backgrounds" (p. 196), and that these characteristics are "determinants of strategic choices" (p. 197). These two factors interact to determine organizational performance levels. To be sure, UET does not propose that demographics cause decision outcomes; rather, demographic attributes are used as measures of unobservable constructs, such as values, cognition, personality factors and other psychological factors that may influence decision behavior. Hambrick and Mason (1984) considered seven observable demography-based managerial characteristics (as proxies for psychological characteristics) - age, functional background, tenure in the organization, formal education, socioeconomic roots, financial position and group characteristics – and proposed 21 hypotheses linking these characteristics with organizational outcomes (strategic choices and performance levels). Below I elaborate on the four managerial characteristics which I utilize in my analysis.

Age

Hambrick and Mason (1984: 198-199) proposed that "firms with younger managers will be more inclined to pursue risky strategies than will firms with older managers. Specific forms of risk include unrelated diversification, product innovation and financial leverage". Empirical evidence has confirmed that executives' age influences firms' strategies, organizational outcomes and performance (Datta & Rajagopalan, 1998; Daily et al., 2000). Bantel and Jackson (1989) suggested that older executives may be less willing to adapt to new ideas and behaviours and Bantel and Wiersema (1992) pointed out that these executives lean toward less risky strategies and actions and tend to be more resistant to change.

Functional Background

Executives from different functional backgrounds are likely to have different frames of reference, which, reflected in different knowledge, attitudes and perspectives, lead to the identification of different problems and the generation of different solutions. The relationship between functional background and strategic decisions can be traced back to Dearborn and Simon's (1958) study which revealed that executives interpret complex business situations in a way that reflects their own functional background. Hambrick and Mason (1984: 199) proposed that there is "a positive association between the degree of throughput-function experience of top managers and the extent to which the firm emphasizes throughput in its strategy". Indictors of a throughput emphasis include automation, plant and equipment newness and backward integration (Hambrick & Mason, 1984). Research has provided evidence that firms tend to emphasize functional areas that are critical to the strategy they have opted for (e.g. Hitt et al., 1982; Litschert et al., 1991; Hambrick & Michel, 1992).

Tenure in the Organization

Hambrick and Mason (1984) argued that managers' career experiences influence their cognitive maps and that years of inside service by top managers are negatively related to strategic choice involving new terrain, and negatively associated with profitability and growth when the organzation faces a severe environmental discontinuity. Bergh (2001) and Datta and Herrmann (2005) provided evidence that tenure influences firm strategies and organizational outcomes. New product market entry (Bocker, 1997) and strategic change (Bantel & Wiersema, 1992) have also been linked to tenure. Kor (2003) argued that managers with existing (industry-specific) experience typically possess solid knowledge of the conditions, regulations, opportunities and threats characteristic of the industry. This existing knowledge increases the cognitive abilities to match existing resources and opportunities (Kor & Mahoney, 2000). Longer-tenured executives have been found to be strategically persistent, conforming with industry norms of conduct and restrictive in their information processing (Finkelstein & Hambrick, 1990), often lacking fresh information possessed by their less-experienced counterparts (Miller, 1991), exhibiting inertia (Fukutomi & Hambrick, 1991) and being loyal to prior strategies (Fredrickson et al., 1993). Shorter tenured executives, on the other hand, are more willing to experiment (Hambrick & Fukutomi, 1991) and are more willing to pursue innovative strategies (Bantel & Jackson, 1989; Litschert et al., 1991), as they are less socialized into accepting their company's existing policies, norms and values (Murray, 1989; Finkelstein & Hambrick, 1996)

Formal Education

Hitt and Tyler (1991) highlighted evidence suggesting that the type of formal education a person receives affects the cognitive models developed, and thereby the strategic choices made. These authors, as well as Bantel and Wiersema (1992), found support for the differential effects of education types on organizational outcomes. Others have suggested a positive link between a higher level of education and, respectively, a higher level of receptivity to change and innovation (Becker, 1970), higher capacity for information processing (Bantel & Jackson, 1989; Bantel & Wiersema, 1992), better ability to interpret more complex information leading to faster strategic decision making (Baum & Wally, 1994), greater tolerance towards ambiguity and more boundary spanning behaviour (Kimberly, 1981) and the extent of innovation in organizations (Evansko & Kimberly, 1981; Bantel & Jackson, 1989), as well as a positive relationship between the amount (but not type) of formal education of top managers and innovation (Hambrick & Mason, 1984).

Unit of Analysis and Data Sources

While some research that has utilized UET has studied top management teams, many studies have opted for analyzing demographic characteristics of company Presidents and/or CEOs (for a discussion see Carpenter et al., 2004). I study the demography of Presidents/CEOs instead of entire top management teams (the latter would include positions such as CFO, COO and even non-executive directors in supra-top management teams (Finkelstein & Hambrick, 1996) in the 15 Chinese companies. Three reasons explain my choice. First, it is meaningful to distinguish between CEOs and non-CEO corporate elites to provide a more accurate examination. The CEO is a less ambiguous unit of analysis as compared to aggregate units of analysis (e.g., board of directors or top management teams) when studying the influence of corporate elites on corporate strategy (Jensen & Zajac, 2004: 521). Including other top managers' demography naturally complicates the analysis as their different backgrounds and the combination thereof would introduce noise to the link between which demographic factors lead to what outcomes. Second, the CEO/President is the key manager and the main decision-maker in the company. She/he is also the most visible top manager and the one most exposed to public attention (Jensen & Zajac, 2004: 511-512). Third, the UET model is "inherently individual-level in focus" (Cannella & Holcomb, 2005).

Data for the present study were gathered from China Vitae, an online database that provides biographies of current Chinese political, military, academic, economic and business leaders. This database contains information about leaders' nationality, year of birth, educational background, professional achievements, and current and past career experiences. Data were also collected through carefully studying the 15 companies' annual reports from various years, the companies' websites, and company news available on the internet and in other media.

An Overview of the 15 Largest Companies in PRC

As evident from the title of this chapter, this study focuses merely on the largest companies in the PRC. Firm size is an important dimension in theoretical and empirical research into organizations (Baum, 1995; Scott, 1992). Firm size has been studied in relation to, among others, interaction with the environment (Freeman & Hannan, 1984), firm death rate (Aldrich & Auster, 1986; Cooper et al., 1989), organizational survival and diversity (Feeman & Hannan, 1989), competition (Baum & Mezias, 1992; Christianson et al., 1992) and firm growth (Breckenridge et al., 1995).

Firm size is commonly measured by firm employment or by output. I opted for the latter measure and identified the 15 largest companies in the PRC on the basis of their 2006 revenue. Annual revenue is an objective measure that provides a solid indication of the scale of company activities. Company profits would not be an appropriate measure in the present study as different types of firms in the PRC apply different profitability criteria. A direct comparison of state-owned enterprises (SOEs) and non-state firms is in itself problematic, as they play different roles in shouldering social welfare burdens (Zhang et al., 2002) and have different capital and tax structures (Lu & Tang, 1997).

Sector and History

Three of the 15 companies operate in the manufacturing sector, eight of them are in the services sector and the remaining four companies are engaged in both manufacturing and service. Consistent with the fact that the state has remained in strong control of strategic industries while privatizing primarily non-strategic industries, five of the companies in the sample operate in the energy sector (e.g. oil and electricity power), another five are finance companies (e.g. banking and insurance), two operate in the communication sector while the remaining three are classified as others. The companies' profiles and how their activities are distributed among industries are presented in Figure 1 and Table 1.

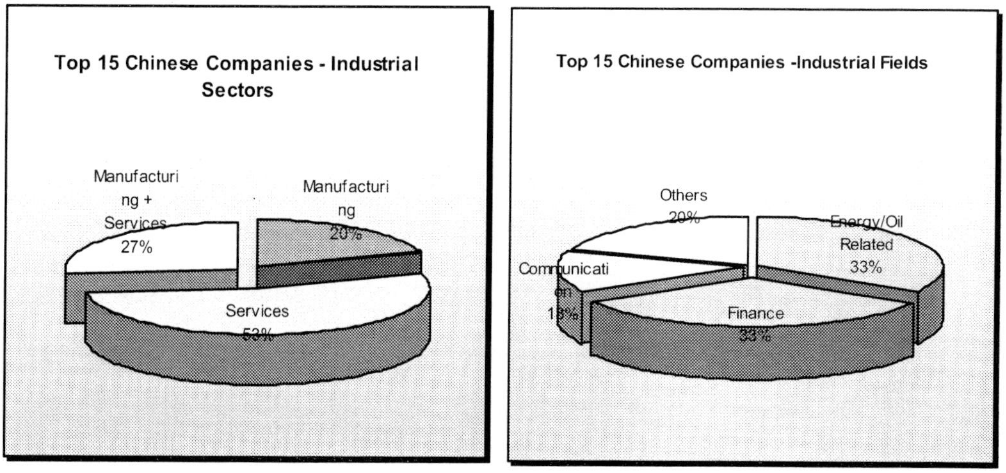

Figure 1. Top 15 Chinese Companies – Industrial Sectors and Fields

Table 1. Overview of top 15 companies

Ranking by Revenue (2006)	**Company Name**	Manufacturing/Services	**Industry Fields**
1	Sinopec Group	Manufacturing + Services	Energy/Oil related
2	State Grid Corporation of China	Manufacturing + Services	Energy/Oil related
3	China National Petroleum Corporation	Manufacturing	Energy/Oil related
4	Industrial and Commercial Bank of China Limited	Services	Finance
5	China Mobile Communications Corporation	Services	Communication
6	China Life Insurance Co. Ltd.	Services	Finance
7	China Southern Power Grid Co., Ltd	Manufacturing + Services	Energy/Oil related
8	China Construction Bank	Services	Finance
9	China Telecommunications Corporation	Services	Communication
10	Bank of China	Services	Finance
11	Baosteel Group Corporation	Manufacturing	Steel
12	Sinochem Corporation	Manufacturing + Services	Energy/Oil related
13	Agricultural Bank of China	Services	Finance
14	Bailian Group	Services	Retail and Investment
15	China FAW Group Corporation	Manufacturing	Auto-mobile

Most companies in the sample have a more than 50-year long history, some with a considerably longer past. For instance, Bank of China's history can be traced back to 1919 as a replacement of Da Qing Government Bank, the Agricultural Bank of China was established in 1949, the Sinochem Corporation was born in 1950 and FAW was founded in 1953. While some other companies officially have a shorter history, the establishment of most of them is based on older companies, or they have been re-established and re-organized by combining several old companies. CNPC, for example, was officially founded in 1988, but its history can be traced back to 1949 when the Chinese government formed a Fuel Industry Ministry dedicated to the management of fuel (Wikipedia, 2008). China Life Insurance was founded in 2003 by reforming the China People's Insurance Company, which was established in 1949. The Baosteel Group Corporation was established in 1998 with the former Baoshan Iron and

Steel (Group) Corporation as its core, also absorbing the former Shanghai Metallurgical Holding Group Corporation and the former Shanghai Meishan Group Co., Ltd. The former Baoshan Iron and Steel was founded back in 1978. Another example is Bailian (Group) Co. Ltd. which was established in 2003 through the merger of four companies with long histories: Shanghai Yibai (Group) Co. Ltd. Hualian (Group) Co. Ltd, Shanghai Youyi (Group) Co. Ltd and Shanghai Wuzi (Group) Co, Ltd.

Ownership

All companies in the sample are SOEs and under the supervision of State Council. These are "non-marketized firms" that differ on several dimensions from "marketized firms" (collectively owned enterprises and private firms) (Nee, 1992) and do not have a structural analogue in the West (Henley & Nyaw, 1986; Tan, 2001). SOEs were earlier defined by China's State Administration for Industry and Commerce as belonging to "the whole people", and through the reform re-defined as "owned by the whole people and managed by the state" (Li & Xia, 2008: 43). As a result, central authorities can invoke these property rights, in the name of the people, to closely intervene in SOEs managers' decision-making (Child & Lu, 1996).

Contrary to (Western) market logic, not only have SOEs not disappeared from the Chinese economic landscape, but they have successfully survived the economic reforms of the last 30 years and are playing an important role in today's Chinese economy (Li & Xia, 2008). This SOE longevity has been attributed to various factors. First, the Chinese authorities have opted for a gradual approach to SOE reform, summarized by Deng Xiaoping as "crossing the river by feeling the stones". Second, SOEs gain access to disproportionally more resources from the state compared to non-state firms (Nee, 1992), due to their "cosy relationship" with the government (Yang, 2004: 76). Additionally, letting loss-making SOEs go bankrupt can lead to mass unemployment and, subsequently, to instability in society (Chow & Fung, 1996: 500). Another important reason for SOEs thriving in PRC's transition economy is that they are not merely enterprises, but important administrative units of the state bureaucracy (Freund, 2001). SOEs tend to follow state policy more closely, are better protected by the state (Li & Xia, 2008: 43), and the Communist Party is strongly represented in their management structures and actual decision-making through the enterprise Communist Party secretaries (Nyaw & Schermerhorn, 1991). Consequently, SOE managers are not merely firm managers, but also government officials (Freund, 2001; Zhu, 1999) subject to tight control by government.

The process of gradually decentralizing control over SOEs started in 1984, with a large-scale SOE reform/privatization in 1997-1998. In 1997 the Chinese government started cutting excess labor and selling off the bulk of loss-making enterprises with the objective of transforming SOEs from purely production units to profit and investment centers with a separation of ownership and control, and with increased levels of management autonomy (Qian, 1996; Zhu, 1999). The reform included measures such as: 1) a higher degree of autonomy for the CEO in input, output, and pricing decisions; 2) linking managers' rewards to the enterprise's performance; 3) providing workers with profit-related bonuses and 4) adding more flexibility to the labor force in a firm (e.g. employing contract workers to replace permanent ones) (Groves et al., 1994).

There is evidence that SOE reforms have not substantially changed SOE behavior and that at present SOEs still perform worse than non-state firms*; although SOEs continue to receive serious support from the central and local government(s), their performance incentives and criteria do not follow a purely market logic. In other words, they are halfway between a centralized command system and a market system (Perkins, 1994). While communication, coordination and monitoring costs between principals and agents can be high for any ownership type and size of firm, the agency costs are particularly high for large SOEs (Chow & Fung, 1996; Groves et al., 1994).

In a recent study Lin and Zhang (2008) assessed the effect of bank ownership on performance using a panel of Chinese banks over the 1997-2004 period. Distinguishing between (domestic) private, foreign and state ownership, the authors found that the "Big Four" state-owned commercial banks are less profitable and less efficient, and have worse asset quality than other types of banks. My analysis of the big four commercial banks in my sample confirms Lin and Zhang's (2008) conclusion. Bank of China, China Construction Bank, Agricultural Bank of China, and Industrial and Commercial Bank of China Limited continuously receive capital injections from the central government to reduce the level of non-performing loans. In 2007 the Hong Kong Trade Development Council stated the following:

> "In 1998, the Big Four received capital injections totalling RMB 270 billion from the government, boosting their equity from 2.45% to 6.15% of their combined assets in one stroke. Four asset management companies were set up, which purchased a total of RMB 1,400 billion in non-performing loans from the Big Four, equivalent to about 18% of their total loan portfolio. […] The second working conference in 2002 went a step further. Reforms began to turn the Big Four into modern financial enterprises with adequate capital and better internal control. Shareholding reforms were executed through a pilot program that saw BOC and CCB receive a total capital injection of US$ 45 billion on 30 December 2003. In 2005, the program was extended to ICBC, which benefited from a US$ 15 billion capital injection. […] Recently, some sources are reporting that Agriculture bank, the only big-four state owned bank yet to be re-structured, is likely to receive US$ 40 billion capital injection from the government."

Sinopec, the largest company in the sample, provides a good example of the fact that pursuing state interests can be a stronger incentive for company management than being economically efficient and profitable. Sinopec received state subsidies of CNY 9.42 billion and CNY 5 billion in 2005 and 2006 respectively (Poon, 2008) and another CNY 12.3 billion in March 2008 for its loss in the oil refining business (Trading markets, 2008). While media and investors argued that Sinopec, as a publicly listed company, should be responsible for all shareholders' interests, the fact remains that being subsidised is strongly related to closely following strategic state interests.

* This chapter is not concerned with firm performance and differences in performance between state-owned and non-state-owned firms. I only mention performance in relation to outlining some key specificities of SOEs that can contribute to explaining their CEOs' behavior.

International Engagement

As evident from Table 2, all 15 companies (with the exception of Bailian Group) have engaged in overseas operations. This is a reflection of the overall Chinese firm internationalization picture – if internationalization is defined as "the crossing of national boundaries in the process of growth" (Buckley & Ghauri, 1999: ix) – then "China is currently the most active internationalizing economy among the developing countries" (Child & Rodrigues, 2005: 382). The companies in oil and oil-related business, such as Sinopec, CNPC and Sinochem, have been frequently engaged in overseas investment and acquisitions over a number of years. All banking corporations operate branches overseas. Telecommunication companies have either engaged in acquisitions or worked on obtaining operation licences to provide international telephone and Internet data services between China and the target countries. The power grids and steel/automobile manufacturing companies have all joint-venture projects with overseas companies both inside and outside PRC.

Table 2. Overview of the top 15 Chinese companies' main overseas activities

Company	Overseas Activities
Sinopec Group	Wholly owned subsidiaries in Middle East, Russia, Iran, North Africa, Singapore. Various overseas joint venture projects and acquisitions. Examples: October 2004: signed a Memorandum of Understanding with the Iranian government to acquire 51% in the large Yadavaran oil field. May 2005: acquired 40% in an oil sands project in Canada for $ 83 million. June 2006: acquired 97% in Udmurtneft, a unit of BP's Russia vehicle TNK-BP, for $ 3.5 billion. June 2006: acquired offshore blocks in Angola for about $1 billion. August 2006: acquired Columbian oil-firm Omimex de Columbia for $ 850 million through its 50:50 joint venture with India's Oil and Natural Gas Corp. Dec 2007: invested around $ 2 billion to develop Iran's Yadavaran oilfied. March 2008: acquired 60% interest in three blocks of two oilfields owned by Australia-based AEO Oil Ltd, through its wholly-owned arm Sinopec International Petroleum Exploration & Production Corp. of China.
State Grid Corporation of China (SGCC)	SGCC is the first power grid company in China to expand internationally: March 2006: SGCC and Russian Joint Stock Company-Unified Energy System of Russia signed an Agreement on Making Feasibility Research of Russia-to-China Electricity Supply between SGCC and Russian Electric Power System Co. Ltd. November 2006: joint venture with Vietnam National Coal Corporation to build a thermal power plant in Vietnam with about 6.8 billion RMB investment from SGCC. Up to 2007, invested 5 billion RMB to build three power plants in Indonesia. Electricity projects with Vietnam, Laos, Myanmar, Thailand, and Cambodia.
China National Petroleum Corporation (CNPC)	30 international exploration and production projects with operations in Azerbaijan, Canada, Indonesia, Myanmar, Oman, Peru, Sudan, Thailand, Turkmenistan, and Venezuela. 1993: signed a service contract with the government of Peru to manage the Talara oilfield. Contract with the government of Sudan to manage a block in the Muglad oilfield. June 1997: acquired 60.3% in the Aktobe Oil Company of Kazakhstan. July 1997: won an oil contract for the Intercampo oilfield and East Caracoles oilfield in Venezuela. April 2002: acquired an Indonesian oil stake from Devon Energy for $216 million. October 2004: began construction of a pipeline from Middle East to Xinjiang. October 2005: completed its acquisition of PetroKazakhstan for $4.18 billion, the largest overseas acquisition by a Chinese company. December 2005: Completed the 600-mile Sino-Kazakh oil pipeline. February 2006: together with Sinopec Group acquired oil and pipeline interests in Ecuador for $1.42 billion from Canada's EnCana Corp. February 2006: joined with ONGC to acquire an asset in Syria from Petro-Canada for $580 million. November 2007: acquired a stake in a new Malaysian oil refinery in the northern state of Kedah (no further details publically available).

Table 2. (Continued)

Company	Overseas Activities
Industrial and Commercial Bank of China Limited	Branches in USA, UK, Luxembourg, Germany, Russia, Kazakhstan , Korea, Japan, Singapore, Australia. October 2007: announced the bank has reached an agreement to acquire 20% in South Africa's Standard Bank for $ 5.46 billion.
China Mobile Communications Corporation	2007: acquired Pakistan's mobile phone firm Paktel Ltd for $284 million, which is the first major overseas acquisition. 2006: tried to bid for Millicom, which controls mobile networks in 16 countries across Latin America, Africa and Asia, but failed.
China Life Insurance Co. Ltd.	September 2007: signed a strategic cooperation memorandum with General Electric of the US to explore joint venture opportunities in financial businesses. Currently in talks to buy into some Western financial firms hurt by the U.S. loan crisis. According to company chairman Yang Chao, the company tries to diversify into non-insurance businesses and turn itself into financial holding company with global reach.
China Southern Power Grid Co. Ltd	Operations started in Vietnam in September 2004. September 2006: the largest power network connection project between China and Vietnam put into operation - the largest electricity project China had carried out with a foreign country. By the end of 2007: transferred 1.84 billion kilowatt hours of electricity to Vietnam via four power lines which generated a sales volume of $80 million.
China Construction Bank	Overseas branches in Hong Kong, Singapore, Germany, South Africa, Japan, Korea, Australia; representative offices in the UK and USA. 2006: acquired Bank of America (Asia) based in Hong Kong.
China Telecommunica-tions Corporation	2002: awarded a licence by the US Telecom authorities to provide international telephone and Internet data services between the two countries. 2004: set up office in London. 2007: failed in its efforts to bid for Saudi Arabia's second fixed-line telephone license.
Bank of China	Wholly owned subsidiaries in Hong Kong, Macau, Singapore and UK. 2006: through its subsidiary, Bank of China Group Investment Limited acquired 100% of the share capital of Singapore Aircraft Leasing Enterprise Pte. Ltd for cash consideration of $ 978,000,000.
Baosteel Group Corporation	22 wholly owned subsidiaries (including 9 overseas subsidiaries), 14 holding companies (including 2 overseas subsidiaries) and 24 equity-sharing companies. Among the wholly owned subsidiaries and share holding companies, 11 are iron and steel companies, 2 financial companies, and 8 trading companies. 2007: joint venture with Brazil CVRD to build a manufacturing plant in Brazil, Baosteel holding more than 60% control.
Sinochem Corporation	Various overseas joint venture projects and acquisitions, mainly on oil retrieve. 2003: fully acquired two Petroleum companies, Atlantis Holding Norway AS and CRS Resources (Ecuador) LDC. November 2006: the Tunisia's Oudna offshore petroleum field, in which Sinochem possesses 40% of interests, was put into operation. June 2007: successfully installed the offshore production platform of UAQ gas-field project in United Arab Emirates, of which Sinochem owned 100% interests. February 2007: purchased 100% shares of the US company New. February 2008: agreed to buy London-listed exploration company Soco International's stake in a Yemen oilfield for $ 465 million.
Agricultural Bank of China	Branches in Singapore and Hong Kong and representative offices in London, Tokyo, New York. No overseas acquisitions so far
Bailian Group	No overseas activities
China FAW Group Corporation	Joint ventures with overseas companies (e.g. Toyota and Mazda Motor Corporation from Japan, TRW from US, Deutz AG, Volkswagen, ThyssenKrupp from Germany, Valeo from France) November 2007: announced plans to establish factories in Mexico through joint ventures with Mexican companies.

Sources: Companies' annual reports and websites; Energy Information Administration, Ministry of Commerce -The People's Republic of China, Ningbo Foreign Trade & Economic Cooperation Bureau; Asia Energy Today; Newspaper and stock market news (e.g. Asia Plus, People Daily, Xinhua News and Business Time Online)

Note: all amounts in dollars are in US dollars

It is beyond the objectives of this chapter to discuss Chinese SOEs' internationalization motives, strategies and routes. I only make reference to the fact that there are several reasons for cross-border expansion and span, from following Party and Government policy and directions (Nolan, 2001), through searching for more flexibility and management autonomy (Van Den Bulcke & Zhang, 1996) to satisfying managers' and their families' personal interests (Salem, 1988). On one hand, the ownership advantages of Chinese multinational enterprises have been attributed to the monopoly status and/or privileged position from which they benefited in their sectors, and on the other hand to the technologies they have acquired with governmental assistance (Nolan, 2001; Van Den Bulcke & Zhang, 1996: 157-158). Recent research has shown that SOEs tend to formulate strategies that make long-term investment as compared to short-term investments favored by non-SOEs (Li & Xia, 2008). Cross-border expansion is a long-term investment and, as evident from my sample, Chinese SOEs utilize both joint ventures, acquisitions and organic expansion when going international. Similarly to Van Den Bulcke and Zhang (1996) and Child and Rodrigues (2005), I argue that the 15 largest companies have been so active in their international expansion not despite, but because of their executives' links with government officials. As evident from Table 2, the international activities of the studied companies are frequent and impressive. Along with Ng et al. (2004) I speculate, although cannot document on the basis of a limited size sample, that many of these activities are either directly initiated or heavily supported by the state bureaucrats. This, however, does not mean that executive elites of these enterprises are left with a very limited strategic choice. I argue that the very decision to keep fertile ties with state authorities is made by CEOs and it is also largely their choice whether to lead their companies on the internationalization route or stay domestic. As observed by Child and Rodrigues (2004: 405), since the beginning of this century, the government's role is related to encouraging and supporting key firms to globalize "within the rationales of their own needs and policies".

TOP MANAGERS' OBSERVABLE CHARACTERISTICS

Age

Among the 14 companies where data on this dimension was available, only four CEOs are younger than 50 years*. The youngest top manager is Mr. Wang Tianpu from Sinopec Group who is 45 years old, and was appointed as President of the company in 2006. The oldest top manager in the sample is Mr. Wang Jianzhou, 59 years old, from China Mobile Communications Corporation. He has served as chairman and president of the company since 2004.

According to Hambrick and Mason (1984: 197), "the occurrence of a particular set of executive backgrounds in a firm is not a random process" and "executives often are chosen precisely because they have the 'right' background or temperament to carry out actions hoped for by the board of directors or other controlling parties". These authors also hypothesized that younger managers are more willing to take risks. In the examined sample the top

* The 15 companies' CEOs' age is calculated as of 2007. The retirement age for men in China is 60.

managers in the manufacturing sector are in general younger than those in the services sector. Most of the top managers in the manufacturing companies are below 50; while very few are below 50 in the services sector. In manufacturing and services, the number of managers below 50 is the same as the number of managers above 50. Figure 2 summarizes the statistics related to top managers' age in different industrial sectors.

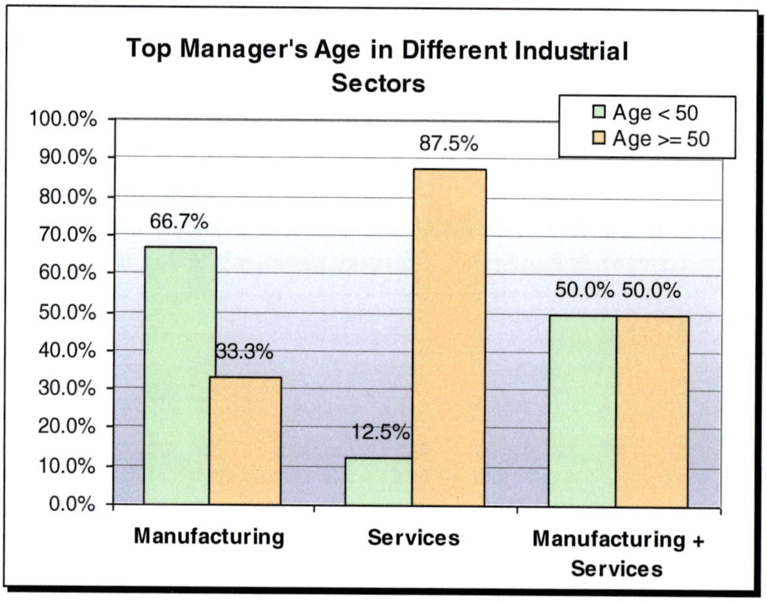

Figure 2. Top Manager's Age in Different Sectors

China opened its market for commodities before opening its services sector, and this led the manufacturing sector in the country to become more competitive. China FAW Group Corporation's and Baosteels' top managers are relatively young, 47 and 48 years old respectively. After China joined the WTO, FAW was exposed to automobile manufacturing competitors from Japan and Europe. Baosteel, too, faces strong competition as steel can be easily substituted by other materials such as aluminium, synthetic materials, engineered plastics and high-tech fibres. Two of the 15 companies support the UET proposition that younger managers are more willing to pursue more risky firm strategies. Baosteel stated in its 2007 fact-book that to achieve its strategic target "to be the most competitive steel manufacturer in the world" the company pursues the following key strategies:

1. "Operation scale expansion, e.g. to further expand the 30 million ton production capacity and strive to be the leading player at home in terms of both production scale and quality;
2. sustained innovation and renovation through developing a market-oriented competitive entity and achieve integrated operation of backbone steel;
3. best Capital Operation through acquiring from the Group quality steel and related assets, and
4. become an internationally listed public company." (Baosteel Co. Ltd., 2007)

FAW also articulated that innovation is "the soul of its development. Our passion for innovation and creative thinking runs deeply in the company's culture, giving our employees the support to turn exciting concepts into reality."

Functional Track

Combining the service and manufacturing sector together, 12 of the Presidents/CEOs are from "throughput function areas" (engineering or production) while three are from "peripheral function areas" (finance, economics, administration or law). There are no Presidents/CEOs with background in the "output functions" (marketing, sales or product research and development).

In the manufacturing sector alone, 11 Presidents/CEOs are from the throughput function area and the rest are from the peripheral function area. This is not different from what Hambrick & Mason (1984: 199) proposed in their original theory, namely that "there will be a positive association between the degree of throughput-function experience of top managers and the extent to which the firm emphasizes throughput in its strategy". Indictors of a throughput emphasis include automation, plant and equipment newness and backward integration. Strategies of automation, plant and equipment newness are emphasized more in the manufacturing sectors than in the services sectors.

In the services sector, only a few Presidents/CEOs are from the throughput function with the majority representing a peripheral function area. This is in line with Hambrick and Mason's (1984: 199) proposition that "the extent of peripheral-function experience of top managers will be positively related to administrative complexity, including thoroughness of formal planning systems, complexity of structures and budgeting detail and thoroughness, and complexity of incentive-compensation schemes".

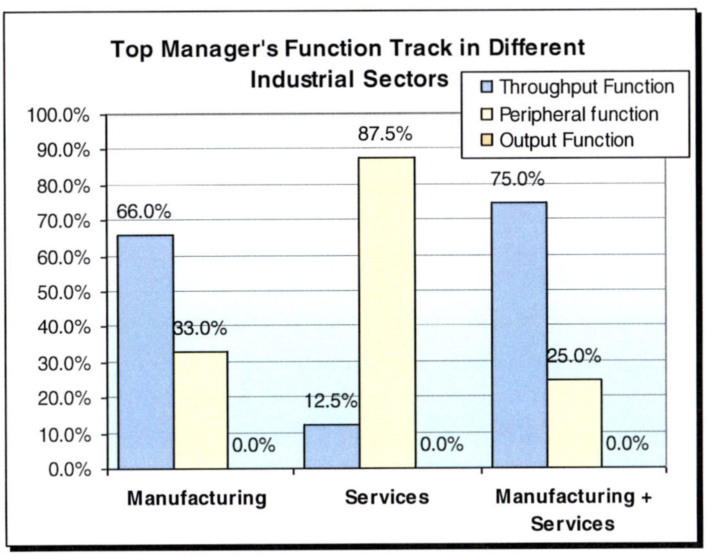

Figure 3. Top Manager's Function Track in Different Industrial Sectors

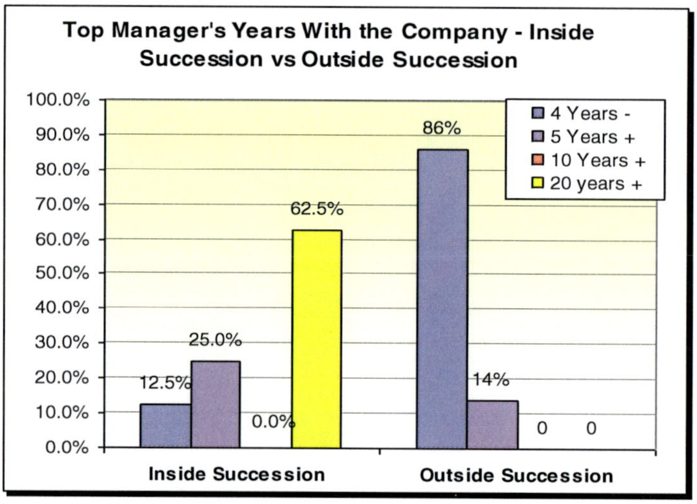

Figure 4. Top Manager's Years with the Company – Inside Succesion vs Outside Succession

Tenure in the Organization (Other Career Experience)

Eight Presidents/CEOs were promoted from inside the company while the other seven were external appointments. Among those promoted inside the company, five have been serving for more than 20 years inside the company and two have been serving for 8 years, while the eighth has been serving for 3 years. Most CEOs promoted from inside the company had held a Vice President position before they were promoted further.

As illustrated in Figure 4, among the outside successions, only one has been serving in the company for nine years while the other six have been serving in the company for less than five years. Although externally appointed, most of them have been working for many years in similar industries; Mr. Xue Quanrong from Bailian Group and Mr. Liu Deshu from Sinochem Corporation being the exceptions. Mr. Xue Quanrong worked in the farm catering industry and as a governor in Shanghai city before he was appointed President of Bailian Group, an investment, trading and real estate company. Mr. Liu Deshu worked in foreign trade before he was appointed CEO in Sinochem Corporation, a chemical materials manufacturing/distribution/import and export company.

The internally promoted Presidents/CEOs tend to have stayed for a number of years with their respective company. All three Presidents/CEOs in the manufacturing sector have been promoted internally. Two of them have been serving inside the company for more than 20 years and the third one for eight years. In contrast, only two of eight Presidents/CEOs from the services sector are internal promotions and they all served in the company for more than 20 years. The other six are all external appointments and they have been serving in their respective company for less than five years.

Three out of four Presidents/CEOs of companies operating in both manufacturing and services sector were promoted from inside. One has been working in the company for only three years, another one for eight years and the third one for 30 years. One President/CEO was appointed from outside, where he was company president for nine years. To sum up, the majority of Presidents/CEOs in the manufacturing sector are inside appointments while most Presidents/CEOs in services represent outside successions.

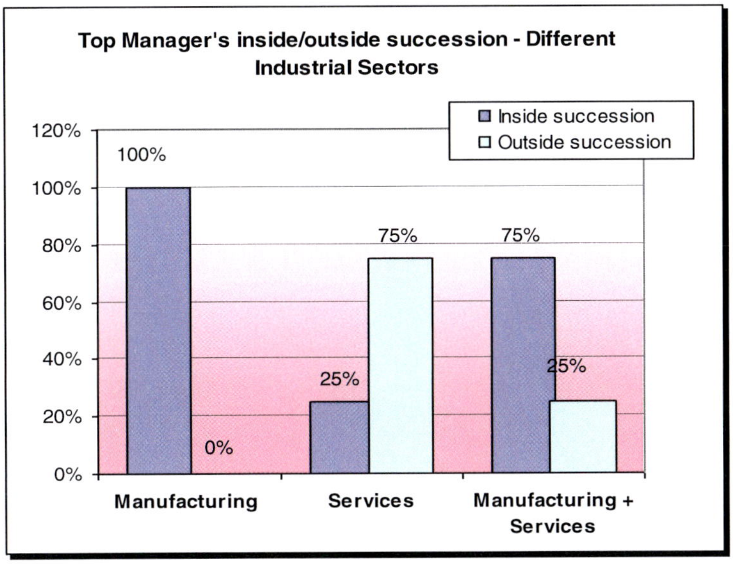

Figure 5. Top Manager's Inside/Outside Succession – Different Industrial Sectors

Hambrick and Mason (1984) proposed that years of inside service by top managers are negatively related to strategic choice involving new terrain and negatively associated with profitability and growth when the organization faces a severe environmental discontinuity. Longer-tenured executives have been found to be restrictive in their information processing and strategically persistent (Finkelstein & Hambrick, 1996), often lacking fresh information possessed by their less-experienced counterparts (Miller, 1991), exhibiting inertia (Fukutomi & Hambrick, 1991) and being loyal to prior strategies (Fredrickson et al., 1993).

This is not supported by the data in my sample. With the exception of Bailian Goup, the other 14 companies engaged in various international activities (please refer to Table 2), no matter how long the CEO had been with the company and no matter whether he represents an inside or outside succession. One explanation for the lack of confirmation of Hambrick and Mason's (1984) theory on this dimension could be that all companies I studied are SOEs and, as such, their international activities are monitored and directed by the central government rather than being at the discretion of the CEO. For example, China's rapid economic development is associated with a high demand for oil. According to IWAAS (2008), "China is abundant in oil resources and is one of the major oil producers in the world. Yet the per capita oil resources are not plentiful enough. As the economy develops fast since the 1990s, the scarcity of oil supply has been more and more prominent." The Economist (2008) also reported that "The international Energy Agency expects China's imports of oil to triple by 2030." This may contribute to Sinopec and CNPC's frequent overseas oil resources expansion through acquisitions and joint venture projects. Due to political reasons, it is risky to be conclusive about whether years of inside service affect the company's overseas expansion or not. Also, since all 15 companies are SOEs, I find it hard to define what exactly "organizations facing a severe environmental discontinuity" (Hambrick & Mason, 1984: 200) implies in the Chinese context: whenever a strategically important SOE (such as the ones in the sample) faces a severe environment, the state always supports it.

As illustrated in Figure 6, the Presidents/CEOs in the manufacturing sector serve longer years with their company than those in the service sectors. One explanation for this tendency is that the service sector in China is younger than the manufacturing industry. Another reason could be that the manufacturing industries are more technically-based and oriented, so companies prefer the selected President/CEO to have long years with them to assure the executive elites have a thorough understanding of technical manufacturing issues.

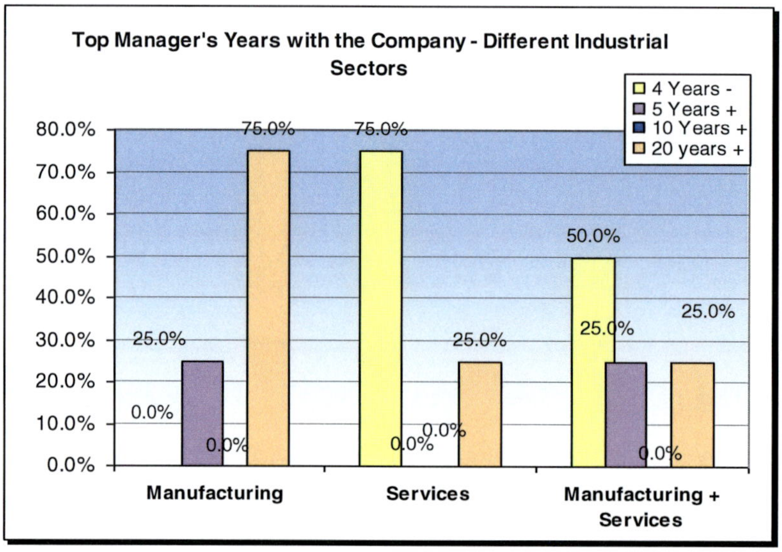

Figure 6. Top Manager's Years with the Company – Different Industrial Sectors

Formal Education

Research has suggested a positive link between a higher level of education and a higher level of receptivity to innovation (Becker, 1970), between formal education of top managers and the extent of innovation in their organization (Kimberly & Evansko, 1981; Bantel & Jackson, 1989), and the amount (but not type) of formal education of top managers and innovation (Hambrick & Mason, 1984).

All 15 top managers in the sample hold a higher education degree – ten have a masters degree and five also have a PhD degree. As illustrated in Figure 7, four of the top managers with a PhD degree work in the services sector while the fifth one is employed by a company that operates in both manufacturing and services. The distribution of executives with a masters degree in the three industry sectors is relatively even. However, half of the CEOs in the service sector and a quarter of the CEOs in both services and manufacturing hold a PhD degree while none of the top managers in manufacturing sectors have gone through a PhD education. This leads me to carefully conclude that top managers in the service sector tend to have higher levels of education compared to top managers in manufacturing. This may be associated with the fact that service firms in general are more innovative than manufacturing firms (Sheehan, 2006). Thirteen of the top managers in the sample received their higher education in China and two, Mr. Yang Chao from China Life Insurance Co. Ltd. and Mr. Ai Baojun from Baosteel Group Corporation, earned their degrees overseas.

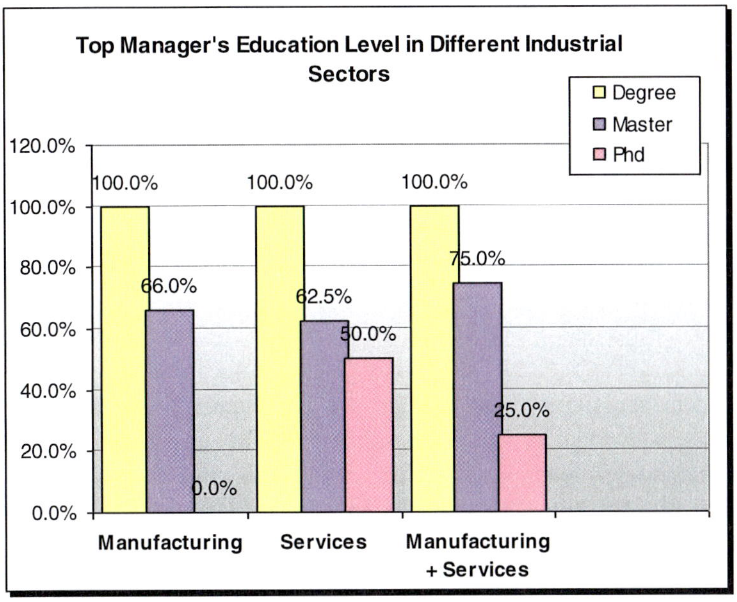

Figure 7. Top Manager's Education Level in Different Industrial Sectors

Political Affiliation

This demographic attribute has not been proposed in Hambrick and Mason's (1984) UET. At the same time, these authors have highlighted that executives are chosen because they have the "right" background (Hambrick & Mason, 1984: 197). Being politically loyal is an important part of having the "right" background in the PRC. Indeed, all 15 Presidents/CEOs in the studied sample are not only Chinese Communist Party (CCP) members, but are also involved in leading Party positions: six served as Secretaries of CCP Committees, the others served as Provincial Governors*. The CCP has never wanted to recruit cadres on the basis of expertise alone (Zang, 2001); political reliability and loyalty has always been (at least) equally important. Due to the fact that the government plays a vital role in resource allocation, China's institutional environment has traditionally favored executive elites who have good connections with officials (Li et al., 2004).

The importance of business-government ties has, however, been debated in relation to economic liberalization. While some researchers argue that the value of these ties would be reduced as liberalization progresses (Guthrie, 1998; Guthrie, 1999; Keister, 2002; Nee, 1989), others, and I subscribe to this latter view, maintain that their influence would remain and even increase (Heath & Peng, 1996; Luo & Park, 2001; Michailova & Worm, 2003; Peng, 1994),

* Some studies (e.g. Walder, 1995) have used CCP membership while others (e.g. Zang, 2001) relied on CCP seniority as a measure for political loyalty. On both dimensions the 15 CEOs subject in this chapter are politically loyal.

as institutional uncertainty stays relatively high. During the economic reforms, political reputation remains a crucial form of capital within the non-market sector of the economy (Tan, 2001: 370). As observed by Zang (2001: 73): "[...] party cadres and technocrats need each other to stay in office. Party bureaucrats rely on the technocrats for their advice and expertise and share power with them. Technocrats cooperate with the bureaucrats to climb up the political hierarchy controlled by the communist elites." Maintaining a good relationship with the Party representatives in their firms is important for SOE managers as it also helps in getting access to resources (e.g. input materials, energy, loans from the central government, information) and interpreting policy guidelines issued by the Party and state ministries (Litschert & Tan, 1994). Business-politics connections and networks were revitalized to enable companies to survive and succeed in an uncertain and volatile environment (Heath & Peng, 1996; McDermott, 2002).

State Council is the major shareholder of the SOEs. Selecting Presidents/CEOs with a strong political background allows the State Council to carefully monitor whether these enterprises work in accordance with and satisfy the State's interests. Strong connections between CEOs and the State can be very helpful in achieving change and other desirable outcomes, but being a SOE can also have the opposite negative effect. In a detailed study of three SOEs in a South China City, Huang and Snell (2003) provided evidence that top managers' strong political connections can be utilized to achieve different objectives. In one of the cases the CEO persuaded the supervisory bureau to allow him to replace the old top management team with managers chosen on merit, and who supported his desire for reforms. He exercised transformational leadership, established internal rule of law, cultivated a spirited moral climate, and achieved turnaround. In another case the CEO exploited the strong political connections to enfeeble the governance structures and destructively exploit company resources while in the third company the equity sensitive CEO was prevented from improving performance.

Over the past several years the Chinese government has undertaken massive anti-corruption campaigns. For example, it punished 97,260 members of the Communist Party of China in 2006 (Embassy of the People's Republic of China in the United States of America, 2007). The government also publicly lists a certain percentage of SOEs' shares. Twelve of the 15 SOEs I studied were public-listed in the Shanghai, Hong Kong or New York stock market exchanges. Once the company has been listed, the State is not its only (although it remains the major) shareholder and the listed company becomes responsible for all of its shareholders' interests and for managing potential conflicts between the various interests. To be listed, the SOE also has to maintain a certain level of transparency and this further helps to improve SOE efficiency and profitability. The Chinese Government, too, is working on further improving the transparency and governance of the listed companies. After a careful study of international experience over the last few years, in December 2007 the Shanghai Stock Exchange (SSE) officially introduced the "SSE Corporate Governance Sector" (Mondo Visione, 2007).

DISCUSSION AND CONCLUSION

In this study I utilized UET to analyze the demographic characteristics of the executive elites of the 15 largest companies in the PRC. Following this theory's logic, I examined the nature of these enterprises (e.g. sector, history, ownership) and their strategies (e.g. international expansion), and linked those to these firms' CEOs' and Presidents' age, functional track, other career experience, and formal education. Hambrick and Mason (1984: 197) highlighted evidence suggesting that "the occurrence of a particular set of executive backgrounds in a firm is not a random process" and "executives often are chosen precisely because they have the 'right' background or temperament to carry out actions hoped for by the board of directors or other controlling parties". Bearing in mind that China's emerging system of capitalism has its own specific institutional and cultural characteristics (Boisot & Child, 1996; Child & Tse, 2001), I extended the theory and suggested that beyond the demographic attributes initially suggested in the UET, executives' political affiliation is a characteristic that is important in the Chinese context and, indeed, part of the "right background" of Chinese executive elites.

I argued that Chinese SOEs' internationalization can, to a certain extent, be explained by the demographic attributes of these enterprises' top managers. I also made the point that in the Chinese context the role of the State is inherent in the key decisions these managers make, and the State's wider interests are integral to the enterprises' own interests. While these two explanations might appear as being relatively distant from one another, I suggest that they are actually closely and logically intertwined. Moreover, the link as such might be decisive in Chinese SOEs' successful internationalization and also a feature that distinguishes those enterprises from multinationals in both developed and other emerging countries. It could, however, also be that Chinese SOEs' internationalization will be slowed down due to inertia and legacy in the entire system, that are likely to inhibit forward-oriented strategic action.

China's institutional environment is changing rapidly. Although it might not be likely, one cannot completely exclude the possibility of changes in the political regime in China, which could lead to repositioning of the SOEs and their executive elites. Siegel (2007) provided evidence that business-government ties, particularly in emerging economies, can be either assets or liabilities, and examined how unexpected changes in political regime could quickly change the nature and impact of these ties. Siegel (2007) concluded that just as positive ties can lead to favor exchange and other benefits for companies, negative ties (having the "wrong friends" at the wrong time) can lead companies to be victims of discrimination, resource exclusion and even occasional expropriation and sabotage between rival socio-political networks. While the SOEs that have extensively relied on their links with the authorities to secure their own survival might end up as the ones with "wrong friends", those SOEs that have also developed a real entrepreneurial logic along with their networks with officials will be able to provide new insights and food for thought for researchers and executives alike.

The present chapter is an effort to stimulate discussion, rather than provide well-defined findings and conclusions, on the relationship between Chinese firm behavior and the characteristics of the executive elites of these firms. I contend that China provides a good example of the need to extend UET to take into greater consideration factors and features that operate within a national context.

Implications for future research arise from the limitations of the presented study. First, I only presented a pilot, primarily descriptive, study that includes the 15 largest companies in the PRC. Formulation of theoretical propositions and testable fine-grained hypotheses as well as a larger sample of companies would be a promising avenue to explore. Second, and similarly to most studies that have utilized UET, I only made use of some of the observable managerial characteristics proposed by Hambrick and Mason (1984). The databases with which I have worked did not provide information on Chinese executive elites' socioeconomic roots, financial position and group characteristics. I realize that these are important attributes and if no readily accessible databases exist, the effort of collecting original data on these dimensions would be worthwhile. Similarly, I have analyzed a characteristic that has not been considered in original UET work, namely executives' political affiliation. While this attribute appears to be very important in the context of China, it is worth considering whether there are other context-specific variables that warrant serious research attention.

ACKNOWLEDGEMENT

I acknowledge and appreciate the research assistance provided by Nicole Siu Kwan Sze.

REFERENCES

[1] Aldrich, H. E., & Auster, E. R. (1986). Even dwarfs started small: Liabilities of age and size and their strategic implications. In B. Staw, & L.L. Cummings (Eds.), *Research in Organizational Behavior, 8*, 165-198. CA: JAL Press.

[2] Bantel, K. A., & Jackson, S. E. (1989). Top management and innovations in banking: Does the composition of the team make a difference? *Strategic Management Journal, 10*, 107-114.

[3] Bantel, K. A., & Wiersema, M. F. (1992). Top management team demography and corporate strategic change. *Academy of Management Journal, 35*(1), 91-121.

[4] Baosteel Co. Ltd. (2007). Company fact-book 2007. http://tv.baosteel.com/ir/pdf/factbook/factbook2007en.pdf

[5] Barber, B. M., & Palmer, D. (2001). Challengers, elites, and owning families: A social class theory of corporate acquisitions in the 1960s. *Administrative Science Quarterly, 46*, 87-120.

[6] Baum, J. A. C. (1995). Organizational ecology. In S.R.Clegg, C. Hardy, & W. Nord (Eds.), *Handbook of Organization Studies*, 77-115. Newbury Park, CA: Sage.

[7] Baum, J. A. C., & Mezias, S. (1992). Localized competition and the dynamics of organizational failure in the Manhattan hotel industry. *Administrative Science Quarterly, 37*, 580-604.

[8] Baum, J. R., & Wally, S. (1994). Personal and structural determinants of the pace of strategic decision making. *Academy of Management Journal, 37*(4), 932-956.

[9] Becker, M. H. (1970). Sociometric location and innovativeness: Reformulation and extension of the diffusion model. *American Sociological Review, 35*, 267-304.

[10] Bergh, D. D. (2001). Executive retention and acquisition outcomes: A test of opposing views on the influence of organizational tenure. *Journal of Management, 27*(5), 603-622.

[11] Bocker, W. (1997). Executive migration and strategic change: The effect of top manager movement on product-market entry. *Administrative Science Quarterly, 42*, 213-236.

[12] Boisot, M., & Child, J. (1996). From fiefs to clans and network capitalism: Explaining China's emerging economic order. *Administrative Science Quarterly, 41*, 600-628.

[13] Breckenridge, R. S., Jones, D. L., & Ranger-Moore, J. (1995). Patterns of growth and size-localized competition in the New York State life insurance industry, 1860-1985. *Social Forces, 73*(3), 1027-1045.

[14] Buckley, P. J., & Ghauri, P. N. (Eds.) (1999). *The Internationalization of the Firm*. London: Thomson Business Press.

[15] Cannella, A. A. Jr., & Holcomb, T. R. (2005). A multi-level analysis of the upper-echelons model. *Research in Multi-Level Issues, JAI, 4*, 197-237.

[16] Carpenter, M. A., Geletkanycz, M. A., & Sanders, W. G. (2004). 'Upper echelons revisited: Antecedents, elements, and consequences of top management team composition'. *Journal of Management, 30*(6), 749-778.

[17] Child, J., & Luo, Y. (1996). Institutional constraints on economic reform: the case of investment decisions in China. *Organization Science, 7*, 60-77.

[18] Child, J., & Rodrigues, S. B. (2005). The internationalization of Chinese firms: A case for theoretical extension? *Management and Organization Review, 1*(3), 381-410.

[19] Child, J., & Tse, D. K. (2001). China's transition and its implications for international business. *Journal of International Business Studies, 32*, 5-21.

[20] Chow, C. K. W., & Fung, M. K. Y. (1996). Firm dynamics and industrialization in the Chinese economy in transition: Implications for small business policy. *Journal of Business Venturing, 11*, 489-505.

[21] Christianson, J. B., Sanchez, S. M., & Wholey, D. R. (1992). Organizational size and failure among health maintenance organizations. *American Sociological Review, 57*, 829-842.

[22] Cooper, A. C., Dunkelberg, W. C., & Woo, C. Y. (1989). Entrepreneurship and the initial size of firms. *Journal of Business Venturing, 4*, 317-332.

[23] Daily, C. M., Dalton, D. R., Ellstrand, A. E., & Tihanyi, L. (2000). Composition of the top management team and firm international diversification. *Journal of Management, 26*(6), 1157-1177.

[24] Datta, D. K., & Herrmann, P. (2005). Relationships between top management team characteristics and international diversification: An empirical investigation. *British Journal of Management, 16*, 69-78.

[25] Datta, D. K., & Rajagopalan, N. (1998). Industry structure and CEO characteristics: An empirical study of succession events. *Strategic Management Journal, 19*, 833-852.

[26] Dearborn, D. C., & Simon, H. A. (1958). Selective perception: A note on the departmental identifications of executives. *Sociometry, 21*, 140-144.

[27] Embassy of the People's Republic of China in the United States of America. (2007). *China punishes 97,000 Party members in anti-corruption campaign*. http://big5.fmprc.gov.cn/gate/big5/www.china-embassy.org/eng/gyzg/t297513.htm

[28] Finkelstein, S., & Hambrick, D. (1996). *Strategic leadership: Top executives and their effects on organizations*. West: St Paul, NM.

[29] Freeman, J., & Hannan, M. T. (1984). Structural inertia and organizational change. *American Journal of Sociology*, 82, 929-964.

[30] Freeman, J., & Hannan, M. T. (1989). *Organizational ecology*. Cambridge, MA: Harvard University Press.

[31] Fredrickson, J. W., Geletkanycz, M., & Hambrick, D. C. (1993). Top executive commitment to the status quo: Some tests of its determinants. *Strategic Management Journal, 14*, 401-418.

[32] Freund, E. M. (2001). Fizz, froth, flat: The challenge of converting China's SOEs into shareholding corporations. *Policy Studies Review, 18*(1), 96-111.

[33] Fukutomi, G. D., & Hambrick, D. C. (1991). The seasons of a CEO's tenure. *Academy of Management Review, 16*, 719-742.

[34] Groves, T., Hong, Y., McMillan, J., & Naughton, B. (1994). Autonomy and incentives in Chinese state enterprises. *Quarterly Journal of Economics, 109*, 183-209.

[35] Guthrie, D. (1998). The declining significance of gianxi in China's economic transition. *China Quarterly, 154*, 254-282.

[36] Guthrie, D. (1999). *Dragon in a Three-piece Ssuit: The Emergence of Capitalism in China.* Princeton, NJ: Princeton University Press.

[37] Hambrick, D. C., & Mason, P. A. (1984). Upper echelons: The organization as a reflection of its top managers. *Academy of Management Review, 9* (2), 193-206.

[38] Hambrick, D. C., & Michel, J. G. (1992). Diversitifaction posture and top management team characteristics. *Academy of Management Journal, 35*, 9-37.

[39] Heath, P. S., & Peng, M. W. (1996). The growth of the firm in planned economies in transition: Institutions, organizations and strategic choice. *Academy of Management Review, 21*, 492-528.

[40] Henley, J. S., & Nyaw, M. K. (1986). Introducing market forces into managerial decision-making in Chinese industrial enterprises. *Journal of Management Studies, 23*, 635-656.

[41] Hitt, M. A., Ireland, R. D., & Palia, K. A. (1982). Industrial firms' grand strategy and functional importance: Moderating effects of technology and uncertainty. *Academy of Management Review, 25*, 265-298.

[42] Hitt, M. A., & Tyler, B. B. (1991). Strategic decision models: Integrating different perspectives. *Strategic Management Journal, 12*(4), 327-351.

[43] Hong Kong Trade Develop Council (2007). Deepening banking reform on the mainland. http://www.tdctrade.com/econforum/hsb/hsb070301.htm

[44] Huang, L. J., & Snell, R. S. (2003). Turnaround, corruption and mediocrity: Leadership and Governance in three state owned enterprises in mainland China. *Journal of Business Ethics*, 43(1/2), 111-124.

[45] IWAAS (Institute of West Asian and African Studies). (2008). China depends on oil of the Middle East. http://iwaas.cass.cn/en/others/show_fruit.asp?id=166

[46] Jensen, M., & Zajac, E. J. (2004). Corporate elites and corporate strategy: How demographic preferences and structural position shape the scope of the firm'. *Strategic Management Journal, 25*(6), 507-524.

[47] Keister, L. A. (2002). Guanxi in business groups: Social ties and the formation of economic relations. In T. Gold, D. Guthrie and D. Wank (Eds.), *Social Connections in China: Institutions, Culture, and the Changing Cature of Guanxi*. 77-96. Cambridge: Cambridge University Press.

[48] Kimberly, J. R. (1981). Managerial innovation. In P.C. Nystrom & W. H. Starbuck (Eds.), *Handbook of Organizational Design*. NY: Oxford University Press.

[49] Kor, Y. Y. (2003). Experience-based top management team competence and sustained growth. *Organization Science*, *14,* 707-719.

[50] Kor, Y. Y., & Mahoney, J. T. (2000). Penrose's resource-based approach: The process and product of research creativity. *Journal of Management Studies*, *37*(1), 109-139.

[51] Li, S., & Xia, J. (2008). The roles and performance of state firms and non-state firms in China's economic transition. *World Development*, 36(1), 39-54.

[52] Lin, X., & Zhang, Y. (2008). Bank ownership reform and bank performance in China. *Journal of Banking & Finance*, forthcoming.

[53] Litschert, R. J., Ramaswamy, K., & Thomas, A. S. (1991). The performance impact of strategy-manager coalignment: An empirical investigation. *Strategic Management Journal*, *12*, 509-522.

[54] Litschert, R. J., & Tan, J. (1994). ‚Environment-strategy relationship and its performance implications: An empirical study of Chinese electronics industry'. *Strategic Management Journal*, *15*, 1-20.

[55] Lu, D., & Tang, Z. (1997). *State Intervention and Business in China.* Cheltenham, UK: Edward Elgar.

[56] Luo, Y., & Park, S. H. (2001). Guanxi and organizational dynamics: Organizational networking in Chinese firms. *Strategic Management Journal*, *22,* 455-477.

[57] McDermott, G. A. (2002). *Embedded politics: Industrial networks and institutional change in postcommunism.* Ann Arbor, MI: University of Michigan Press.

[58] Michailova, S., & Worm, V. (2003). Personal networking in Russia and China: Blat and guanxi. *European Management Journal, 21*(4), 509-519.

[59] Miller, D. (1991). Stale in the saddle: CEO tenure and the match between organization and environment. *Management Science*, *37*, 34-52.

[60] Mondo Visione. (2007). Shanghai stock exchange corporate governance sector officially launched.http://www.mondovisione.com/index.cfm?section=news&action=detail&id=71557

[61] Murray, A. I. (1989). Top management group heterogeneity and firm performance. *Strategic Management Journal*, *10*, 125-141.

[62] Nee, V. (1989). A theory of market transition: From redistribution to markets in state socialism. *American Sociological Review*, 54, 663-681.

[63] Nee, V. (1992). Organizational dynamics of market transition: hybrid forms, property rights and mixed economy in China. *Administrative Science Quarterly*, *3*, 293-310.

[64] Ng, S.H., Xu, X., & Warner, M. (2004). Late development experience and the evolution of transnational firms in the People's Republic of China. *Asia Pacific Business Review*, *10*, 324-345.

[65] Nolan, P. (2001). *China and the global economy*. Basingstoke, UK: Palgrave.

[66] Nyaw, M. K., & Schermerhorn, J. R. Jr. (1991). Managerial leadership in Chinese industrial enterprises. In O. Shenkar (Eds.), *Organization and Management in China: 1979-1990*, 9-21. Armonk, NY: M.E. Sharpe Inc.

[67] Peng, M. W. (1994). 'Organizational changes in planned economies in transition: An eclectic model. In J. L. C. Cheng and R. B. Peterson (Eds.)', *Advances in International Comparative Management, 9,* 223-251. Greenwich, CT: JAI Press.

[68] Perkins, D. (1994). Completing China's Move to the Market. *Journal of Economic Perspectives, 8*(2), 23– 45.

[69] Poon, A. (2008). Sinopec to get Chinese government subsidy for 2007 refining loss. http://www.marketwatch.com/news/story/sinopec-get-chinese-government subsidy/story.aspx?guid=%7BAE99D43F-8E11-460B-885C-6E4E40C4E2FF%7D

[70] Qian, Y. (1996). Enterprise reform in China: Agency problems and political control. *Economics of Transition*, 4(2), 427-447.

[71] Salem, E. (1988). The China syndrome: Peking pours money into Hong Kong – for its own benefit. *Far Eastern Economic Review*, 23, June, 64-66.

[72] Scott, W. R. (1992). *Organizations: Rational, Natural and Open Systems* (3rd ed). New York: Prentice Hall.

[73] Sheehan, J. (2006). Understanding service sector innovation. *Communication of the ACM*, *49* (7), 43-48.

[74] Siegel, J. (2007). Contingent political capital and international alliances: Evidence from South Korea. *Administrative Science Quarterly*, *52*, 621-666.

[75] Tan, J. (2001). Innovation and risk-taking in a transitional economy: A comparative study of Chinese managers and entrepreneurs. *Journal of Business Venturing*, *16*, 359-376.

[76] The Economist. (2008). Leaders: The new colonialists. March 2008, 386, 13.

[77] Trading Markets. (2008). Sinopec Gets CNY12.3bn Subsidies for Oil Refining Loss. http://www.tradingmarkets.com/.site/news/Stock%20News/1232166/

[78] Walder, A. (1995). Career mobility and the communist political order. *American Sociological Review*, *65*, 191-209.

[79] Wikipedia. (2008). China National Petroleum Corporation. http://en.wikipedia.org/wiki/CNPC.

[80] Yang, Y. (2004). SOE reform and private sector development in China. In R. Garnaut and L. Song (Eds.), *China's third economic transition,* 72-90. NY: RoutledgeCurzon.

[81] Zang, X. (2001). University education, party seniority, and elite recruitment in China. *Social Science Research, 30*, 62-75.

[82] Van den Bulcke, & Zhang, H. Y. (1996). International management strategies of Chinese multinational firms. In J. Child & Y. Lu (Eds.), *Management Issues for China,* Volume II: International enterprise, 141-164. London: Routledge.

[83] Zhang, A., Zhang, Y., & Zhao, R. (2002). Profitability and productivity of Chinese industrial firms: Measurement and ownership implications. *China Economic Review*, *13*, 65-88.

[84] Zhu, T. (1999). China's corporatization drive: An evaluation and policy implications. *Contemporary Economic Policy*, *17*(4), 530-539.

In: Thirty Years of China's Economic Reform
Editors: Yue Wang and Prem Ramburuth ISBN: 978-1-60876-908-7
© 2010 Nova Science Publishers, Inc.

Chapter 8

THE RISE OF FEMALE ENTREPRENEURS IN CHINA

Wenxian Zhang* and Ilan Alon+
Rollins College, Winter Park, Florida, USA

Women can hold up half the sky. – Mao Zedong

ABSTRACT

Women entrepreneurs have been playing an increasingly significant role in the Chinese economic reform of the past thirty years. Through historical review and case studies, this paper examines the development of female entrepreneurship in the People's Republic of China. Faced with both challenges and opportunities, aspiring Chinese women must have a clear vision, sheer determination and perseverance to move forward, and they must also possess a sense of aggressiveness and decision-making competence in order to achieve desirable business objectives. In addition, successful female entrepreneurs in China appear to be well educated, mostly married and politically shrewd, they seem to enjoy strong family support and benefit greatly from extensive personal networks.

Keywords: Female entrepreneurs; entrepreneurship; Chinese economic reform; women and gender; characteristics; personal profile.

INTRODUCTION

* Email: wzhang@rollins.edu.Wenxian Zhang is Professor and Head of Archives & Special Collections at Rollins College, Winter Park, Florida, USA
+ Email: ialon@rollins.edu. Ilan Alon is Petters Chair of International Business, Executive Director of China Center at Rollins College, and Visiting Scholar of the John F. Kennedy School of Government at Harvard University.

Ever since the founding of the People's Republic of China, women's participation in employment has been a large-scale phenomenon. During those early years of the PRC, based on a misunderstood notion of equal opportunity, Mao's slogan "women can hold up half the sky" was widely promoted. Dubbed "iron girls", women were encouraged to perform all kinds of work that were traditionally reserved for men. Consequently, the country has had a far higher womens' employment rate than the world average, with women representing 47 percent of its total workforce (*China Statistics Yearbook*). China has the largest population in the world, with more than half a billion women, over 50 percent of whom are in full-time employment; its female workforce contributed 38 percent of the country's GDP in the year 2000 (Liu, 2001). The country as a whole is seen to have a higher level of gender equality than Japan, the UK and the USA, with permanent full-time work being the norm for all adults irrespective of sex, and a high degree of egalitarianism in family roles (Stockman, et al., 1995). Clearly, women have been playing an increasingly significant role in China's economy.

However, this remarkable achievement has been criticised by some as a hollow victory. According to Cooke (2004), the state's role during the past decades has been limited to protecting women's labor rights and increasing their share in employment, with little provision aimed to ensure and improve the quality of women's employment prospects - a lower proportion of women are professionals or managers, and a much higher proportion are in clerical and lower-level manual work. Among the 60 million workers who worked in private and individual businesses, over 50 percent were female; such sectors are often associated with lower wages and pensions, less job security, lower employment welfare, reduced training opportunities and fewer promotions (Jiang, 2000).

Entrepreneurship is the best way to empower women. Entrepreneurs are defined as individuals who are opportunistic, proactive, action-oriented, value-driven, risk-accepting, and whose creative ideas take the form of organizational birth, growth, and transformation (Tan, 1996). A female entrepreneur can be described as a "woman who has initiated a business, is actively involved in management, owns 50% of the firm, and has been in operation for one year or longer" (Moore and Butler, 1997: 13). For the purpose of this study, a few top female executives are also included, as they are the representatives of millions of women working in various industries today. Through the recent ownership reform in China, many of them have become large shareholders, as their enterprises went public.

Since 1995, the number of women involved in the private economy has risen by 60%, reaching nearly 10 million, and women entrepreneurs make up 20% of the total Chinese entrepreneurial population (Tan, 2008). The growth of female entrepreneurs in the private sector is driven by women who are unwilling to compromise themselves through employment that is not conducive to career progression. The profile of women entrepreneurs in the future will continue to match their changing situation, and move closer to their male counterparts. However, women entrepreneurs may not be able to completely eliminate discrimination against them, as they are still surrounded by a male-dominated society.

Although more women are becoming entrepreneurs in the non-state sectors at an increasing speed, their numbers are still lagging behind men. According to the second national sample survey of womens' social position in China (2001), 6.1 percent of women in urban employment, compared with 8 percent of men, were in managerial positions. Another survey by the All-China Women's Federation (2000) indicated that the majority of entrepreneurs surveyed were younger women, had higher levels of education than the national average for women, and most worked in private-owned enterprises. A large majority of them were married and felt that their husbands were a great source of support in their career, and many of the couples operated the business together. They felt they were inferior to men in their physical strength, readiness to face challenges, strategic decision-making, analytical ability and innovativeness. According to them, the quality deficiency of women themselves and social bias were the major causes for the lack of women entrepreneurs in China.

Despite the advancement in female entrepreneurship, current research offered inconsistent predictions and empirical evidence is far from being conclusive. Because of the complex nature of the subject and competing conclusions in the existing literature, a framework is needed that should include both internal factors, such as personal characteristics, and external factors such as values, regulations, and family and support systems. Furthermore, according to one study, 64 percent of articles were based in the US, and 83 percent of studies on women in entrepreneurship came from the Anglo-Saxon sphere (Ahl, 2003). Those findings are useful but limited, and such observations should not be over-generalised or stereotyped. In order to gain a comprehensive understanding of this important subject, the following section of the paper will present the brief profiles of nine women entrepreneurs (Zhang and Alon, 2009). Through those case studies, this research seeks to examine the development of female entrepreneurship in the People's Republic of China, the challenges and opportunities faced by aspiring women, and various social, economic and cultural factors that influence the growth of female entrepreneurship in China.

Brief Profiles of Female Entrepreneurs in China

Ranked the second richest woman, worth US$2.6 billion by *Hurun Report* (2008), *Chen Lihua* (Chan, Laiwa 陈丽华1941-) is one of the wealthiest business people in China. Growing up in a poor family living in Beijing appears to have been a source of great encouragement to her. After finishing high school, Chen began a furniture repairing business in 1976. Having an interest in international trade, and with an entrepreneurial spirit, she sought opportunities in Hong Kong and in 1988 founded the Fuhua (Fu Wah) International Group in Beijing, which conducts real estate, hospitality, international trade, and tourism business among others. She has since worked as president and chairwoman of the multi-billion dollar corporation, and was able to benefit from the growing real estate market in Beijing through connections with leaders within the Communist Party. By targeting high-end consumers, Fuhua has become one of the most successful real estate companies in China. In 1995, Chen founded the Changan Club, a luxurious first-class club for top business people who have self-made fortunes. With 800 members, the project provided much strength, success and popularity for the company. In recent years, she also donated millions towards disaster relief and contributed to education and poverty-relief efforts. Closely associated with her business, Chen is politically active and is recognised as a loyal member of the State Unification Commission, the National Committee of Chinese People's Consultative Conference (CPPCC) and the China Association of Industry and Commerce.

Dong Mingzhu (董明珠 1954-) is vice-chairperson and general manager of Zhuhai Gree Electric Appliance, and has built Gree from a small, local company into a leading air conditioner manufacturer globally, and is widely recognized as one of the most respected and successful businesswomen in China today. In 1990, 36 year-old Dong joined Gree, and rose steadily from marketing and sales manager to director of operations and general manager. In 1995, when China's young air conditioning industry experienced a crisis, Dong successfully convinced top management not to jump into the price war, believing that the slip in sales was related more to the unseasonably rainy and cool weather. By leaving prices untouched, Glee was able to maintain a healthy profit margin. A year later, when another price war broke out, Dong's stubborn refusal to slash prices helped Gree to gain ground against major competitors, a strategic move that eventually led to Gree's dominance in the market. In 2001, Dong again found out that she had to stand up and say no, this time to China's powerful home appliances retailers, who preferred to squeeze the profit margin of suppliers in order to provide the lowest possible price to consumers. Instead, Dong started to build her own distribution network. Dubbed "the Gree Model", she has kept retail partners satisfied through a win-win rebate system, which is one of China's most successful and innovative business practices in recent years. As a result, Gree achieved enviable revenue of RMB13.8 billion that year, an increase of nearly 38% over previous sales. For her vision, innovation and entrepreneurship, Dong was twice named among the World's 50 Most Powerful Women in Business by *Fortune*, the Top Ten Chinese Business Figures of the Year by CCTV in 2006, and ranked number 93 of the World's 100 Most Powerful Women by *Forbes* in 2007. Dong is also the deputy director of the Chinese Household Appliances Association, vice-chair of the Women Entrepreneur Association of Guangdong Province, and chairperson of the Women Entrepreneur Association of Zhuhai.

Shi Xiaoyan (史晓燕 1962-) is the CEO of the Beijing-based Illinois Investment Limited, a furniture company targeting middle-class, white-collar workers. Along the course of Chinese economic reform, Shi has made a huge leap forward in her life: from a nurse in a Beijing hospital to a student studying abroad, from a housewife to a millionaire and the boss of a famous furniture company, and from owning a small shop to running a large auto theme park. After graduating from a nursing school, Shi first worked as a nurse at the Beijing Union Medical College Hospital. However, she not only was frustrated by the tedious and boring nature of her assignment, but also could not bear her low monthly salary of RMB70 yuan while struggling to make a living in the Chinese capital. Being a woman who could not be content with a stable life, Shi job-hopped to a foreign company in 1984, although at that time changing careers was quite unimaginable in China. Working for the new company, she did not even know how to use a typewriter. But as a smart, capable, and quick minded individual, she still won the appreciation of her employer. After marriage, she still was not satisfied to be a housewife. A trip abroad inspired her to enter into the furniture industry. In 1989, her husband moved to Singapore to work for an IT company. There, she realised that personal values are usually embodied in ones' lifestyles, and noticed the delicate design of furniture and other household appliances in developed countries. Hence she decided to major in interior design at the University of Chicago, while keeping an eye on both international fashion trends and China's economic development. Shi returned to China in the mid-1990s; after losing US$3 million and a few other setbacks, she, together with her husband, established a small furniture factory and imitated the design and style of foreign brands. Because of its low price and novel style, her Illinois brand was gradually accepted by customers in Beijing. Yet this strategy did not last long, and Shi started to think about setting up her own furniture design shop. Since 2000, after researching the international furniture market, she has defined and developed Illinois' unique style - new classic, postmodernism. This soon became a real hit, which attracted not only Chinese customers, but also many from abroad. Her insight into the market and sense of aesthetics enables her company to stay at the cutting edge of furniture design. Shi never stops expanding her business. Apart from running a furniture company, Shi has also established China's first auto theme park located near Beijing Capital International Airport.

Wang Jiafen (王佳芬 1951-) is the president and CEO of the Shanghai-based Bright Dairy Co. Ltd., and has been instrumental in turning the company from a local brand into one of the leading national dairy producers. A native of Shanghai, during the Cultural Revolution Wang joined millions of urban youths and left for a farming community to be "reeducated" through physical labor. In 1974, due to her outstanding performance, she was named deputy party secretary of the farm in charge of over 20,000 people. When the Cultural Revolution concluded, Wang trekked back to the city and in 1992 chose to leave behind the security of a government office job to take over the leadership of Shanghai Dairy Company. Wang visited dairy manufacturers in a number of countries and was determined to carry out reforms in order to make the company competitive. In 1996, the company formed a joint venture with a company from Hong Kong and changed its name to Bright Dairy Co.; Wang introduced a new slogan for the firm: 'let brightness (bright dairy) shine all over China'. Since 1996, Bright Dairy has been ranked number one in sales of dairy products, such as fresh milk and yogurt, with a comprehensive market share and strong profits. While *Fortune* named Bright Dairy as "China's most admirable joint venture", Wang was nicknamed the "Queen of Dairy Products". In 2002, Bright Dairy became a listed company. However in 2005, Wang experienced a low point in her career when a branch milk manufacturer was exposed of reprocessing overstocked milk for sale as fresh milk in the market. The subsequent wide coverage of this devastating news, and the discovery of other Bright Dairy products failing to meet the desired quality, put Wang and the company on the defensive. With her usual toughness and determination, she made repeated claims and promises about the company's full attention to the quality of dairy products. The incident cast a dark shadow over Wang's otherwise brilliant career at Bright Dairy. In 2007, the company went through reorganization. During the subsequent personnel changes, Wang resigned from the position of general manager, although she remained CEO of the company.

Chairwoman of Shanghai Baosteel Group, *Xie Qihua* (谢企华 1943-) has made a tremendous contribution to the development of China's largest steel manufacturer. Known as China's "Woman of Steel" or "Iron lady", Xie is one of a handful of female CEOs in Chinese state-owned enterprises, and a dominant force in an industry ruled mostly by men. Her influence has been in step with China's insatiable need for iron and steel over the past thirty years. While China is the world's largest producer and consumer of steel, Xie is the industry's public face. After graduation from Tsinghua University in 1968, she first worked as a technician at the Shaanxi Steel Plant. A decade later, Xie joined Baosteel while it was still under construction, heading up the technical division and gradually rising through ranks to become company president in 1994, and board chairperson in 2000. As a role model for many Chinese women, Xie dedicated herself to the development of Baosteel, implemented the acquisition and merger as a corporate strategy for expansion, and successfully transformed the Baosteel Group into the largest iron and steel conglomerate in China. In 2004 Baosteel, under Xie, signed a cooperation agreement with France's Arcelor and Brazil's Companhia Vale do Rio Doce to jointly build a steel plant in Brazil. This was regarded as China's largest direct investment in an overseas project at the time, and became the entry point for Baosteel into the international market. Under her leadership Baosteel also became the first Chinese manufacturer to enter the rankings of the world's top 500 companies. In 2005 Xie was ranked second of the 50 most powerful women outside the US by *Fortune*, among the top ten of 50 Businesswomen in the World by *Forbes*, and was listed by the *Wall Street Journal* in its Top 50 Businesswomen to Watch rankings. Since, according to Chinese regulations, the mandatory retirement age for senior executives in state-owned enterprises is 60, Xie stepped down from the chairmanship of Baosteel Group Corp in 2007, making a full exit from China's biggest mill at age 64. Still regarded among the most powerful women in the nation's corporate world, as well as its steel industry, Xie boasts a string of other titles that include alternate member of the 16th Central Committee of the Chinese Communist Party, president of the China Iron and Steel Association, and board member of the China Business Council for Sustainable Development. At end of her tenure, Xie oversaw 100,000 workers who roll out 21 million tons of steel each year, ranked the world's sixth-largest steel company in terms of capacity, with profits rising to $22 billion.

Cofounder and director of Sun Television Cyber Networks Holdings Limited, *Yang Lan* (杨澜 1968-) enjoys a high reputation as a TV personality and studio manager in China. She is also regarded as one of China's 50 most successful entrepreneurs and ranks among China's wealthiest self-made woman. After graduating from the Beijing Foreign Language University, where her father taught English literature, Yang was selected in 1990 from over 1,000 candidates as the host of a new entertainment program on CCTV. Yang's style, talent and personality made her stand out among Chinese presenters and, within a year, her primetime Saturday celebrity quiz and talk show was China's top-rated TV program, with an audience of 220 million, making Yang a household name. In 1994, Yang was honored with a Golden Microphone award at the first National Hosts Competition. However, setting her sights even higher, in late 1994 Yang gave up her position at CCTV to go to the USA and study international media; two years later, she received her Master's degree from Columbia University. In 1997, Yang became a studio producer and host for Hong Kong's Phoenix Satellite Television Company, an experience that greatly benefited her professionally. The relaxed production environment allowed her to create a series of important programs, which also made her well known in Hong Kong and Taiwan. Then in 1999, with her career flourishing, Yang left Phoenix in search of greater production freedom. Yang's TV skills are matched by a keen mind for business. With her husband, Bruno Wu, she started her own media company, Sun Television Cyber Networks, with which she hoped to help promote both China's splendid culture and the world's great historic achievements. Going to air internationally in 2000, Sun TV's programs about figures, science and civilization, and unsolved mysteries have since attracted large audiences. Traded on the Hong Kong Stock Exchange since April 2002, Sun TV was valued at US$179 million by November 2002, of which Yang owns 35 percent, worth $63 million. The couple's accumulated fortune was later estimated to be $400 million, ranked among China's top 100 richest people by *Forbes*. In 1999, Yang was named by *Asia Week* as one of the top 20 most influential leaders of the great Asia region, and in 2001 she was appointed as an image ambassador for the 2008 Beijing Olympic Games, joining three other Chinese women to be so honored.

An outstanding female executive, *Yu Shumin* (于淑珉1951-) is the president of the Qingdao-based Hisense Group. Prior to this post, Yu also served as vice-president, general manager, deputy secretary and secretary of the party committee of Hisense Group. With her strong determination, Yu is famous for her leadership and management skills; at the same time, her unique feminine gentleness and carefulness also helps her a great deal in a field dominated by male executives. In recent years Yu has been making special efforts to achieve sustainable growth for her large corporation. As a remarkable businesswoman, Yu was recognised several times as a National Model Worker, and in 2007 she was elected one of the Ten Outstanding Women in China, which is the country's top honor for women in the professional world. Yu believes that the only way to keep a leading position in market share is through independent technological innovation with newly launched products. Under her leadership, Hisense founded the first chips R&D group in 2000 and, in 2005, China's first video-processing chips with proprietary intellectual property developed by Hisense, which has set a good example as China's top whitegoods maker. During Yu's eight-year tenure as the executive president of Hisense Group, the company expanded at a rate of over 40 percent every year, profits went up 35 percent annually, and income from sales raised from RMB 10.6 billion to 43.5 billion yuan. Hisense TV has already occupied the largest share in the domestic market, and its flat-panel TV has also been ranked the first in the nation three years in a row. After a successful merger with Kelon in 2006, Hisense has become the only enterprise in China that owns three famous brands - Hisense, Kelon, and Rong Sheng - and was listed in three places: Shanghai, Shenzhen and Hong Kong.

Yu Yu (俞渝1965-) is the co-founder and co-president of Dangdang.com along with her husband Li Guoqing. Founded in 1999, Dangdang is China's largest online retailer and the world's leading online seller of Chinese language books, movies and music. Yu returned to China in 1998 after eleven years in the U.S. to start Dangdang.com, a successful online bookstore dubbed as the Amazon.com of China. Yu received her bachelor degree in English literature from Beijing Foreign Studies University in 1986. She first worked as an interpreter and secretary for a joint venture in Beijing, then went to the U.S. to pursue graduate studies. After receiving her MBA from NYU in 1992, she began to work for a Wall Street consulting firm specializing in mergers and acquisitions and providing an advisory service to corporate clients. Fascinated by the monumental success of online bookstore Amazon.com, she conceptualised the idea of a similar e-commerce website for China. However, upon returning to China she found the country had only a tiny community of Internet users, and no comprehensive, up-to-date database on books in print in China, essential for establishing an online bookstore. As an experienced financial professional, she and her partners began to build such a database in China, which was finished in three years and laid the foundation for Yu's business. While the database was under construction, the Internet community in China grew at a dizzying speed and by late 1999 the country had over 8.9 million of Internet users. So, in that year she and her husband founded their Chinese bookstore Dangdang, which quickly became China's leading online destination for retail shopping and has recorded significant growth in just a few years. Managing an online bookstore in China was not an easy job. Since Chinese people lack meaningful online experience, Yu had to struggle with consumers' defiance of online shopping, inhibiting credit card regulations and an ineffectual delivery system. Despite all those drawbacks, Dangdang's business has grown steadily. Within several years, Dangdang grew into the largest Chinese internet bookstore in the world.

By 2005, the company began aggressively transforming itself from an online bookstore to a mass merchandiser, featuring everything from digital products to cosmetics. In 2008 Yu was ranked among the top 50 richest women in China with US$210 million (*Hurun Report*), and her Dangdang has been called the "bellwether" of China's e-commerce.

Chairperson of Nine Dragons Paper, *Zhang Yin* (Cheung Yan 张茵1958-) is regarded by some sources to be China's wealthiest person, and the wealthiest self-made woman in the world, surpassing Oprah Winfrey of the United States and J.K. Rowling of the United Kingdom. Her fortune was estimated at $10 billion in 2007. Meanwhile, Nine Dragons is currently on pace to become China's number one producer of packaged paper. Zhang is considered a pioneer among female leaders, breaking gender barriers in China and leading a very successful business from start-up to immense growth. Zhang was born the oldest of eight siblings in Guangdong Province. Her father was a military officer, who later became general manager of a local metallurgy company. His contacts and connections with the Communist Party would help along her business career. Upon reaching adulthood, Zhang relocated to Shenzhen in the 1980s, accepted a job as a finance associate with a paper-products company, and developed a keen interest in the industry. After realizing its enormous market potential, she decided to enter the recycling sector. Based in Hong Kong and with only $4,000 in savings, she launched Nine Dragons, a company that buys scrap paper from the United States and reproduces the commodity for use in China. Upon growing Nine Dragons as a major Chinese corporation, her goal was to develop the firm and its brand equity globally. In building the company, Zhang endured numerous financial difficulties, unethical practices from unstable business partners, and intimidating acts by local organised mafia organizations. She persevered through the challenges by moving to the United States to build her empire and establish herself as a tycoon in the paper recycling industry. To date, she has retained a nearly 75% equity stake in the company that she founded. Her husband, Liu Mingchung, currently helps run the company as a senior executive. The success of the company has springboarded Zhang to the top of *Hurun Report*'s list of the richest people in China, as shares of Nine Dragons have nearly tripled since they were initially introduced on the Hong Kong Stock Exchange. What is perhaps most noteworthy is the fact that Zhang has succeeded as an entrepreneur in an economic and political system that is heavily skewed toward male dominance.

Analysis of Female Entrepreneurship in China

Research on modern entrepreneurship has studied behavioral characteristics such as personality and traits, gender, educational and individual background, and how these attributes have been associated with entrepreneurial decisions and outcome. The existing literature has confirmed certain common characteristics for all entrepreneurs, regardless of gender, which include the need for achievement, risk-taking propensity, innovativeness, independence and inner locus of control (Tan, 2008). Entrepreneurs must have a vision, understand proactivity, seize the moment and take initiative. Some of the common traits among women entrepreneurs: they are more frequently married, have children, are well educated, and are somewhat older than their counterparts; they are highly capable and productive, possess a greater amount of autonomy, power and extended financial parameters, and illustrate their business in family terms and envision business relations as a network. Those women are usually multi-tasking individuals, having the ability to balance chores and priorities, being flexible and adaptable. In the following section of this paper, those key factors that have significant impacts on the development of female entrepreneurship in China are further examined.

Vision and Motivation

Among factors that contribute to the success of women entrepreneurs in China, a clear vision and personal motivation are probably the most important. Existing research indicates that men are more likely than women to pursue opportunity entrepreneurship, while women are more likely to pursue necessity entrepreneurship (Reynolds, et al., 2002). According to Tan (2008), men and women share many entrepreneurial orientations such as futurity, proactiveness, aggressiveness and innovativeness, but women are more prepared to take risks than men, and women entrepreneurs are more willing to accept higher risks for higher return, and pursue greater opportunities despite high uncertainty.

As previously noted, Zhang Yin decided to enter the recycling sector after realizing the enormous market potential; Chen Lihua seized the opportunity and was able to benefit from the growing real estate market; Shi Xiaoyan, Wang Jiafen and Yang Lan gave up secure employment to seek risky new adventures, and Yu Yu rode the wave of the internet revolution to build Dangdang; all of them have demonstrated a forward-looking vision, seized the moment and taken initiatives to ensure business success. As with their male counterparts, they possessed a sense of aggressiveness and showed decision-making competence. Furthermore, they have also displayed great personal perseverance in reaching desirable outcomes, such as Dong Mingzhu's stubborn refusal to engage in price wars, Yu Yu's struggles with consumers' defiance of online shopping, inhibiting credit card regulations and an ineffectual delivery system, and Zhang Yin's endurance through numerous financial difficulties, unethical practices from unstable business partners and intimidating acts by local organised mafia organizations.

Despite recent progress, the growing number of female entrepreneurs still make up a small proportion of all entrepreneurs in China. According to national surveys on private businesses done by the China Women Entrepreneurs Association (2002), women entrepreneurs only made up 8 to 13 percent of the sample. Another study indicated that women entrepreneurs accounted for about 20 percent of the total Chinese entrepreneurial population (Tan, 2008). Many women entrepreneurs in self-employment chose to enter business because of the lack of quality employment opportunities available to them, rather than because of a flair for entrepreneurship. Women were often motivated to start their own venture when they felt they were "displaced"; they may also be "pulled" into an entrepreneurial venture to leverage resources, pursue an opportunity to develop an idea, to receive high income, to fulfill oneself, and to be their own boss and not have to take orders from others. This study confirms that many of them are increasingly driven by the "pull" elements, such as being the decision-maker, self-actualization, financial benefits, the desire to achieve a more comfortable balance between family and work responsibilities, and capitalizing on network resources and opportunities.

Family Support System

One common characteristic among successful women entrepreneurs is that most of them are married to a supportive husband, who is equally well-connected to an extensive social network, as in the cases of Yang Lan, Shi Xiaoyang, Yu Yu and Zhang Yin mentioned above. In the traditional Chinese setting, family offered a reliable supportive system that significantly improved the women entrepreneurs' capacity to endure hardship and uncertainty. They provide added network resources to secure funding, technical assistance, and business connections (Tan, 2008). As Chinese believe that family is the basic fabric of society and that the benefit of this extends beyond family boundaries, such support systems have led to a much-improved chance of success for women entrepreneurs. It should be noted that family support is also extended from parents, as illustrated by Zhang Yin and others. Women, more so than men, tend to enter their business careers by a route dependent on personal and family networks. According to an early study, 90 percent of those women entrepreneurs surveyed felt that the support and understanding of family members, especially their spouses, played an important role in their success (Hisrich and Zhang, 1991).

Notwithstanding the benefit of family support, Chinese women entrepreneurs still face the challenge of balancing the need for business advancement with family obligations. For historical reasons, management jobs in the West have been specifically designed for married men who were able to cope with the long hours and dedication that careers demand because they had the support of their full-time home-making wives. Similarly, in a typical Chinese family, couples often decide that the man's career takes precedence (Korabik, 1993). As a result, China's growing ranks of career women are facing increasing difficulties in attracting the country's eligible men, whose idea of the perfect wife remains a homemaker, not a breadwinner (Cooke, 2004). In recent years, technological advances in the workplace and the home, the one-child policy, and the marketization of housework and domestic care mean that women's working and domestic lives are becoming less physically demanding and time-consuming. Despite the progress, successful businesswomen with supporting husbands are still exceptions rather than a general rule in China. For aspiring women, a primary frustration has been the competing needs of running business and taking care of a family, which often mean that they will have to make some personal sacrifices in order to move forward.

Guanxi Network

Probably more so than their male counterparts, a *guanxi* (关系) network is another key contributing factor to the business success of female entrepreneurs in China. *Guanxi*, an informal social relationship, provides the lubricant for the Chinese to get through life. The cultural emphasis on personal relationships means that Chinese business connections and deals are built on *guanxi* ties. Strongly influenced by Confucian teachings, Chinese view other individuals in terms of particularistic relationships. *Guanxi* is "an informal, unofficial relationship utilised to get things done, from simple tasks to major life choices" (Ruan, 1993). Simply put, *guanxi* is an interpersonal network that Chinese use as a crucial social resource to pursue their personal interests (Brown, 2002). *Guanxi* is not just something mechanical, or simply a Western version of networking. It is about "affectual relations" among people. *Guanxi* is an emotional bond, and requires cultivation over time (Gold, 2001). In the business world, *guanxi* practice has evolved into a powerful and flexible tool that allows people to create trustworthy, expansive business networks in the absence of adequate legal guarantees (Hsu, 2005).

In review of the cases of Chinese female entrepreneurs, it is clear that the concept of *guanxi* has a very profound influence on the growth of their businesses, whether it be Chen Lihua's relationship with party officials and her Changan Club, or the vast business connections possessed by Yang Lan and Zhang Yin. Along the course of their business development, those women have also demonstrated a keen sense of political intelligence. Many of them have served as delegates to the National People's Congress, or are members of the Chinese People's Consultative Conference, and held leadership positions in the China Association of Industry and Commerce or other semi-official organizations, which not only enhanced their personal profiles but also greatly extended their business connections and influence.

The importance of harmonious interpersonal relationships also reflects the core value of Confucianism, which emphasises the order among relationships, having a sense of shame, saving face and respect for traditions (Gerrard, et al, 2003). This virtue, combined with other features of Confucianism such as persistence, thrift and self-respect, has become an important part of Chinese womens' value systems (Deng, et al), and is found to be correlated with broad measures of economic growth (Hofstede and Bond, 1988).

Challenges and Discriminations

As Tan (2008) summarised, for centuries Chinese women have been separated from social and economic life by a "bamboo curtain," and found themselves under a "glass ceiling" like women elsewhere in the world. Although the country's economic transformation over the last three decades has generated new opportunities for women, equality still remains an elusive ideal in China, and women still face considerable challenges in a period of radical social, economic and institutional change.

This study only highlights nine high-profile cases of businesswomen running large enterprises; behind them there are at least another 1.5 million female entrepreneurs working in small and medium-size businesses in China (Wang, 2004), and on daily basis they face enormous hurdles moving forward. Despite this recent progress, deep down China is still a society with the Confucian tradition of male dominance that has kept women in subservient roles for more than two thousand years. The success of a few female entrepreneurs should not hide the fact of gender discrimination existing in China today, which begins in the cradle where baby boys are prized more than girls in many areas of the country. Under heavy social and cultural influences, images of women entrepreneurs are usually stereotyped in China. According to a survey of university students, a far higher proportion of men than women surveyed believed that women leaders were emotional, trivial, incompetent, lacked innovativeness, and were respectable but cold, un-feminine and not lovable (Jin, 2002).

In practice, many female entrepreneurs are at a disadvantage compared to their male counterparts, as they usually face discrimination when it comes to financing. In addition, since much of the business discussions are conducted over dinner tables and in entertainment facilities, many women find it quite offensive when men start to make dirty jokes and engage in other entertainment activities. Furthermore, since there are few women in senior positions to act as role models, an aspiring female may have to look for a man as a mentor to establish her network relationship in a system dominated by men. Given the level of intimacy that the relationship naturally engenders, women may find themselves embraced by rumors, which can be highly damaging to their career, because of the relatively low tolerance in Chinese society of close relationships between men and women outside of marriage (Vinnicombe and Colwill, 1995).

Despite all the challenges and discriminative measures, education and economic progress still offer the best hope for Chinese women, and entrepreneurship is the best way to empower them. Given the numerous hurdles they have had to jump, it is really remarkable for those high-profile female entrepreneurs to achieve the success as described above. They have effectively served as a model for millions of Chinese women to follow, in this new age of economic development.

Conclusion

Women entrepreneurs have been playing an increasingly significant role in the Chinese economic reform of the past thirty years. Behind their accomplishments are several trends, as observed by Cooke (2005), among them: the level of female participation in employment has been steady and relatively high; the educational levels of employed women have been getting closer to those of men; and a sectorial shift from the manufacturing and other secondary industries towards the service industries, a new area of focus in China's economic development, and one in which women may be at an advantage compared to men. More significantly, the rapid expansion of private companies and the growth of self-employed businesses have brought new opportunities for women to develop their entrepreneurship and managerial careers.

Based on the case studies of nine high-profile female entrepreneurs, the common factors that contributed to their success include a forward-looking vision, sheer determination and perseverance. To achieve desirable business objectives, they must possess a sense of aggressiveness and decision-making competence. Furthermore, they have to become multitasking individuals and balance career commitment with family responsibilities. In review of the brief profiles described above, notwithstanding that these factors should be further tested through empirical studies, successful female entrepreneurs in China appear to be well-educated, mostly married and politically shrewd. They seem to enjoy strong family support and benefit greatly from extensive personal networks.

In the current business environment, aspiring businesswomen still face numerous challenges - notable among them are some discriminative measures in education, recruitment and promotion policies and many questionable business practices that occur in China today. To overcome the prevailing stereotypes, women entrepreneurs need to not only demonstrate vision and leadership, but also portray themselves as professionally competent, physically elegant, and feminine in disposition; they need to both show their toughness and persistence and display their feminine gentleness and empathy at the same time; and they need to be flexible, multitasked individuals and relationship builders while still balancing their work with family responsibilities. In other words, as Cooke (2005) appropriately noted, they need to be both an angel and superwoman.

REFERENCES

[1] Ahl, H. (2003). The scientific reproduction of gender inequality: A discourse analysis of research articles on women's entrepreneurship, paper presented at *Gender and Power in the New Europe: The 5th European Feminist Research Conference*, Jonkoping University, Sweden.

[2] All-China Women's Federation (2000). The situation of women entrepreneurs in non-public sectors, *Research in Women, 2*, 34-39.

[3] Brown, B. (2002). Entrepreneurship and ethics in the Chinese context, *Ruffin Series in Business Ethics*, 219.

[4] China Women Entrepreneurs Association (2002). A survey of the situation of women entrepreneurs in China, *Capital China, 9*, 43-44.

[5] *Chinese Statistical Yearbook* (2008). Edited by the State Statistical Bureau, Beijing: China Statistics Press.

[6] Cooke, F. L. (2004). Women in management in China, in M.J. Davidson, & R. J. Burke (Eds.), *Women in Management Worldwide: Facts, Figures and Analysis*, Hants, England: Ashgate Publishing, 243-258.

[7] Cooke, F. L. (2005). Women's managerial careers in China in a period of reform, *Asia Pacific Business Review, 11*(2), 149-162.

[8] Deng, S., Wang, X., & Alon, I. Women entrepreneurship in China: Looking back and looking forward. To appear in *International Journal of Business and Emerging Market.*

[9] Gerrard, P., Schoch, H., & Cunningham, B. (2003). Values and skills of female entrepreneurs in Vietnam: An Exploratory Study, *Asia Pacific Business Review, 10*(2), 138-159.

[10] Gold, T. (2001). In China – bonding gone bad? *Christian Science Monitor*, 10 January, 6.

[11] Hisrich, R. D., & Zhang, F. (1991). Women entrepreneurs in the People's Republic of China, *Journal of Managerial Psychology, 6*(3), 3-12.

[12] Hofstede, G., & Bond, M. H. (1988). The Confucius connection: From cultural roots to economic growth, *Organizational Dynamics, 14*(4), 4-21.

[13] Hsu, C. (2005). Capitalism without contract versus capitalists without capitalism: Comparing the influence of Chinese *guanxi* and Russian blat on marketization, *Communist and Post-Communist Studies, 38*(3), 309.

[14] *Hurun Report* (2008). Richest women in China list, available at http://www.hurun.net/listen134.aspx.

[15] Jiang, Y. P. (2000). State intervention in the employment of urban women, Paper presented at the *International Seminar on the Legal Protection of Women's Employment Rights*, April, Shanghai, China.

[16] Jin, Y. H. (2002). Media's influence on women's participation in politics as seen from the public perception, *Collection of Women's Studies, 2*, 15-22.

[17] Korabik, K. (1993). Managerial women in the People's Republic of China: The long march continues, *International Studies of Management and Organization, 23*(4), 47-56.

[18] Liu, Y. (2001). Chinese women in politics in the new century, *China National Conditions and Strength, 107* (11-12), 28-29.

[19] Moore, D. P., & Buttner, E. H. (1997). *Women Entrepreneurs: Moving Beyond the Glass Ceiling*. Thousands Oaks, CA: Sage.

[20] Reynold, P. D., Bygrave, W. D., Autio, E., & Hay, M. (2002). *Global Entrepreneurship Monitor 2002 Summary Report*. Wellesley, MA: Babson College.

[21] Ruan, D. (1993). *Social Networks in Urban China* [dissertation]. New York: Columbia University, 19.

[22] Second national sample survey of women's social position in China: Project report (2001). *Collection of Women's Studies, 42*(5), 4-12.

[23] Stockman, N., Bonney, N., & Sheng, X. W. (1995). *Women's Work in East and West: The Dual Burden of Employment and Family Life*. London: UCL Press.

[24] Tan, J. (2008). Breaking the 'Bamboo curtain' and the 'Glass Ceiling': The experience of women entrepreneurs in high-tech industries in an emerging market, *Journal of Business Ethics, 80*(3), 547-564.

[25] Tan, J. (1996). Regulatory environment and entrepreneurial strategic orientation: A study of Chinese private entrepreneurs, *Entrepreneurships: Theory and Practice, 21*, 31-46.

[26] Vinnicombe, S., & Colwill, N. (1995). *The Essence of Women in Management*. London: Prentice Hall.

[27] Wang, A. (2004). Holding up half the sky, *Fortune, 150* (7), 170.

[28] Zhang, W., & Alon, I. (2009). *Biographical Dictionary of New Chinese Entrepreneurs and Business Leaders*. Cheltenham, England: Edward Elgar Publishing.

PART III: INWARD AND OUTWARD FDI

In: Thirty Years of China's Economic Reform
Editors: Yue Wang and Prem Ramburuth ISBN: 978-1-60876-908-7
© 2010 Nova Science Publishers, Inc.

Chapter 9

THE CHINESE DRAGON ENGAGES AFRICA

***Prem Ramburuth**[*,1]**, Paul N. Buatsi**[+,2]** and Richard Owusu**[¥,3]*

[1]Australian School of Business, University of New South Wales, Sydney, Australia

[2]Office of the Chief Director, Ministry of Education, Accra, Ghana

[3]Swedish School of Economics and Business Administration, CERS-Department of Marketing and Corporate Geography, Helsinki, Finland

ABSTRACT

China and Africa have been trading partners for centuries, and China is now Africa's third-largest trading partner. This chapter explores the extent of China's economic engagement in Africa, its strategies and approaches, and implications for African development. The interpretative approach adopted in this chapter involves a comprehensive review of current literature, and draws on recent data to highlight China's activities in Africa and identify areas of expansion and development. Specifically, it draws attention to China's bilateral trade with Africa, and its growth from under $10 billion in 1995 to $106 billion in 2008. Currently, 80% of China's imports from Africa are from the extractive industry, and the most significant import is oil. China's intentions seem to be divided between acting as a facilitator for Africa's development and an extractor of its resources. It has adopted a 'soft diplomacy' strategy in its pursuit of global growth, and is supporting the increased presence of Chinese SOEs and privately owned enterprises in Africa. Clearly, there are benefits to Africa's development. However, in weighing the benefits of China's engagement in Africa, African countries must consider issues of sustainability for long-term economic development and develop strategies to leverage the benefits of their rich resources, without being dependent on external agencies for their development.

* Email: p.ramburuth@unsw.edu.au.

INTRODUCTION AND BACKGROUND

China and Africa have been trading partners for centuries, dealing with each other through complex networks of economic engagement and diplomacy. More recently, the partnership has intensified with an exponential growth in trade and investment across the countries of Africa. China is now Africa's third-largest trading partner after the US and the European Union. On the home front, China continues its strong economic growth, surge in home-grown markets, attraction of inward FDI, and support for the entrepreneurial development of its SOEs and private sector enterprises. On the global front, it continues its aggressive search for resources to fuel its economic growth, targeting of foreign markets for its products, strategic growth of outward FDI, and implementation of its 'soft diplomacy' policy to underpin and expand global growth. These global strategies are clearly evident in its economic engagement in Africa. This paper provides insights into China's strategic expansion in Africa, and its targeted trade and investment activities across the continent. It draws attention to specific industry sectors (for example, energy and oil), the role and impact of Chinese SOEs and private sector enterprises in Africa, and long- and short-term implications for African economic growth and development. The paper explores the contentious issue of China's 'intentions' in Africa, and whether it is a benevolent facilitator of African development or an extractor of much needed African resources. The paper advocates the need for research into the impact and implications of China's strategic engagement in Africa, so that countries in Africa can better leverage the benefits of their rich resources for the sustained improvement of trade and investment, and the betterment of their countries and people.

Sino-African relations are not new and go as far back as the Ming Dynasty in the fifteenth century, when the ancient Chinese mariner, Zheng He, sailed the coast of East Africa. The intention then was to win the allegiance of people from distant lands, an act thought to have brought prestige and recognition to the emperor. On his visits in 1963-1964, the late Chinese Premier Zhou En-lai reinforced the notion of 'friendship', declaring that his delegation essentially came "to renew acquaintance with old friends" (Snow, 1988, p.75). He set in place the principles that would govern Sino-African relations, including the intention to promote friendship; to respect the sovereignty of each African country and, therefore, adopt a policy of non-intervention; to facilitate development on the basis of equality and for mutual benefit; to establish foundations for consultation in international affairs; and to cooperate to create a stable and prosperous world (Le Pere, 2008; Snow, 1988).

These sentiments continue to be reflected in Sino-African relations today and in the Chinese rhetoric about mutual economic benefits, international co-operation and advancement, and assistance for development and progress in Africa. They underpin the diplomatic relations that China currently has with 49 of Africa's 53 countries, evident in individual country dealings, and reinforced in highly publicised forums such as the 2006 Forum on 'China-Africa Cooperation' (FOCAC) (Le Pere, 2008).

CHINA'S STRATEGIC INTENTIONS

As China firmly sets its footprint across Africa, there are many who question the intentions of its global policy on this continent. In reviewing the literature (albeit limited in this area), two seemingly contradictory perspectives emerge. The first presents a positive view of China's presence in Africa. Broadman (2007, p.1), for example, asserts that "China and India's newfound trade and investment in Africa presents a significant opportunity for growth and integration of the Sub-Saharan Continent into the global economy". Supporting this perspective, (Naidu, 2008, p.1) suggests that "China's increased trade, investment and aid will assist in achieving sustainable development across the continent". Other researchers offer more specific indications of China's engagement in Africa bringing multiple levels of economic benefits - for example, through investment in industries and infrastructure (Corkin, 2007a), development assistance (Davies, 2007), affordable commodities (Burke, 2008), and the intangibles of respect and recognition – *for* developing countries *by* a developing country. The latter is an important factor to add to the equation in discussing China's intentions, with researchers (Davies, 2007; Large, 2008; Van Dijk, 2007) pointing to the lack of recognition given to countries in Africa in the post-colonial period, and neglect by the West in developing mutual relations with these countries. This gap has been strategically filled by China, giving it the opportunity to establish a strong presence in Africa. Two decades ago, Snow (1988, p. xv-xvi) observed that Sino-African relations "is a reminder that we in the West can no longer always expect to occupy centre stage…", a truism that continues in Africa today.

The second perspective presents a less positive view, suggesting that China's strategic aim is essentially to gain raw materials for its booming economy and new markets for its products (Kondapalli, 2005; Van Dijk, 2007). This view tends to capture the notion of China as a new 'imperial power', leading the scramble for the world's much needed resources in Africa, especially in relation to commodities such as oil, gas and metals. This perspective has resulted in growing concern that the nature of China's engagement in Africa may have the potential to undermine rather than facilitate its growth and long-term development. Some are more critical than others, viewing China's economic engagement of Africa as essentially opportunistic.

As researchers ponder the competing perspectives and seek answers to the question of just what are the impacts and sustained benefits of China's increasing presence in Africa, perhaps the answer lies in *how* leaders in Africa engage with China, how they define their business relationships and manage their political interactions. It also lies in just how effectively African leaders are able to leverage the benefits of the rapid growth in trade with China.

CHINA – AFRICA TRADE AND INVESTMENT FLOWS

The strong growth in trade and investment between China and Africa in the last decade or so is evident in the dramatic rise in bilateral trade (approximately 45%) from 2007 to 2008 (Foster, Butterfield, Chen and Pushak, 2008), with estimates of China's export to Africa at US$50.84 billion, China's imports from Africa at US$56 billion, and a total bilateral trade value of approximately US$106 billion (Administration of Customs of the People's Republic of China, 2008). China's imports from Africa increased significantly by 54% between 2007 and 2008, whilst China's exports to Africa also increased, but at a lesser rate of 36% (Foster *et al* 2008; Trade Law Centre for Southern Africa, 2009).

It is hardly surprising that 80% of China's imports from Africa are from the extractive industries, with the most significant import being oil (70%), followed by iron ore, cotton, wood and agricultural products. Conversely, the most significant export to Africa is heavy machinery (10% in 2008), required for infrastructure building projects as outlined later in the paper, followed by transport equipment, textiles and clothing, footwear and plastics. Whilst researchers (Corkin, 2007; Van Dijk, 2007; Wang and Bio Tchane, 2008) identify several other industries that reflect the nature and extent of China's engagement in Africa, discussion in this paper will focus mainly on key commodities exported to and from China, and those impacting most on trade and development activities in Africa.

Energy Resources and China's Search for Oil

Like most industrialised countries, China is feeling the impact of the oil crisis. In this context, China's relentless pursuit of oil resources in Africa is understandable. To many, who are concerned about China's search for oil, "Africa has become a tempting territory" (Lafargue, 2005, p.5) following the US intervention in Iraq and its control over oil-supplying countries in the Middle East. It is also tempting because the African continent possesses 8.9% of global oil reserves and represents 11% of global production – a commodity that is bound to attract interest from other countries as well.

It seems that China's pursuit of oil sources in Africa has two main purposes: (a) short-term acquisition of oil supplies to fulfil the growing demand in China; and (b) long-term investment as a global player in the international oil market. Hence, the strong focus on the oil rich countries of Africa – Angola, Sudan, Nigeria, Equatorial Guinea and Chad. These five oil- and mineral-rich countries account for 85% of Africa's exports to China (Broadman, 2007). It is also interesting to note that, in 2006, Angola surpassed Saudi Arabia as China's largest source of crude oil imports. Africa and the oil deals and partnerships also provide a fertile context for the growth, development and refinement of China's multinational enterprises. China's SOEs play a significant role in targeting and pursuing opportunities for acquisition of African oil, developing multiple approaches to 'partnering' with oil-rich African countries, depending on the country, the richness of the resources and the negotiating climate. The impact of one such SOE is evident in the activities of the China National Offshore Oil Corporation (CNOOC).

China's search for African oil seems to have gained greater momentum after the CNOOC failed in its bid for American Unocal in August 2005, driving greater Chinese multinational activity in Africa. In her study of 'China's Emerging Multinationals in Africa', Corkin (2007a) points to the heightened activity in this area - for example, CNOOC's $2.27 billion payment to a Nigerian company, South Atlantic Petroleum Ltd., for a 45% stake in Nigeria's oil fields (January 2006); CNOOC's expansion in Nigeria with the purchase of a 35% stake in a contract to further explore oil in Nigeria; and CNOOC's subsidiary, CNOOC Africa Ltd. signing oil production sharing contracts in Kenya. In addition, joint ventures have begun to proliferate in the oil sector - for example, Chinese SOE Sinopec and Angolan state-owned

Sonangol's formation of Sonangol-Sinopec International (SSI), a joint venture to develop a new refinery in Angola, with a total investment of $3 billion (March 2006).

In a partnership 'package' that incorporates infrastructure building, in 2008, China's state oil company, China National Petroleum Corp (CNPC) won a $5 billion deal to develop oil reserves in eastern Niger. The CNPC will build a refinery with a capacity of 20,000 barrels of oil per day and a 2,000 km pipeline to export the oil. China National Petroleum Corporation, (CNPC) has begun operations at two oil blocks in Sudan, with annual output estimated at 10 million metric tons of crude oil (Corkin, 2007; Foster *et al*., 2008). And so the oil sourcing continues. It is interesting to note that China's oil companies are all state-owned and work in concert with China's Exim Bank (the Export-Import Bank of China), established in 1994 to promote foreign trade and support overseas investment projects (Wang, J. Y. & Bio-Tchane, A., 2008). In terms of gains, China is now the second major importer of African oil, after the United States (Naidu, 2007), and acquires 30% of its oil resources from Africa. China's target is to acquire 40% of its oil and gas from Africa in the next five to ten years.

Building Infrastructure in Africa

A major challenge for both sustained economic development in Africa and African development per se is the poor infrastructure – the lack of transport networks including roads, railways and ports; poor technology and communication systems; and erratic power supplies. For any level of economic advancement, existing infrastructure would have to be vastly improved and new systems created. China's solution to managing the challenges has been to build its own infrastructure and import its machinery and transport equipment to achieve its aims, to the benefit of its own economic agenda and the development agenda in Africa.

In this area, China has made significant contributions to Africa in many of the countries, as indicated in the extensive report on 'China's Growing Role as Infrastructure Financier for Africa' (Foster *et al*, 2008). The report highlights the array of infrastructure projects that has involved active engagement in 35 African countries on an unprecedented scale. The authors estimate that China's financial commitments to African infrastructure projects rose from less than US$1 billion per year between 2001-2003, to approximately US$1.5 billion in 2004-2005, and reached a peak of US$7 billion in 2006 (in the 'Year of Africa'), although it did fall to US$4.5 billion in 2007 (Foster *et al*, 2008, p.vii), perhaps indicative of more challenging times in the global financial markets. Sectors that have been strategically targeted and most supported are power (mainly hydropower) and transport (mainly railways). Foster *et al* (2008) and Sebastian (2008) estimate that China is responsible for rebuilding 1,350 km of rail, building 1,600km of new rails throughout the continent, and increasing total hydropower in Sub-Saharan Africa by a significant 30%.

China's SOEs and, more recently, its rising private sector enterprises, are the drivers of the infrastructure projects. In a booming Chinese construction industry in Africa, they have been building railways across the African continent, including railways across Angola, Zambia and Mozambique, and creating rail networks from the West to the East coast. They have also engaged in post-war reconstruction - for example in Angola, the Democratic Republic of the Congo and Mozambique, and in a range of other infrastructural projects such as the building of dams, roads, schools and hospitals.

It is interesting to observe, that whilst 35 countries in Africa have benefited from China's engagement in infrastructure projects, in terms of the actual dollars spent, 70% of the funding goes to Nigeria, Angola, Sudan and Ethiopia, countries where China has either oil rights or oil and mineral rights. Despite this observation, there is no doubt about the infrastructure gains to Africa and the potential for Africa's economic development. There is no doubt, too, of gains to the dynamic global development of China's construction industry, as Wang and Bio Tchane (2008, pp. 7-8) note:

> *"Africa is quickly becoming a key market for Chinese construction and engineering enterprises…the number of private Chinese construction companies is growing rapidly, as are their size and capacity. They compete actively for construction contracts in Africa".*

The information technology and telecommunications sector has also been a beneficiary of infrastructure projects, although China's involvement is mainly in the role of equipment provider. It is here that benefits to Africa occur in the form of more diversified infrastructure and affordable equipment and services, controlled by Chinese companies such as the SOE Zhong Xing Telecommunication Equipments Company (ZTE) and the emerging Chinese private sector company Huawei. These new arrivals in Africa are serious competitors to the more traditional companies dominating the telecommunications landscape of Africa - namely, Britain's Vodafone, France's Telecom, and South Africa's Vodacom and MTN. (Corkin 2007a). Of particular significance is Huawei, the first Chinese private sector telecommunications company to successfully launch its global operations. Its stunning success is being upheld as a model in China, and an example of the "next wave of aspirant multinational firms" (Davies, 2007: 4). It can be viewed as a pre-curser of what is to come in the way of China's highly competitive emerging MNEs. Across Africa, there were 674 officially registered Chinese companies in early 2005, and these have risen to over 800 Chinese companies at the end of 2006, with many using Africa as a practice run before entering the more competitive markets of the US and Europe (Sebastion, 2007).

On another dimension, and an important one for geopolitical perspectives, China's policy on infrastructure building has created comparative advantage in Africa. It seems that Western investors and donors have not seen this as a high priority, and their neglect has created opportunities for China to fill the gap and firmly set its footprint in Africa (Lafargue, 2005; Naidu, 2007b). There is, however, growing concern about the sustainability of the pace and cost of infrastructure building in the current economic climate, and evidence to suggest that China may be tempted to modify aspects of its policies or drive harder bargains with its African partners, as the global financial crisis intensifies (Polgreen, 2009).

Impact of China's Exports to Africa

Whilst Africa benefits from cheaper exports from China, there is growing concern about some of the more 'contentious' exports from China to Africa, and the implications for local industries and employment. For example, Wang and Bio-Tchane (2008) and Naidu (2007b) and others note that the disconcertingly high percentage of China's textile, apparel and footwear exports to Africa have had an impact on local manufacturers and small business in Africa. Such imports seem to be 'a double edged sword'. On the one hand, they offer cheaper Chinese products that enable greater affordability, especially amongst the poor in Africa, but on the other hand, they create situations where local businesses cannot compete with the lower-priced imported products, leading to closures and unemployment. The question that arises is whether the African countries are prepared or able to raise such problems in their dealings with China. Naidu (2007a, p.290) points to a "larger power house like South Africa", which can influence the trade agenda. She cites the example of the Chinese government making concessions and imposing restraints on clothing and textile exports to the South African market, a decision probably due to pressure from the Congress of South African Trade Unions (COSATU) to counter the impact of the influx of cheap Chinese textiles, price distortions and job losses. It is uncertain whether smaller and less powerful African nations can have the same expectation, suggesting, therefore, the need for stronger African leadership and proactive measures to ensure two-way economic benefits.

Davies (2007, p.5) alludes to the South African steel tank manufacturers which once controlled half of global production and now no longer exist, having been forced out by competition from China. He also points to more recent threats in the automobile components sector and, indeed, the automobile industry itself, which are almost certain to be "hollowed out" in the next decade through competition from China. He argues that an impacting factor is the inability of governments to provide the competitive advantage in funding support that China provides its SOEs and private sector enterprises in its 'Going Global' strategy. The latter encourages Chinese entrepreneurial companies and corporate 'winners' to compete for resources and markets outside the country.

CHINA'S SOFT DIPLOMACY POLICY IN AFRICA

China's strategic expansion policy seems to be an interweaving of trade and investment, with infrastructure building for economic development, underpinned by aid and soft diplomacy. With regard to aid and soft diplomacy (and 'soft power'), there are multiple strategies that China employs when engaging with Africa, some attracting praise and others attracting criticism. If we are to consider the qualities attached to the notions of 'soft diplomacy' and 'soft power', then it would seem to include working with people, understanding people and using the understanding to influence decision making; being aware of culture and identity and using it for comparative advantage; and engaging with communities and using that engagement to win support. Kapelus (2007) asserts that many governments use the strategy of 'soft power' in their engagement in Africa - for example, in the form of development assistance to create opportunities for economic linkages.

China has a long history of providing aid and soft loans to Africa. Since 2000, Beijing has extended or waived approximately US$1.3 billion in the debt of at least 30 of the poorer African countries, drawing strong criticism (and even suspicion as to the intentions of the action) from Western countries, which see this as going against practices for ensuring fiscal responsibility on the part of African countries. Critics of China's debt waivers to African countries tend to advocate more stringent debt recovery strategies adopted by the West and the IMF (Broadman, 2007; Naidu 2007a; 2007b).

In contrast, there is widespread recognition of, and praise for, China's aid initiatives in Africa. It has engaged in capacity-building activities that go beyond trade and investment, with examples of engagement including the training of more than 10,000 African personnel in both the civilian and security sectors; engaging in peace keeping operations on the continent by contributing several hundred peace-keepers to operations in the DRC and Liberia; providing 1,200 scholarships per year for Africans to study in China; dispatching 16,000 doctors to work in rural areas (between 2000 and 2005); deploying 700 teachers to work in rural schools across the continent (2000 to 2005); and contributing US$5 million to the NEPAD (New Partnership for Africa's Development) Secretariat for medical purposes. In addition, China initially granted zero-tariff rates for 190 products exported to Beijing from poorer Sub-Saharan economies. No Western country or cluster of Western countries has invested to such an extent to support capacity-building in Africa, and in donations and soft loans to improve education, health, and the availability of water, food, security and other such commodities. Many (for example, Broadman, 2007; Edinger, H., Herman, H., and Jansson, J., 2008; Naidu, 2007b) assert that this must be to China's credit.

More recently, at the FOCAC meeting in 2006, China strengthened this strategy and set in place a humanitarian aid and development program on an even grander scale, further entrenching its presence and leaving its 'footprint' in Africa. At the 2006 FOCAC, President Hu Jintao offered a multi-billion dollar package to Africa. The 2006 aid package doubled China's commitment to the African continent by 2009; provided US$3 billion in preferential loans and US$2 billion in preferential buyer's credits to Africa over the next 3 years; set up a China-Africa development fund that will reach US$5 billion and encourage Chinese companies to invest in Africa; cancelled debt arising from the interest-free government loans that matured at the end of 2005 and owed by the least developed African countries; and opened up the Chinese market to African products by increasing from 190 to 440 the number of export items to China receiving zero-tariff treatment from the least developed countries in Africa (Broadman, 2007; Lafargue, 2005; Naidu 2007a).

Are there downsides to these actions of generosity in aid and 'soft power'? Naidu (2007a) and Lafargue (2005) point to the move away from an 'aid only' approach, and the incorporation of commercial initiatives in China's partnership arrangements with countries in Africa. In this approach, for example, at the 2006 FOCAC meeting, in what was meant to be a 'development' initiative, the largest contract was signed with Egypt for the construction of an aluminium smelter worth US$938 million, to be undertaken by China's state-owned China International Trust and Investment Company (CITIC). On another dimension, Polgreen (2009) expresses concern about just how much the current global economic climate will impact on China's delivery and good intentions in Africa, and whether there will be a tightening of expectations on the part of China, and the driving of harder bargains. She argues that China's strategy in Africa is changing, and points to issues of political instability, shrinking economies and heightened risk factors in Africa, which might cause China to back away from some of its aid and development ventures in the more risk-ridden countries of Africa.

WEIGHING THE BALANCE

Mutual Benefits

African countries have received tremendous benefits from China's engagement in their vast, diverse and, in some places, impoverished continent. Researchers (Broadman, 2007; Davies, 2007; Naidu, 2007a; 2007b; Van Dijk, 2007) highlight some of the benefits which include the rapid facilitation of African economic development through China's complex array of bilateral trade agreements and investment; the extensive and invaluable contribution to infrastructure building to advance and sustain development; the generous access to aid and 'soft' loans; the accessibility to affordable goods (tailored by Chinese multinationals to the economic status of people in Africa); and the creation of opportunities for Africa to capitalise on the world's need for its key resources, particularly in the extractive industries.

For China, through its increasing levels of outward FDI and its 'Going Global' strategy, it has opened up the potential for Africa's growth and development in an alternative approach that appealed to the African countries. As described by Polgreen (2009, p.2), "China espoused a new model for African investment: mutually beneficial trade between sovereign nations with none of the meddling so common among Western donors and investors...". In doing so, it has not only increased the short term revenue of African countries, but created opportunities for future growth and development. It has, in fact, brought to countries in Africa levels of economic development, infrastructure building and aid that no other country or cluster of countries have provided, although it also sought and gained a considerable share of the outcomes. Wang and Bio-Tchane (2008) point to the fact that China has, in the process of engaging in Africa, taken risks in a continent that is fraught with problems (political, economic, and social) and has ventured where others have been cautious. In terms of a geopolitical agenda, China has stamped it's footprint on Africa and, in doing so, has access to some of the world's richest resources, especially in terms of extractive resources (oil, gas, minerals). It has also acquired thriving markets for its home-grown products and practice grounds for its increasingly competitive SOEs and private sector enterprises, where it is also spawning the growth of MNEs (Corkin, 2007a).

Challenges and Questions Arising

Despite these and other contributions, questions do arise in relation to the status of African countries in their 'power' relationship with China. Perhaps one of the most important questions is whether African countries can be satisfied with just simply being the source of extractive resources, or whether they should be demanding more equitable economic relations with China. And if they are not satisfied, are their leaders in a position to challenge unfair or unequal decisions, or, as expressed by Lafargue (2005), are they able to say 'No'? Yet another important question relates to the extent to which African countries are being given opportunities to participate in China's 'Going Global' strategy, and whether their omission from the strategy hinders Africa's economic advancement rather than promoting it. Furthermore, researchers and commentators (for example, Coonan, 2008; Harris, 2007; Naidu, 2007b) report on the settlement of Chinese migrants in Africa, and the importation of skills and industry expertise from China, in the absence of local skills in Africa. The question then arises as to whether African countries would be better served if there were more opportunities for skills building, training and technology transfer as a key component of economic and human resources development for sustainable workforces in Africa.

China also faces challenges in its ventures in Africa, and, despite its well-meaning efforts and endeavours in Africa, there are some negative perceptions that China must overcome. An important issue it has to manage is that of international perceptions of its agenda in Africa being mainly that of an extractor of resources (Lafargue, 2005), despite its parallel agenda of aid and development. Linked to resources extraction are the sensitive issues of sustainability and management of the environment. Currently, neither China nor countries in Africa have a good track record of managing environmental issues and there is concern about the strongly focused extractive nature of China's activities (Corkin, 2007b; Davies, 2007; Polgreen, 2009). Kapelus (2007) suggests that China is coming to terms with issues of corporate social and environmental responsibility, and beginning to see CSR as an attractive feature for its 'soft power' packages. Other challenges facing China are criticisms of its links with African countries where there is an absence of good governance, and the potential for corruption with the seemingly lax terms of accountability on the part of some leaders in Africa. There is the belief that China's tacit support conveys the message of legitimization of African regimes that may engage in human rights contraventions, and its policy of non-intervention does not enable change in practices (Van Dijk, 2007). China's lax loan conditions could also be viewed as detrimental to many countries in Africa, particularly at a time of global financial downturn. Another challenge that China is facing is the increasing dissatisfaction amongst African countries with the displacement of local, small business enterprises and industries such as the textile industry, and perceptions of cheaper Chinese products, especially in relation to the 'made in China' label (Lafargue, 2005; Naidu, 2007; Van Dijk, 2007). On yet another dimension, China will need to manage the growing tension arising from the relocation of Chinese managers and personnel to Africa, and local perceptions of loss of jobs to Chinese expatriates. As unemployment rises in most of the African countries, so too are the levels of tension between locals and Chinese expatriates.

Conclusion

China's footprint in Africa is well and truly stamped, and its engagement in bilateral trade and development in Africa continues to grow. The short-term impacts of the engagement have been briefly outlined in the context of this paper. The long-term impacts are yet to be seen and will, as alluded to earlier in the paper, depend largely on how Africa and each of its countries engage with China, and how each leader manages the relationship. There is little evidence of sustained research in this area. As Large (2008) and Kornegay assert, despite growing interest in this area, and concerns of a geopolitical nature arising from the renewed interest in Africa, little is understood about the impact of Sino-African relations. More research is required as the global reconfiguration of economic relationships change and China becomes a global power.

Africa needs to explore the dynamics of how to create a more enabling environment and devise more empowering strategies to effectively engage with China and participate in the global supply chain. A more pro-active response is required if Africa is to manage China's scramble for African resources, and there is also the reminder (Lafargue, 2005) of India's foray into Africa to contend with as well. It, therefore, needs to set a clear agenda for moving forward and in doing so, must consider the question posed by Kornegay (2008, p.4): "Whose agenda? An African agenda for Africa or a Chinese (and/or other external actors) agenda for Africa?" - a question that is bound to raise vigorous discussion and debate.

REFERENCES

[1] Asamadu, K., & Ramburuth P. (2007). The slow growth of SMEs in Sub-Sahara Africa: Market, leadership and policy failure, In Littrell, R. and Ramburuth, P. (Ed.), *Leadership and Management Studies in Sub-Sahara Africa.* University Readers, San Diego, CA, 178-198.

[2] Broadman, H.G. (2007). *Africa's Silk Road: China and India's New Economic Frontier*, The World Bank, Washington.

[3] Burke, C. (2007). China's entry into construction industries in Africa: Tanzania and Zambia as case studies. *China Report*, *43,* 3, 323-336.

[4] Carmody, P., & Taylor, I. (2009). *Flexigemony and force in China's geoeconomic strategy in Africa: Sudan and Zambia compared.* Discussion paper, Institute for International Integration Studies.

[5] Coonan, C. (2008). China's new export: Farmers. *The Independent*, 29 December 29, 4-6.

[6] Corkin, L. (2006). Chinese MNCs' strategy and success. *The China Monitor*, August 2006, 4-6.

[7] Corkin, L. (2007a). China's emerging multinationals in Africa: Re-branding Africa. *The Africa Journal*, Spring, 20-22.

[8] Corkin, L. (2007b). China's contribution to the development of African infrastructure through investment in the extractive industries. *AFRODAD Occasional Papers*, 8, December 2007.

[9] Davies, M. (2007). Who are the new champions?. *The China Monitor*, 22, 4-6.

[10] Davies, M., & Alden, C. (2006). A profile of the operations of Chinese multinationals in Africa. *South African Journal of International Affairs*, *13*, 1, 83-96.

[11] Edinger, H., Herman, H., & Jansson, J. (Ed.) (2008). *New Impulses from the South: China's Engagement of Africa.* Stellenbosch University, Centre for Chinese Studies, SA.

[12] Foster, V., Butterfield, W., Chen, C., & Pushak, N. (2008). *Building Bridges: China's Growing Role as Infrastructure Financier for Africa.* The World Bank, Washington DC.

[13] General Administration of Customs of the People's Republic of China, available at: http://www.haiguan.info/CustomData/CustomData.aspx. Accessed 20 April 2008.

[14] Guerrero, D., & Manji, F. (2008). *China's New Role in Africa and the South: A Search for New Perspectives*. Fahamu, Cape Town, South Africa.

[15] Harris, K. (2007). Waves of migration: A brief outline of the history of Chinese in South Africa. *The China Monitor*, *21*, 4-5.

[16] Kapelus, P. (2007). China and 'Soft Power'. *The China Monitor*, *22*, 7-8.

[17] Kitissou, M. (2007). *Africa in China's Global Strategy*. Adonis & Abbey Publisher Ltd., London.

[18] Kondapalli, S. (2005). *The Rise of China and the Impact on Africa.* Institute for Defence and Analysis, India.

[19] Kornegay, F. A. (2008). Africa's strategic diplomatic engagement with China. *The China Monitor*, May, 3-12.

[20] Lafargue, F. (2005). China's presence in Africa. *China Perspectives*, available at URL: http://chinaperspectivea.revives.org/documents519.html. Accessed 02 May 2008.

[21] Large, D. (2008). Beyond 'dragon in the bush': The study of China-Africa relations. *African Affairs, 107*, 45-61.

[22] Le Pere, G. (2007), (Ed.), *China in Africa: Mercantilist Predator or Partner in Development,* Institute for Global Dialogue & South African Institute for International Affairs. Braamfontein, SA.

[23] Littrell, R.F. & Ramburuth, P. (2007). *Leadership and Management Studies in Sub-Sahara Africa.* University Readers, San Diego CA.

[24] Lotta, R. (2008). China's rise in the world economy and the erosion of US hegemony. *Global Research*, available at: http://www.globalresearch.ca/index.php?context=va&aid=10173. Accessed 14 September 2008.

[25] Naidu, S. (2007a). The forum on China-Africa cooperation (FOCAC): What does the future hold? *China Report*, *43*, 3, 283-296.

[26] Naidu, S. (2007b). China-African relations in the 21st Century: A 'win-win' relationship. China in Africa. *Current African Issues*, *33*, 41-46.

[27] Naidu, S. (2008). China and Africa's natural resource sector: A view from South Africa. *CSIS Africa Policy Forum*. Centre for Strategic & International Studies, SA.

[28] Naidu, S., & Davies, M. (2006). China fuels its future with Africa's riches. *South African Journal of International Affairs*, *13*, 2, 69-83.

[29] National Bureau of Statistics of China, 2009. Available at: http://www.stats.gov.cn/tjsj/ Accessed 02 April 2009.

[30] Ndumbe, J. & Ifedi, A. (2008). China's ventures in Africa: Patterns, prospects, and implications for African Development, *Mediterranean Quarterly*, *19*, 4, 91-110.

[31] Polgreen, L. (2009). As Chinese investments in Africa drop, hope sinks. *International Herald Tribune* 26 March.

[32] Sebastian, R. (2008). China-Africa investments: An analysis of China's investments in Africa, available at:

[33] http://www.chinavest.com/pdf/China Africa%20Investments.pdf

[34] Accessed 29 April 2009.

[35] Snow, P. (1998). *The Star Raft: China's Encounter with Africa.* Weidenfeld & Nicolson, New York.

[36] Taylor, I. (2006). *China and Africa.* Routledge, London.

[37] Taylor, I. (2007a). China and Africa: The barriers to win-win. *Foreign Policy in Focus*, March 2007.

[38] Taylor, I. (2007b). Unpacking China's resource diplomacy in Africa: China in Africa, *Current African Issues*, *33*, 10-25.

[39] Trade Law Centre for Southern Africa. 2009. Africa-China trading relationship – Update 2009, available at: http://www.tralac.org/cause_data/images/1694/Africa-China09.pdf. Accessed 02 May 09.

[40] Tu, J. (2008). Sino-Africa relations: Historical development and long-term challenges. *China: An International Journal, 6*, 2, 330-343.

[41] Van Dijk, M.P. (2007). The role of China in Africa, in particular Chinese foreign direct investment. Paper presented at the AEGIS European Conference on African Studies, 10 July, Africa Studies Centre, Leiden, Netherlands.

[42] Wang, J. Y., & Bio-Tchane, A. (2008). Africa's burgeoning ties with China: Maximizing the benefits of China's increasing economic engagement with Africa. *Finance and Development, 45*, 1, 44-47.

In: Thirty Years of China's Economic Reform
Editors: Yue Wang and Prem Ramburuth

ISBN: 978-1-60876-908-7
© 2010 Nova Science Publishers, Inc.

Chapter 10

On the Internationalization of China's Big Business Groups After Three Decades of Reform

Dylan Sutherland [*] ***and Ning Lutao*** [+]

School of Contemporary Chinese Studies, Nottingham University, UK
East Asian Studies, University of Cambridge, UK

Abstract

Chinese business groups have grown rapidly in recent years. To date, however, few studies have noted the concentration of assets, sales, profits and R&D expenditures in a small number of super-large trial business groups. These groups are now also responsible for a large share of China's outward foreign direct investment. This is no coincidence, as top leaders have long harboured plans to create internationally competitive business groups, following their East Asian neighbours. In recent years, with rapidly growing OFDI from China, it is of interest to ask what progress these groups have made in internationalizing their operations. There is also a growing interest in the idea of 'strategic-asset-seeking' OFDI from China. This type of OFDI is associated with rapid firm-level catch-up. This chapter therefore considers the extent to which these big business groups have engaged in such OFDI and, more generally, their overall development trajectory to date.

Keywords: business groups, strategic-asset-seeking, outward FDI

* Email: dylan.sutherland@nottingham.ac.uk
+ Email: ln227@cam.ac.uk

INTRODUCTION

Business groups, as opposed to free standing firms, have played prominent roles in the economic growth of many developing economies. This is particularly true for the economies of East Asia, where they have been key microeconomic units of growth in the process of late-industrialization (Amsden, 1989; Wade, 1990). Japan, in the 1950s and 60s, and South Korea in the 1970s and 80s, espoused the development of business groups as a cornerstone of their successful development strategies. They did so despite the severe criticism that these interventionist policies to build big businesses arose from more orthodox economic thinking (World Bank, 1993; World Bank 1997). Interestingly, China has also openly declared policies with somewhat similar intentions. The 'grasping the large and letting go of the small' policy for example, looks in spirit to emulate the policies of these successful East Asian neighbours. Indeed, by the end of 2006, there were already 2,856 officially recognised big business groups in China. They had, according to official statistics, around 27,950 first- tier, majority owned subsidiaries and employed around 30 million people (SSB, 2007). Therefore, the reach and influence of China's business groups is already of undoubted importance. Within these 3,000 or so business groups, around 150 of the very largest were selected to undergo important trials and reforms. As with Japan and South Korea, Chinese policy makers looked to concentrate their efforts and resources in a small number of large groups. One important purpose of these efforts was that these select 'national champion' business groups would lead China's efforts to create internationally competitive TNCs. The prominence of China's big business groups and the interesting similarities with the policies of Japan and South Korea raises numerous questions. Among one of the more interesting is the extent to which China's 'national champion' trial groups have contributed to Chinese outward foreign direct investment (OFDI). A further question, moreover, concerns the nature of this investment. After three decades of reforms, China's OFDI has started to grow at high speeds. There is a notion that Chinese firms are increasingly undertaking 'strategic-asset-seeking' to achieve rapid firm-level catch-up (Child and Rodrigues, 2005). To what extent then are China's trial groups involved in this sort of OFDI?

The chapter is organised as follows. First, we summarize some recent literature on Chinese business groups. Second, in light of this review, we investigate and summarize some of the important policies related to the groups. Third, adding flesh to this description, we provide an overview of the growth of big business groups focusing on the small number of trial national champion groups. Fourth, we consider the extent to which these groups have contributed to Chinese OFDI and their evolution as TNCs. We briefly examine China's largest non-financial TNCs and compare them with their developing country counterparts. We conclude by noting that China's large groups have contributed significantly to China's OFDI. To date, however, most of their international investments are probably in areas unrelated to 'strategic-asset-seeking' and thus less closely associated with rapid firm-level catch-up. Such investments, however, while limited to date, may well increase as greater opportunities emerge in the wake of the global financial crisis.

BUSINESS GROUPS IN CHINA

A range of scholars from business, economics and management have recently become interested in 'business groups'. Capturing this interest, a summary of this growing literature was recently published in the *Journal of Economic Literature*. This summary and review addressed a fundamental question to which much academic research, by and large, has been addressed: are business groups 'paragons' or 'parasites' (Khanna and Yafeh, 2007)? Business groups have been defined in numerous ways. They may, however, in general be thought of as collections of independent firms with both formal and informal ties. They have the tendency to operate in numerous industries and often with the participation of outside investors (though to varying degrees) (Khanna and Yafeh 2007). While there are some reasons why groups may be thought of as paragons, there are also reasons to believe such groups may play a negative and harmful role in economic development. Their roles in rent seeking, monopoly, crony capitalism and misdirection of capital for example, have all been alluded to. As well as this, certain types of business group structures may have negative impacts on the corporate governance of member firms. Pyramidal type structures in particular have been picked out as having particularly negative consequences for economic performance (Morck *et al* 2005). On the other hand, looking at the more positive aspects of business groups' development, it has been suggested that such groups may be instrumental in addressing market failures in product, finance and labour markets. Such groups have also played pivotal roles in some of the most successful late-industrializing countries, Japan and South Korea key among these. Among other things, such groups have played a key part in assimilating advanced technologies through developing 'project execution capabilities' (Amsden and Hikino, 1994). In turn, the largest groups managed to achieve dramatic firm-level catch-up, eventually allowing their big business groups to enter into the ranks of the world's most successful global companies. China too has long harboured aspirations to create its own internationally competitive TNCs. To this end, it has looked to develop a state supported 'national team' of business groups.

While general interest abounds in business groups, a comparatively small (though growing) literature exists on China's business groups. The official definition of the Chinese business group includes those groups with sales or assets of over 500 million RMB and numerous participating member firms at different levels (usually at least five in the first-tier). Firms are only considered to be included as business group members in these official statistics if over 50% of their equity is owned by the parent company (referred to as *mu gongsi*, or mother company). In reality, the boundaries of business groups in China are more porous and are more in keeping with the earlier definition given.

The earliest business group-related work in China can be traced back to research on reforms in large-scale state enterprises, the precursor of today's groups. Nolan (1996) and Lo (1999), for example, showed that large state-owned enterprises, contrary to common perception, had continued to grow during China's early reforms. While most observers thought state-owned enterprises had been performing poorly as a whole, they had overlooked the fact that within the state sector large enterprises had performed considerably better than small enterprises. Thus, contrary to the ideas of the 'transition orthodoxy', there was some evidence that large state corporations could contribute towards a successful economic transition. Later on, Smyth (2000), in one of the earliest studies specifically mentioning groups, was to build on these ideas. He went on to note that the growth of big business had led to the institutional transformation of the large-scale sector into business groups. Smyth (2000) also went on to ask: should China be promoting big business groups? In the light of rather limited evidence, his conclusions were broadly in agreement with the Chinese policy to promote groups. Later works, such as Nolan and Wang (1999) and Nolan (2001, 2002), took a slightly different approach. They were based primarily upon case studies, and looked to answer other questions. For example, they began to investigate the nature of institutional change within China's big business groups in the context of transition and globalization. Importantly, at this time China's imminent entry to WTO led to greater discussion of how such large groups could lead China's integration into the world economy. Nolan (2001), for example, dedicated lengthy work to China's emergence at the time of a 'global big business revolution' and studied the implications for firm-level catch-up.

While there has been considerable interest in the challenges Chinese groups face in catching-up, another interesting area has recently emerged. A new body of research has also examined the microeconomic impact of groups in China (often looking at the impact on subsidiaries). Using approaches commonly found in business group literature for example, studies of Chinese groups have employed quantitative approaches to examine whether, and under what conditions, affiliated members benefit from group membership. Keister (1998, 2000), for example, has examined the performance of 40 of China's largest groups. Yiu *et al.* (2005) have also looked at performance, examining the profitability of 224 business groups (including all subsidiaries). They argued that groups acquire resources and capabilities so that they can become successful agents to promote economic transformation and growth. Thus they find that group profitability is negatively related to what they call 'endowed resources' (including such things as the age of the group, the extent of government ownership and the prevalence of management with government links) but positively related to what they call 'acquired resources'. Such resources they argue are acquired through actions such as acquisitions, internal capability development and international diversification (Yiu *et al* 2005). Ma *et al* (2006), on the other hand, look to examine how business groups fill 'ownership voids' by serving as the direct owners of state-owned enterprises in the absence of other private actors. They find that the combination of business group affiliation and state ownership has a positive effect on subsidiary performance. Therefore, as well as substituting for imperfect markets, they argue that they may also play an important role in ownership reforms.

As well as microeconomic studies, complementary work in the International Business field has also indirectly focused on what it sees as the Chinese groups' tendency to acquire 'strategic assets'. This involves the notion that Chinese groups seek technological and brand assets that in turn may quickly create competitive positions for them in international markets. This is complementary to Nolan's (2001) earlier study on Chinese firm-level catch-up. A number of recent studies use manufacturing industry case studies to illustrate and discuss this process (Lenovo, Galanz and Haier, among others). Luo and Tung (2005) for example, investigate this rapid firm-level catch-up and allude to it as the 'springboard perspective' used by emerging market TNCs. This focuses on the ways in which emerging market TNCs may acquire strategic resources (such as R&D capacity, proprietary technology, design facilities, brands, local distribution networks and so on) embedded in firms in industrialized countries. This literature argues that one way emerging market TNCs can access these assets is by aggressive takeover of the critical assets from advanced TNCs, so overcoming their 'latecomer disadvantages' (Luo and Tung, 2007). International expansion of latecomers, they further argue, may be primarily driven by the need to seek strategic assets. These assets can in turn allow them to catch-up with and counter-attack global rivals' major foothold in their home country market (Luo and Tung, 2007). In China's case, for example, Morck *et al.* (2008) argue that: 'with over a trillion dollars in foreign reserves and increasing economic clout, China can send flagship companies abroad to acquire technologies, brands, resources, and better access to international markets'. Others suggest, along these lines, that China is seeking 'technological and brand assets to create a competitive position in international markets' (Child and Rodrigues, 2005, p.381). In the final analysis, the strategic-asset-seeking perspective argues there may be no relationship between firm-specific ownership advantages and the pursuit of OFDI in the Chinese case. Chinese firms, in other words, engage in OFDI to enhance their competitiveness rather than exploiting an existing set of advantages, as conventional theory would have it. This may allow them to rapidly catch-up.

A number of interesting research questions emerge from this brief review of research on Chinese business groups and strategic-asset-seeking OFDI. Given the apparent centrality of China's champion trial groups to the aspirations to create TNCs, what progress have they made to date? Have these large trial groups been involved in the much discussed 'strategic-asset-seeking' so central to firm-level catch-up?

BUSINESS GROUP POLICY: BUILDING CHINA'S FIRST TNCS?

To answer these questions it is useful to first briefly consider associated government policies to build national champion business groups. Nolan (2001) and Sutherland (2001, 2003) identified and described quite early China's 'national team' business groups. Indeed, the emergence of these trial groups now dates back some time. The very first experimentation or trials started in the auto industry in the early 1980s. Later, the State Council published some key policy documents outlining their objectives. An early policy directive, issued by the State Council in December 1991, for example, endorsed 55 of China's largest business groups to undergo influential trial reforms. The number of trial groups later enlarged to about 120 in 1997. Since this time the number of groups has fluctuated around this level until the creation of the State Owned Assets Supervision and Administration Commission (SASAC) in 2003 (Table 1). At this time a number of further groups were added to the trials. These trial groups have also received a variety of special policies to help improve their performance (Nolan, 2001). Among these policy experiments were: the development of internal group finance companies; the systematic introduction of stock market listings; preferential loans from state banks; the promotion of preferential planning within the groups, giving them greater autonomy in basic decision making; granting of import and export rights; the empowerment of the group's core with special rights to incorporate state assets into the group; and the creation of research and technology centres. These measures were largely of an institutional nature, aimed at freeing the groups from the constraints of the formerly centrally-planned economy and allowing trans-provincial, trans-departmental enterprise groups to emerge (Sutherland, 2001). While it is difficult, if not impossible to gauge the success of these measures, some evidence suggests certain policies may have improved the performance of the groups. Keister (1998, 2000), for example, finds groups with technology and finance companies, far more common in the trial groups, allowed subsidiary companies to outperform. In any case, the trial groups have grown far more quickly than other groups in recent times and their profitability has also greatly improved.

The 'grasp the large' policy accelerated in 1997. At the 15th Party Conference at this time President Jiang Zemin summarized how efforts were to be made to distil the state sector into key 'pillar' industries of the national economy using strategic adjustments to create 'highly competitive large enterprise groups':

> 'The state-owned sector must be in a dominant position in major industries and key areas that concern the life-blood of the national economy....we shall effectuate a strategic reorganization of state-owned enterprises by managing well large enterprises while adopting a flexible policy toward small ones. By using capital as the bonds and relying on market forces, China will establish highly competitive large enterprise groups with trans-regional, inter-trade, cross-ownership and trans-national operations' (New Star Press, 1997, p. 22).

At this time, the "walking-out" (*zouchuqu*) or the "go global" policy, was first officially announced by Jiang Zemin. The 1997 State Council document was very explicit in noting the challenges closer international integration posed for the groups (Sutherland, 2003). A set of policies aimed to achieve integration with the international market through two steps: one step was to increase exports and the second step, following from this, was towards overseas investment from the business groups (Ning 2009). Both the "going-out" and the "big business" policies, therefore, were a part of an interconnected industrial strategy. This detailed how China was to integrate into the world economy and to improve its international competitiveness by moving, eventually, from 'asset exploitation' to 'strategic-asset-seeking'. While implementing Deng's "open-door" policy, Jiang argued that China could not encourage foreign inputs to its economy (including imports and inward FDI) without also developing domestic outputs (exports and OFDI) that would simultaneously flow out to the rest of the world. Although a small number of outward investments were made for political motives, the early implementation of the policy was, for the most part, about "attracting-in" (inward FDI). Recognising the economic and political turmoil at the beginning of China's market reform, Jiang argued that a relatively liberalized regime and adequate financial incentives were necessary to attract inward FDI. The main policy motivations were to use inward FDI "*to lay the foundation, bringing up the [technological, production and management] level*" and to gain finance for production and marketing channels to the advanced economies. The development logic of Chinese leaders was that a well-guided "attracting-in" inward FDI strategy would stimulate the growth of indigenous production capability and in turn achieve the first step of Chinese products export "going-out".

Despite this optimism, however, China's self-financed and self-sufficient science and technology programs (such as the 863, 909, and "Torch" projects) appeared to have rather limited success (in contrast to the "attracting in" of foreign investment). They produced neither substantial commercial spin-offs nor seemed to improve the general capabilities of big business in helping to close the gap with developed countries. Chinese leaders decided to further liberalise the domestic market in the hope of bringing in and acquiring newer and more desirable technologies (known as *shichang huan jishu,* i.e exchange markets for technologies). A regularly revised foreign trade and investment guideline system was therefore established as early as 1995. Since this time, restricted and prohibited areas and trade barriers have been gradually reduced to be consistent with the protocol of China's accession to the World Trade Organization (WTO). The ultimate aims of a more liberal "attracting-in" policy were still to foster the international competitiveness of domestic enterprises. This envisaged, therefore, a transition from the first step of "going-out", namely exporting of products, to the second step, namely of outward investment and development of Chinese controlled transnational production networks. During the first export-led "going out" stage, vertically integrated state-owned enterprises/state-controlled enterprises associated with the Japanese/Korean model were therefore encouraged. One key reason was that they should be able to absorb "attracted" technologies, and to swiftly turn them into a large scale production, to achieve cost comparative advantages over international counterparts. This policy, in essence, encourages a mixture of OFDI activities with an emphasis, in particular, on strategic-asset-seeking activity.

Table 1. Indicators of growth in China's big business groups (billion $US unless otherwise stated)

	1997	1998	1999	2000	2001	2002	2003	2004	2005	2006	Annual growth
Panel A: All business groups											
Total number	2,369	2,472	2,757	2,655	2,710	2,627	2,692	2,764	2,845	2,856	
Total asset value	607	807	1,052	1,289	1,543	1,717	2,050	2,347	2,780	3,268	20.6
Turnover	340	423	527	642	791	929	1,206	1,523	1,874	2,285	23.6
Profits	14.7	13.1	20.8	35.0	38.7	50.3	66.9	99.9	125.2	157.5	30.1
Exports	31.1	32.4	43.2	55.2	65.1	75.7	90.8	120.3	142.1	177.6	21.4
Employees (million)	18.5	20.9	23.4	22.8	25.2	25.2	25.9	26.7	28.3	30.1	5.6
Total R&D	1.9	2.6	4.3	5.8	8.1	9.7	10.9	14.4	18.1	24.8	33.2
Panel B: Non trial business groups											
Total number	2250	2351	2631	2536	2591	2511	2579	2596	2697	2719	
Total asset value	328.4	399.0	504.6	745.0	961.7	1081.9	1335.0	1067.9	1353.4	1676.5	19.9
Turnover	204.7	228.8	264.6	366.1	484.3	571.0	761.7	785.5	1000.8	1289.6	22.7
Profits	9.4	8.9	11.8	17.7	21.1	25.9	34.5	39.6	50.6	69.7	25.0
Profits/assets (%)	2.9	2.2	2.3	2.4	2.2	2.4	2.6	3.7	3.7	4.2	
Exports	22.1	22.5	26.7	37.5	47.4	54.0	67.0	80.3	96.9	126.5	21.4
Employees (million)	10.9	11.0	12.2	12.9	16.0	16.3	16.9	15.7	17.4	19.8	6.9
Total R&D spend	1.3	1.6	2.2	3.1	4.9	5.4	6.3	7.7	9.0	13.4	29.6
Panel C: Trial business groups											
Number of trial groups	119	121	126	119	119	116	113	168	148	137	
Total asset value	278.2	408.1	547.4	544.0	581.0	635.4	715.3	1278.8	1426.9	1591.1	21.4
Turnover	135.1	193.8	262.7	275.6	306.3	358.2	444.3	737.2	872.7	995.2	24.9
Profits	5.3	4.2	8.9	17.2	17.5	24.4	32.3	60.3	74.6	87.8	36.7
Profits/assets (%)	1.9	1.0	1.6	3.2	3.0	3.8	4.5	4.7	5.2	5.5	
Exports	9.0	9.8	16.5	17.6	17.7	21.7	23.9	40.1	45.2	51.1	21.3
Employees (million)	7.6	9.9	11.2	9.9	9.3	8.8	9.0	11.0	10.9	10.3	3.5
Total R&D spend	0.6	1.0	2.0	2.6	3.2	4.3	4.7	6.8	9.2	11.3	38.6
***Panel D:* Trial business group share of total (%)**											
Share of assets	46	51	52	42	38	37	35	54	51	49	...
Share of turnover	40	46	50	43	39	39	37	48	47	44	...
Share of profits	36	32	43	49	45	49	48	60	60	56	...
Share of exports	29	30	38	32	27	29	26	33	32	29	...
Share of employees	41	47	48	43	37	35	35	41	38	34	...
Share of R&D	33	0	48	46	40	44	43	47	51	46	...

Source: SSB (2007a).

More recent policy developments have focused on ownership reforms and led to the creation of the State Owned Assets Supervision and Administration Commission (SASAC) to oversee the trial groups. In 2004, the number of trial groups increased from 113 to 168. Other groups were introduced to the trials with the intention of eventually focusing and consolidating them to 30-50 super groups. An important element of current policy, therefore, is that they should become more focused so as to achieve international competitiveness. Indeed, according to one recent review:

> Increasingly, the SASAC formulates its agenda in terms that a Wall Street investment bank would understand. The SASAC sees its mission as restructuring the large firms under its control, hiving off and discarding non-core businesses, and building strong, competitive firms around a few core businesses. These core businesses should be leaders in their sectors, or they should drop out of the business. SASAC head Li Rongrong repeats the mantra of Jack Welch, the legendary head of General Electric, that each business should be No. 1, 2, or 3 in its market - or else it should be discarded. (Naughton 2005, p.7)

Historically, a feature of the business group, China's included, has been their tendency to diversify into different industries. Indeed, such diversification is a strategy that is probably driven by, among other things, the imperfect market institutions that are found in developing markets (and transition economies in particular in finance, product and labour markets). Anecdotal as well as more formal evidence suggests that diversification is also a common strategy in China. A large survey undertaken in 2003 of all of China's 2,692 groups found only 890 were functioning in a single core area (SSB, 2006a); another 1,200 or so were operating within businesses of only some relevance to their core business, though ultimately outside it; and around one quarter of all groups surveyed had diversified into completely unrelated industries by 2003. It has been noted that 'groups around the world vary considerably in form: some are extremely diversified whereas others are more focused' (Khanna and Yafeh 2007: 331). Group diversification, as measured by the number of two-digit industries in which the group operates, therefore varies considerably between countries (Brazil averages 1.4, Chile 5.1, India 4.2, Indonesia 2.1, South Korea 1.7, Mexico 2.7, Philippines 3.1, Taiwan 1.6, Thailand 3.5)(Khanna and Yafeh 2007, p.334). While it is difficult to make exact comparisons, a review of some of the largest centrally-supported key groups controlled by SASAC - those picked out to develop core businesses - shows that they too are diversified across numerous business activities. More recently, with the establishment of SASAC to oversee these groups, there has been a policy to force the groups to focus on core business. The success of this policy is as yet unknown.

Business Group Expansion

The above description suggests China's trial business groups should play a prominent role in China's OFDI. This is indeed the case. Of total business group-related OFDI (i.e. for all 2,850 groups), a negligible amount has originated from the lower province level and private groups. OFDI from the trial groups has been rising quickly in recent years and a considerable amount of China's total OFDI in the 2002 to 2006 period is explained by OFDI from the trial groups alone (Sutherland 2009). Their share of all officially recorded OFDI from China, for example, stood at 74% in 2003 (SSB, 2007b). Thus by 2003 the majority of China's OFDI was channeled through roughly 113 trial business groups. By 2006 this had fallen to around 21%, though some of this apparent fall was caused by the large flows of outward investment to Caribbean tax havens – a statistical anomaly unique to China's 'round tripping' processes, among other things (SSB 2007b). In nominal terms the volume of OFDI from the trial groups had more than doubled to around $3billion by 2006.

How have these trial groups managed to make such important contributions to China's OFDI? Firstly, it is relevant that China's 3,000 or so business groups as a whole have grown at amazing speeds over the past decade (see Table 1). As such, their internationalization has been supported by rapid domestic growth. Total assets and sales, for example, have grown at around 20% whereas profits and R&D have grown even more quickly, closer to 30% per annum. Within China's business groups, however, an important distinction emerged between the largest centrally-supported trial groups and lower level groups. The former (Table 1, panels C and D), as noted, are far fewer in number but considerably larger in size. For most indicators they have grown at faster rates than the other non-trial groups. By 2006 the 137 trial groups accounted for around one half of all of China's business group assets, sales and profits (Table 1, panel D). On average they employed about 75,000 people, compared with 7,300 in province level and other groups. They had average assets of $11.5 billion compared to $0.6 billion in the other groups, and had also become far more profitable (with profits as a share of total assets improving to around 5.5% by 2006, compared with only 4.2% in other groups). Profits soared in these trial groups, increasing at an average annual compounded rate of nearly 37% between 1997 and 2006. As well as soaring profits, expenditures on R&D increased at similarly dramatic rates in keeping with the strategic objectives of creating internationally competitive groups.

Secondly, this rapid growth has been supported by the industries in which these groups are found. Many of the trial groups are often found within capital intensive industries which have the potential to benefit from economies of scale and scope and rapid productivity growth. Economic historians have identified these specific industries as bastions of big business (Chandler, 1990). For example, mining and natural resources, energy supply, electronics, iron and steel, autos, machinery, pharmaceuticals, aviation and aerospace, oil and petrochemicals are some of the more important. Chinese policy makers refer to these industries as the 'pillar' industries of the national economy. Other industrial sectors, by contrast - those in which large enterprises are now not so dominant - have not received the same level of support as big groups. The big business group yearbook classifies businesses by their main business activities. According to these official definitions most of China's groups were classified in manufacturing (1,303), wholesale and retail trade (310), construction (176) and real estate (136) (SSB, 2007a). The greatest profits were earned in manufacturing, mining, information transmission, computer services and software. Alone they accounted for 75% of all business group profits. Significantly, the trial groups were also very important to these areas: only 4 trial mining groups accounted for 73% of profits for all of China's mining groups, the 65 trial manufacturing groups accounted for 39%, and 4 IT groups accounted for 97% of profits (SSB, 2007a). Clearly, the trial groups make large profits and this is in part related to their strong domestic market positions. Monopolistic positions arguably provide them with high profits, which in turn may drive heavy R&D investments as well as OFDI.

Finally, unlike in Japan and South Korea, China's business groups face the additional challenge of reforming their ownership structures. This presents further challenges for the formation of business groups, particularly given the large numbers of participating firms. As noted, there were around 30,000 participating firms (including parent and first-tier subsidiaries) in all of China's groups; that is, on average, around 11 firms per group (SSB, 2007a). How then has ownership evolved in China's big business groups and what does this mean for internationalisation strategies? As well as rapid growth, various kinds of ownership and institutional transformations have taken place within the groups. This transformation has occurred at both the level of the parent, and also among subsidiaries. Among the parent companies, more and more are now registered as private (*siren*) groups – nearly 1,100 by 2006. Despite this transformation, however, state-owned parent companies still predominated among the groups as a whole. By 2006, for example, around 1,500 state-owned groups still existed. They were, on average, considerably larger than the non-state owned groups. The trial groups, however, with few exceptions, all remained registered as state-owned. As noted they are also the largest groups in China. The trial groups therefore remained closely wed to the state.

Policy makers have increasingly concentrated resources on a small number of big business groups. These trial groups have grown at high speed, are concentrated in a number of 'pillar' industries, are less involved in ownership reforms than other groups, but play an increasingly important role in R&D. They have tapped China's stock markets to raise capital, and have a higher proportion of technology centres and financial arms within the groups. As well as this they are becoming more and more profitable. One purpose of these measures, of course, is that these firms should quickly develop overseas operations and become successful transnational firms. To what extent are these objectives being realized?

INTERNATIONALIZATION AND THE TRIAL BUSINESS GROUPS

To answer this question this section further explores the nature of Chinese OFDI (using national-level data) as well as a sample of China's largest TNCs compiled from UNCTAD's list of top 100 TNCs. This list allows us to compare China's largest TNCs with other developing country TNCs, and is therefore instructive (Table 2).

As previously noted, a significant share of all of China's OFDI was undertaken by these trial groups. Analyzing national trends therefore may shed some light on its nature. Firstly then, it is of interest to note that by 2006 transportation, storage and post (10% of OFDI stock), wholesale and retail trade (17%), leasing and business services (including construction) (26%) were among the most important areas for OFDI from China. In total these sectors accounted for over 50% of total OFDI stock at the end of 2006 (SSB, 2007b). These sectors are, arguably, quite closely related to China's expansion as a vast trading empire. They are, therefore, more likely to be related to market-seeking OFDI than strategic-asset-seeking. This is important as strategic assets are most commonly associated with firm-level catch-up. Transportation (e.g. ships and ports), trading outlets to market exports and business services to facilitate trade purchases are, by contrast, all more closely related to trade expansion than strategic-asset-seeking. Mining and natural resources, which also accounted for a further 24% of OFDI stock by 2006, are arguably also of central importance to China's trade expansion (through the maintenance of low energy prices and basic inputs). Together these four categories accounted for around 80% of the stock of all China's OFDI by the end of 2006. By contrast, only 10% of China's OFDI stock was in the manufacturing industries (SSB 2007b). A general breakdown of China's national total OFDI suggests that most of it is still related to the development of China's international trading empire, rather than to acquiring critical assets to 'springboard' her leading firms to international competitiveness.

Secondly, the destination of Chinese OFDI also confirms this view. It is argued that emerging market TNCs may use 'international expansion as a springboard to counter-attack global rivals' major foothold in their home country market', according to the strategic-asset-seeking perspective (Luo and Tung, 2007, p. 486). The idea of the 'counterattack' suggests that emerging market TNCs, such as those from China, attempt to acquire strategic assets from developed market economies, where such assets are more abundant. Child and Rodrigues (2005) further argue that the internationalization paths followed by leading firms from China are not put off by problems of psychic distance. Rather, these firms explicitly target further-off developed markets so they may learn how to compete globally and, crucially, acquire the technological and brand assets to support the globalization strategy (Child and Rodrigues 2005, p.403). With the exception of Hong Kong and the Cayman Islands, however, China's OFDI has been quite evenly spread across many countries of the world (SSB, 2007b). Many of the regions that might supply critical strategic assets to help firm-level catch-up, namely the developed markets, still received only a minimal share of China's OFDI. Up until 2006 only about 2-3% of China's total OFDI stock was destined for Europe and North America (SSB, 2007b). This is not the kind of pattern we might expect if strategic-asset-seeking were a key motive driving China's OFDI.

Have the 100 or so trial groups played a more significant role in China's strategic-asset-seeking? We might expect this to be so. As noted earlier, the policy measures put in place were designed in part to help them rapidly catch up with their developed country counterparts. By breaking down OFDI from the trial groups by sector, we can establish their approximate national contribution to different areas of business activity. The trial groups are in fact important in many areas that are generally not considered closely related to strategic-asset-seeking OFDI. They are, for example, particularly dominant in mining OFDI (with an un-weighted four-year average between 2002 and 2006 of 90%), but also important in construction and transportation, utilities and information transmission (Sutherland, 2009). Mining investments, for example, are primarily considered to be resource-seeking and state-driven, thus of less interest to the 'springboard' thesis and considerations of firm-level catch-up. With regards to manufacturing, the 50 or so trial groups accounted for around half of China's OFDI in the manufacturing sector between 2002 and 2006 (Sutherland, 2009). They were, therefore, important players. However, it should be noted that by 2006, manufacturing OFDI still only accounted for 10% of the stock of China's OFDI. China's OFDI to date, while concentrated in the trial groups, has been largely oriented towards non-strategic-asset-seeking types of investments, notably those more closely related to market and resource seeking. This would suggest they have played a limited role in spurring rapid firm-level catch-up, as the springboard thesis suggests (Luo and Tung, 2007).

Is this national-level aggregate data reflected in firm level trends? Table 2 is based on UNCTAD'S (2008) listing of largest non-financial TNCs from developing countries. From the top 100 there are nine mainland-listed companies. Seven of these companies, as would be

Table 2. China's largest non-financial TNCs in 2006 (by foreign assets)

Name	Rank			Industry	Assets		Sales		Employment		TNI	No of affiliates		
	Foreign assets	TNI rank	I		Foreign assets	Total assets	Foreign	Total	Foreign	Total		Foreign	Total	II
CITIC Group	7	92	6	Diversified	17 623	117 355	2 482	10 113	18 305	107 340	18.9	12	112	10.7
China Ocean Shipping (Group) Company	13	69	3	Transport and storage	10 397	18 711	8 777	15 737	4 432	69 549	39.2	245	947	25.9
China State Construction Engineering	19	80	5	Construction	6 998	15 986	4 483	18 544	25 000	119 000	29.7	23	70	32.9
China National Petroleum Corporation	21	100	0	Petroleum expl./ref./distr.	6 374	178 843	3 036	114 443	22 000	167 129	2.7	5	65	7.7
Sinochem Corp.	26	55	7	Petroleum expl./ref./distr.	5 326	8 898	19 374	23 594	220	21 048	47.7	31	161	19.3
Lenovo Group	49	58	3	Computers and related businesses	3 058	5 449	9 009	14 590	5 800	25 100	47	22	38	57.9
China National Offshore Oil Corp.	75	98	0	Petroleum and natural gas	1 741h	19 884	1 818i	11 391	1 500	44 000	9.4	8	28	28.6
China Minmetals Corp.	92	97	2	Metals and metal products	1 266	6 813	2 527	17 256	630	32 594	11.7	14	265	5.3
China Communications Construction	96	99	.	Construction	1 162	16 258	2 855	14 712	1 078	78 331	9.3	..	..	..

Source: UNCTAD (2008, p. 220).

Notes: The TNI is calculated as the average of the following three ratios: foreign assets to total assets, foreign sales to total sales and foreign employment to total employment. II is the number of foreign affiliates divided by number of all affiliates (only majority-owned).

expected, have been involved with the business group trials. The exceptions, Lenovo and CITIC, also have close ties to the central government. They remain predominantly state-owned. This sample, moreover, appears to reflect quite closely the aggregate data on Chinese OFDI already described. Mining and natural resources, transportation and construction (captured in business services in national data) have been among the more important areas of OFDI until 2006. COSCO, for example, the transport group, is China's second-largest outward investor, and has more overseas subsidiaries (245) than all the other Chinese TNCs listed here combined. Other construction groups are also important. This picture, therefore, is also somewhat at odds with the view that China's OFDI is focused upon strategic assets, predominantly found in manufacturing firms. In our sample only Lenovo Group enters the top nine.

It is also of further interest to compare China's embryonic TNCs with those from other developing countries. In this regard most of China's groups cannot be considered to be highly trans-national. This is captured by the trans-nationality index (TNI). The average TNI for this sample of Chinese groups was only 24 for these Chinese firms. This compared with an average of 54 for the top 100 non-financial TNCs from developing countries (i.e. their average non-domestic asset, employment and sales shares stood at 54%). In other words, most of the business activities of Chinese TNCs are still predominantly focused on the domestic market. This fact is also reflected in the high TNI rank of these firms. CITIC, for example, China's largest TNC by assets, was ranked at only 92 out of the top 100 TNCs in terms of its TNI. The average TNI rank for these Chinese TNCs stood at 83 out of 100, whereas the average foreign asset rank was 44. By the standards of other developing country TNCs, therefore, China's TNCs remained comparatively dependent upon domestic markets. This suggests that these groups are still in comparatively early stages of trans-nationalization.

Conclusion

This chapter has shown that from within China's 3,000 or so big business groups a small number of trial 'national champion' business groups were selected to become China's pioneering TNCs. A variety of policies were granted to them. The largest groups, sometimes in highly profitable domestic industries, grew quickly in response to this support. Their profitability has also improved markedly. They have also seen rapid increases in their R&D spending, a marker of their future intentions. The trial groups, moreover, have played an important role in China's OFDI to date. This chapter has argued, however, that contrary to the impression generated by some media coverage and promoted also by the *ex-post* observation biases of some academic work, the bulk of OFDI undertaken by these groups is probably not closely related to strategic-asset-seeking investments. This is important, as it is these types of investments that are most commonly associated with firm-level catch-up strategies. By contrast, however, this chapter has argued that, at the national level, much of China's OFDI appears closely tied to China's emergence as a trading nation with a natural resource deficit. This observation is supported by observations at the firm-level. As well as trading groups, construction and natural resource sectors are areas in which China's largest TNCs are more commonly found. Nearly all of China's largest TNCs are large state-owned groups that have been part of the aforementioned business group trials. In many instances they hold favorable domestic market positions. This allows them to subsidize their risky international investments. In this sense the development of the 100 or so trial groups looks more closely related to China's national development plans, as opposed to firm-level internationalization strategies.

Given the close attachment of these groups to the highest decision-making bodies of the Chinese government, currently working under SASAC and the State Council, this is perhaps not surprising. From early on, China's aspirations for the big business groups were clearly articulated. Plans were put in place for them to quickly develop high-tech-focused groups, with the ability to compete with foreign rivals in key manufacturing sectors:

> In reality, international economic confrontations show that if a country has several large companies or groups it will be assured of maintaining a certain market share and position in the international economic order. America, for example, relies on General Motors, Boeing, Du Pont and a batch of other multinational companies. Japan relies on six large enterprise groups and South Korea relies on 10 large commercial groupings. In the same way now and in the next century our nation's position in the international economic order will be to a large extent determined by the position of our nation's large enterprises and groups' (Wu Bangguo, Jingji Ribao, 1st August 1998).

To date, however, there are no Chinese groups that could be considered anywhere near the equivalents of GM, Boeing or Dupont. According to UNCTAD, China's largest TNC (CITIC) is a diversified conglomerate. The second largest (COSCO) is a shipping company. The third is a construction company (China State Construction Engineering). There are, moreover, comparatively few examples of successful strategic-asset-seeking OFDI when balanced against the far larger number of less glamorous internationalization activities related to trade and market seeking, construction and natural resource investments. The jury is still out as regards the success of the most ambitious strategic-asset-seeking ventures. It is clear that China's largest TNCs to date are still considerably less internationalized, even when compared to their developing country rivals. This suggests they are still heavily dependent upon their comparatively sheltered domestic markets. Only time will tell how successful these trial groups will be and whether the 'go global' strategy will achieve its desired objectives. To date, however, we would suggest their success, at least in the perspective of the highly ambitious 'strategic-asset-seeking' and 'springboard' view, has been somewhat limited.

In the future, it is possible that the outward investment of these groups will accelerate and that they may also start to acquire more strategic assets. This is particularly so as the global financial crisis has had an adverse impact on the real economies of the largest developed markets. It has, as a result, devastated the earnings of the world's largest corporations (with a record fall in profits for the Fortune 500 companies in 2008). China's big groups, at least in a financial sense, are now larger than they have ever been, *vis a vis* their international competitors. More importantly, the Chinese banking system remains comparatively solvent. It is also being primed to support the overseas acquisitions of China's largest groups. Recently, for example, a consortium of state-owned banks clubbed together to provide $20 billion dollars to fund Chinalco's pursuit of a significant share of Rio Tinto, the huge global mining group. As such, the global financial crisis provides a unique window of opportunity for China's big groups, particularly those state-supported groups that we have discussed. Future research, therefore, will no doubt need to pay close attention to the ways in which the global financial crisis has influenced their pursuit of strategic assets. It should also take seriously the role of the state, state-owned banks and their interaction with big business groups in China's outward foreign direct investment.

REFERENCES

[1] Amsden, A.H. (1989). *Asia's Next: South Korea and Late Industrialization*. New York: Oxford University Press.

[2] Amsden, A. H., and T. Hikino. (1994). Project Execution Capability, Organisational Know-How and Conglomerate Corporate Growth in Late Industrialisation. *Industrial and Corporate Change*, 3,1, 111-107.

[3] Chandler, A. (1990). *Scale and Scope, the Dynamics of Industrial Capitalism*. Cambridge, MA: Harvard University Press.

[4] Keister, L.(1998). Engineering growth: business group structure and firm performance in China's transition economy. *American Journal of Sociology*, *104*, 404-440.

[5] Keister, L. (2000). *The Structure and Impact of Interfirm Relations during Economic Development*, Oxford University Press, Oxford.

[6] Khanna, T., & Yafeh Y. (2007). Business groups in emerging markets: paragons or parasites? *Journal of Economic Literature*, XLV, 331-372.

[7] Luo, Y., & Tung, R.L. (2007). International expansion of emerging market enterprises: A springboard perspective. *Journal of International Business Studies*, *38*, 481–498.

[8] Morck, R., Yeung, B., & Minyuan Zhao (2008). Perspectives on China's Outward Foreign Direct Investment. *Journal of International Business Studies*, *39*, 3, 337-350.

[9] Ma, X., Yao, X., & Xi, Y. (2006). Business group affiliation and firm performance in a transition economy: A focus on ownership voids. *Asia Pacific Journal of Management*, *23*, 467-483.

[10] Morck, R., Wolfenzon, D., & Yeung, B. (2005). Corporate Governance, Economic, Entrenchment, and Growth. *Journal of Economic Literature*, XLIII, 655–720.

[11] Naughton, B. (2005). SASAC Rising. *China Leadership Monitor,* 14 (Spring), 1-11.

[12] New Star Press, *Selected documents of the 15th CPC National Congress*. Beijing: New Star Publishers, 1997.

[13] Ning, L (2009). China's Leadership in the World ICT Industry: A Successful Story of its 'Attracting-in' and 'Walking-out' Strategy?'. *Pacific Affairs*, *82*, 1, Spring., 67-91.

[14] Nolan, P. (1996). Large firms and industrial reform in former planned economies: the case of China. *Cambridge Journal of Economics*, *20*, 6, 1-29.

[15] Nolan, P. (2001). *China and the Global Business Revolution*, Palgrave, Basingstoke.

[16] Nolan P. (2002). China and the global business revolution. *Cambridge Journal of Economics*, *26*, 1.

[17] Nolan, P., & Wang, X. (1999). Beyond privatization: Institutional innovation and growth in China's large state-owned enterprises. *World Development*, *27*, 1, 169-200.

[18] Rui, H., & Yip, G. (2008). Foreign acquisitions by Chinese firms: A strategic intent

[19] Perspective. Journal of World Business, *43*, 213-226.

[20] Smyth, R. (2000). Should China be promoting large-scale enterprises and enterprise groups?. *World Development*, *28*, 721-737.

[21] SSB (State Statistical Bureau).(2002a– 2007a). *China's Big Business Group Yearbook (Zhongguo Da Qiye Jituan Nianjian)*, Zhongguo Tongji Chubanshe, Beijing:

[22] SSB (State Statistical Bureau). *(2002b.–2007b). China Statistical Yearbook, Zhongguo Tongji Chubanshe*, Beijing.(in Chinese)

[23] Sutherland, D. (2001). Policies to Build National Champions: China's 'National Team' of Enterprise Groups. in P. Nolan (Ed.). *China and the Global Business Revolution*, Palgrave MacMillan, New York.

[24] Sutherland, D. (2003). *China's Large Enterprises and the Challenge of Late Industrialisation*, Routledge, London.

[25] Sutherland (2009). China's National Team and Strategic-Asset-Seeking OFDI. *Chinese Management Studies*, *3*, 1, 1-13.

[26] UNCTAD. (2008). *World Investment Report*. Geneva: UNCTAD.

[27] World Bank. (1993). *The East Asian Miracle: Economic Growth and Public Policy*. Oxford: Oxford University Press.

[28] Wade, R. (1990). *Governing the Market: Economic Theory and the Role of Government in East Asian Industrialization*. Princeton, N.J.: Princeton University Press.

[29] World Bank. (1997). *China 2020*. The World Bank, Washington, D.C.

[30] Yiu, D, Bruton G.D., & Yuan L. (2005). Understanding business group performance in an emerging economy: acquiring resources and capabilities in order to prosper, *Journal of Management Studies*, *42*, 1, 183, 206.

[31] Yiu, D, Lau, C.M., Bruton, G. D. (2007). International venturing by emerging economy firms: the effects of firm capabilities, home country networks, and corporate entrepreneurship. *Journal of International Business Studies*, *38*, 3, 519–540.

In: Thirty Years of China's Economic Reform
Editors: Yue Wang and Prem Ramburuth
ISBN: 978-1-60876-908-7
© 2010 Nova Science Publishers, Inc.

Chapter 11

BARRIERS AND FACTORS AFFECTING THE INTERNATIONALISATION OF CHINESE SMEs

Gaston Fornes*[1] and Guillermo Cardoza+[2]

[1]University of Bristol (UK) and ESIC Business and Marketing School (Spain), Bristol, United Kingdom

[2]Instituto de Empresa Business School (Spain), Madrid, Spain

ABSTRACT

The chapter aims to study the international expansion of SMEs in China. The data was collected from around 500 SMEs and then analysed using multivariate regressions; the models used the firms' export intensity at the regional, national, and international level as dependent variables. The results showed (i) that several factors are hindering the expansion of Chinese SMEs (this was expected, although they seem to face fewer barriers than their Western counterparts), (ii) that finance does not seem to be a barrier to their expansion, (iii) that different barriers apply to crossing the regional and national boundaries, and (iv) that ownership by the state does not seem to play a relevant role in international expansion. The chapter concludes with some closing remarks and contributions for policy-makers and practitioners.

Keywords: Internationalisation from China's firms, Chinese SMEs expansion, factors affecting SMEs' internationalisation.

INTRODUCTION

The Chinese authorities are actively pursuing the development and national and international expansion of small and medium-sized enterprises (SMEs) (Ministry of

---

* Email: g.fornes@bristol.ac.uk.
+ Email: guillermo.cardoza@ie.edu.

Commerce of the People's Republic of China, 2008a, 2008b, 2008c), mainly due to their role in entrepreneurship, job opportunities, technology diffusion, fiscal income, identification and adoption of international best practices, risk diversification, and wealth generation (Cardoza, 1997).

Chinese SMEs, mainly due to the apparent early development stage which they are currently in (Boisot & Meyer, 2008; Ge & Ding, 2008; Liu, Xiao, & Huang, 2008; Nolan, 2001), may be facing factors/barriers that are promoting/hindering this expansion process and which have to be assessed. Managers, academics, and policy makers need to identify and understand the challenges posed by this expansion process, especially as the current literature on the internationalisation of emerging countries' SMEs is scarce. In addition, it has been suggested that the Chinese outward internationalisation process seems to differ from the patterns seen in other countries (Boisot & Child, 1996; Buckley, et al., 2007; Child & Rodrigues, 2005; Child & Tse, 2001; Mathews, 2006; Yamakawa, Peng, & Deeds, 2008). In this context, the international expansion of SMEs from China is worth studying to understand the factors hindering/promoting this internationalisation process.

This chapter is structured as follows. First, a review of the literature on the national and international expansion of Chinese firms is presented; this is followed by a description of the analysis carried out; and third, a discussion of the results is presented. The chapter finishes with some concluding remarks.

LITERATURE REVIEW

Most of the works on the national and international expansion of Chinese companies are based on large companies. Studies on the expansion of Chinese SMEs are scarce. Nevertheless, and due to the pace of change in the Chinese economy, it could be argued that many of the now relatively large companies were small or medium-sized organisations only a few years ago. Examples of this rapid transformation worth mentioning are what Zeng and Williamson (2003, pp. 3-4) called "competitive networks", a group of companies that "have taken on world markets by bringing together small, specialized companies that operate in close proximity", and "technology up-starts", firms exploiting technology developed by research institutes owned by the government. As a consequence, it would be relatively safe to assume that some of the characteristics found in previous studies on China's international companies may also be applicable, to some extent, to small and medium-sized firms.

The Internationalisation of Chinese SMEs: Conceptual Framework

Mainstream internationalisation theory assumes the existence of prior competitive advantages (Porter, 1980), firm-specific advantages (FSA) (Rugman, Collinson, & Hodgetts, 2006), or ownership-specific advantages (Dunning, 1977) and the company's ability to exploit them abroad (Buckley & Casson, 1976). However, recent works have questioned the applicability of these theories in the context of Emerging Economies (EE).

For instance, Wright et al. (2005, p.2) suggested that the analysis of companies from less developed countries should take a different perspective, as they argue that emerging markets are "a new context in which to understand the relative strengths and weaknesses of the different [conceptual] perspectives" used in conventional theory. These authors added that "domestic firms competing within emerging economies face a 'high velocity' environment of rapid political, economic, and institutional changes that are accompanied by relatively underdeveloped factor and product markets" (p.7). This changing environment presents different challenges for firms operating in these countries, which have been widely documented in the literature (see for example Filatotchev, Wright, Hoskisson, Uhlenbruck, & Tihanyi, 2003; Fornes, 2008; Fornes, 2009; Fornes & Butt-Philip, 2009; Fornes & Cardoza, 2009; Guillen, 2000; Hoskisson, Eden, Lau, & Wright, 2000; Khanna & Palepu, 1997; Khanna & Palepu, 2000; Peng, 2003). Most of these works on emerging markets' firms suggest that firms from these countries develop a set of specific advantages needed to cope with a changing environment and the relatively low development of the markets. When crossing the border, these specific advantages can help companies to successfully exploit opportunities in other emerging markets, or to create a framework for developing the necessary resources to acquire and also manage assets in other countries.

In this context, Child and Rodrigues (2005, pp. 384-385) claimed that the specific characteristics of the Chinese outward internationalisation process need to be analysed on their own merits. The first point supporting their claim is that China's emergence as an industrial power falls within the late development thesis (also applied to other East Asian countries) as China's companies need to catch up in "terms of technology and know-how, as well as in the development of business environments supportive of international competitiveness". They argue that Chinese firms need to use outward FDI to close the gap with "leading companies through acquiring appropriate assets and resources", rather than firms wishing to exploit their prior competitive advantages, the main assumption in mainstream theory (Buckley & Casson, 1976; Dunning, 1977).

Their second point concerns the Chinese government's role in its companies' internationalisation process, as many firms have received financial support and protection from the authorities to reduce their "late-coming disadvantage" and "acquire assets that enable [them] to compete in the world market" (Child & Rodrigues, 2005, pp. 384-385).

The third point is the counterpart of the second: the companies receiving support and aid as described "could be weakened by the way they remain beholden to administrative approval and bear a legacy of institutional dependence", which may suggest that their strategic options are limited from a "heavily institutionalised environment" (Child & Rodrigues, 2005, pp. 384-385).

The fourth point supporting their claim (Child & Rodrigues, 2005, pp. 384-385) concerns the Chinese "distinctive cultural and institutional legacy" including, for example, their reliance on close personal relationships (guanxi) or their management styles, which may increase their psychic distance (Johanson & Wiedersheim-Paul, 1975). This liability of foreignness could eventually compromise the effectiveness of the strategy of acquiring resources abroad.

All in all, the relevant question seems to be whether the internationalisation of companies from emerging economies "and, specifically, from China, requires a special theory nested within the general theory" (Buckley, et al., 2007).

In an attempt to answer this question, Mathews proposed an extension of the OLI paradigm (Dunning, 1977), as this traditional model uses "a 'push-oriented' concept" from Western MNEs where the firm's internationalisation "is propelled by some strategic objective", rather than by a pull and push process that seems to be the reality for most Asian Pacific companies (Mathews, 2006, p.16). This extended model, LLL, is supported by the idea that the internationalisation of "EE-based firms is not necessarily based on the possession of overwhelming assets, but rather on firms' ability to leverage its capability in organisational learning" (Yamakawa, et al., 2008, p.68).

Yamakawa et al. (2008) continued the analysis of EE's firms and found that the three main perspectives that have traditionally been used to study the internationalisation of companies – industry-based view (Porter, 1980), resource-based view (Barney, 1991; Penrose, 1959), and institution-based view (Meyer & Peng, 2005; North, 1990; Williamson, 1975) – need to be put together in the context of EE, as "none of them is likely to be strong enough to sustain on its own; rather, it is the combination of their insights that leads to a better and more insightful understanding" of this emerging phenomenon (p.64).

They claim that this combination is necessary as: (i) the industry-based view allows the examination of external opportunities, threats, and barriers; (ii) the resource-based view identifies internal strengths and weaknesses; and (iii) the institution-based view takes into account the interaction between organisations and institutions (Peng, Wang, & Jiang, 2008; Yamakawa, et al., 2008). Within this context, the factors driving the internationalisation of Chinese SMEs have been analysed through the study of small and medium-sized firms from four provinces/autonomous regions – Ningxia Hui (Cardoza & Fornes, 2008), Jiangsu (Xu,Fornes, & Cardoza, 2009), Anhui (Xu, Fornes, &Cardoza, 2009) and Shandong (Li, Fornes, & Cardoza, 2009) – with a focus on the combination of the three views mentioned above.

The Analysis

The definition of internationalisation was comprised of that proposed by Leonidou (2004, p. 281): "the firm's ability to initiate, to develop, or to sustain business operations" outside their local market, plus that proposed by Mathews (2006, p. 16): "the process of the firm's becoming integrated in international economic activities" (which covers export activities as well as foreign direct investment). This combined definition intends to take account of the process that takes SMEs from local to international markets (within Learning, the third L in the LLL model (Mathews, 2006)). It also considers the specific situation of an "unusually fragmented" Chinese market, where it has been reported that "access to foreign markets is easier and cheaper than access to most of the country's domestic markets" (Boisot & Meyer, 2008, p.354 and p.356). In this context, barriers for the national and international expansion of SMEs are those hindering this internationalisation process (Leonidou, 2004).

The definition taken for SMEs is the one given by the National Bureau of Statistics of China and can be seen in Table 1.

Table 1. Definition of Small and Medium-sized Enterprises

	Employees	Sales	Total Assets
Industry	2,000	3,000	4,000
Construction	3,000	3,000	4,000
Wholesale	200	3,000	
Retail	500	1,000	
Transportation	3,000	3,000	
Postal Service	1,000	3,000	
Accommodation & Restaurant	800	3,000	

Source: (National Bureau of Statistics of China, 2009)

The factors affecting internationalisation were operationalised using Leonidou's (2004) recollection of factors/barriers hindering the international development of SMEs. Leonidou (2004) found two main types of barriers: (i) internal barriers are "associated with organisational resources/capabilities and company approach to export business" and can be broken down into Informational, Functional, and Marketing; on the other hand, (ii) external barriers are those "stemming from the home and host environment within which the firm operates" and can be classified as Procedural, Governmental, Task, and Environmental.

The data was collected using a questionnaire based on the set of barriers also presented by Leonidou (2004). The questionnaire contained different 5-point Likert-type scale questions designed to measure the perception of the barriers examined. It was applied to a convenience sample of around 500 senior managers and directors of SMEs in Ningxia Hui, Jiangsu, Anhui, and Shandong between July 2007 and July 2009. The definition of the barriers can be seen in Table 2.

Table 2. Definition of Variables (Scale variables using a 5-point Likert-type scale)

Internal Barriers		External Barriers	
Info Sources	The company does not have access to the relevant information sources to identify external markets for the company's products and services	Paperwork	It is considered that the paperwork related to exports are complicated and costly
Data	The company does not have the relevant data to assess the possibilities that the international markets are offering	Communication	Communication difficulties affect the normal development of business abroad
Contacts	The company has difficulties to identifying and contacting potential customers in markets overseas	Payment	The payment collections make export activities more difficult
Time	The daily management of the company does not give enough time to think about exports	Assistance	The government does not offer adequate assistance and incentives to carry out export activities
Skills	There are no persons in the company with the right skills to manage export-related activities	DomRegulations	The regulations in place make it more difficult to capitalise on opportunities in international markets
Facilities	Limited production facilities do not allow the company to consider exports	Preferences	The different preferences, patterns, prices, and communication of customers in international markets make exports more difficult

Table 2. Continued

Internal Barriers		External Barriers	
Finance	The company does not have access to the necessary financial resources to fund an export-oriented plan	Competitiveness	The target international markets are perceived as highly competitive
Product	The current product portfolio is not adequate to serve the identified international markets	EconEnvironment	The deterioration of the countries' economic environment is an additional barrier to exports
Design	The design of the firm's products is not adjusted to the needs and tastes of customers in markets overseas	ExchRate	Exchange rate variations represent an important risk for the company's exports
Quality	The products' quality standards do not meet the needs of customers in international markets	PolInstability	The political instability in external markets is seen as a barrier to exports
Labels	The products' labels and packaging do not meet the requirements of the target markets	HostRegulations	The different regulations in external markets make access and operations more difficult
PostSale	The company does not have the means to offer an adequate post-sale service to its customers overseas	Tariff&NTB	The tariff and non-tariff barriers in international markets restrict export activities
Price	The retail price of the company's products are not adequate for the final consumers in international markets	Familiarity	The lack of familiarity with commercial practices abroad affect the company's operations
CompPrice	The company finds it difficult to meet the competitors' prices in the targeted international markets	Socio-cultural	The socio-cultural differences (religion, values, customs, attitudes, etc.) are considered obstacles to export activities
Credit	It is difficult for the company to give credit to customers in international markets	Verbal	The differences in verbal and non-verbal language affect the activities carried out in external markets
Distribution	The company finds the distribution channels complex to serve international markets		
DistAccess	It is complex and costly to access the distribution channels to export the company's products		
Representatives	It is difficult to find reliable representatives abroad		
Control	It is difficult to exercise effective control over the middlemen in international markets		
Supply	The company finds many difficulties in supplying adequately international markets		
Warehouses	The countries where the company exports to do not have adequate warehouse facilities		
Transport	The company considers that the transport and insurance costs related to exports are excessive		
Promotion	It is difficult to adjust the promotional activities to international markets		

Source: (Cardoza & Fornes, 2008; Li, et al., 2009; Xu, et al., 2009; Xu, et al., 2009)

Discussion of the Results

Although as can be expected the analysis from each region showed different results, it was possible to find some common patterns that seem to be specific to the Chinese business reality. First, the companies in the sample do not perceive *Finance* as a barrier to their expansion, a barrier mentioned widely in the literature on Western SMEs. This could be explained by the strong support from the government in terms of ownership and loans from state-owned banks (one of the characteristics of Chinese international firms identified in previous works). A similar conclusion was reached by Ge and Ding (2008) in their study of Galanz.

Second, the SMEs in the study face fewer barriers (between 30 to 40% of the total recollected by Leonidou (2004) assuming an equal weighting) to their expansion than their Western counterparts. This finding was not expected, as it can be thought that companies from an emerging country would face more barriers than companies operating in more developed economies. Possibly, due to the fact that the barriers used in the analysis were collected in advanced economies, studies based on barriers developed specifically for the Chinese environment may be needed.

Third, the results show that there are different barriers to crossing regional and national boundaries; this suggests that different barriers apply to regional, national, and international expansion, and supports Mathews' (2006) idea of leverage of organisational learning. Also, these findings are among the first to provide empirical support to Boisot and Meyer's propositions (2008) related to the barriers in the domestic Chinese market.

On the other hand, the findings suggest that ownership by the state does not play a significant role in SMEs' international expansion. However, the support from the state in the form of funding seems to be instrumental in the first stages of their (local and regional) expansion. In addition, the evidence shows that support from private sources is relevant to cross-national boundaries. These findings are in line with the conclusions from previous works (Cai, 1999; Child & Rodrigues, 2005; Fornes & Butt-Philip, 2009; Ge & Ding, 2008; Mathews, 2006; Yamakawa, et al., 2008; Zeng & Williamson, 2003; Zhang & Van Den Bulcke, 1996) and adds a new dimension by showing that different stages in the expansion process are fuelled by the support of different sources. In other words, the first push seems to be given by financial help from the government, and the second by financial support from private sources. This private support is also usually linked to a transfer of the knowledge and skills needed to operate in international markets (Linkage in Mathew's (2006) LLL framework); it also seems to provide support to Mathews' (2006) claim that the internationalisation of companies from China is based on a push and pull process (from the local SMEs and from the government or international partner in this case, respectively), rather than propelled only by a push process based on strategic objectives as in Western companies.

In this sense, the fact that state ownership does not play a relevant role in the firms' expansion could be interpreted from the findings of Child and Rodrigues (2005), that Chinese state-owned companies' strategic position "could be weakened by the way they remain beholden to administrative approval and … a legacy of institutional dependence". To this, Liu, Xiao, and Huang (2008, p. p. 505) added that "Chinese entrepreneurs are bounded by… unfavourable institutional arrangements". The results obtained in this analysis are the first to provide empirical evidence of the effects of state ownership and financial support in Chinese SMEs.

Concluding Remarks

First, the factors affecting the internationalisation of Chinese SMEs can be grouped into three main areas: (i) *Knowledge of International Business*; (ii) *International Operations and Logistics*; and (iii) *Skills and Internal Capabilities*. This grouping shows that the barriers are related mainly to weak management skills and knowledge regardless of the difference between internal and external. These findings suggest that SMEs in the provinces/autonomous region under study share this characteristic with other Chinese international companies as identified by previous works (Ge & Ding, 2008; Liu, et al., 2008; Nolan, 2001; Rugman & Li, 2007).

Second, from the results presented in this work, it seems that mainstream internationalisation theories do not appear to entirely fit the case of Chinese firms, similar to what previous theoretical papers have suggested. In particular, the evidence seems to suggest that competitive advantages (Porter, 1980), firm-specific advantages (FSA) (Rugman, et al., 2006), or ownership-specific advantages (Dunning, 1977) play a different role than that in Western companies; rather, it appears that the combination between internal and external factors is the main driver behind their internationalisation. In this process, the role played by the institutions is not clear, it may be negative, as suggested by Child & Rodriguez (2005), or it could be a "cognitive effect" (very pragmatic and the result of balanced efforts between markets and government intervention) as proposed by Santiso (2005a, 2005b); the fact that finance does not seem to be a factor affecting these companies' international expansion may be a back-door way to explain their role. In other words, as Buckley et al. put it, the internationalisation of Chinese firms appears to have "both a conventional and an idiosyncratic dimension" (2007, p. 514).

Third, there are also opportunities for policy-makers and SMEs' managers to improve the effectiveness of their policies and decisions. The results show that they need to establish a specialised infrastructure offering value-added information services, to act as an active interface between the international market and the local SMEs. In addition, companies, unions, and public and private institutions need to develop management training programmes in international business, including studies on partnerships, joint ventures, marketing, payment methods, etc. These programmes should aim at filling the skills gap in the professional profile of entrepreneurs and managers.

All in all, the internationalisation of companies from EE is still an area in need of further research, although there seems to be agreement in recent literature that mainstream internationalisation theories developed from companies based in Western economies do not entirely apply to the specifics of EE. From the evidence presented in this paper it appears that recently published theoretical models (mainly Mathews, 2006; Yamakawa, et al., 2008) are the most suitable approximation, but the literature on EE-based companies still needs to reach a better understanding of the interaction among the external factors, internal factors, and the institutions, as it is evident that the three play an important role in the firms' internationalisation process.

To conclude, and more broadly, the national and international expansion of emerging countries' SMEs presents interesting routes for developing the IB agenda. In this sense, Buckley (2002) suggested that one of the potential areas for IB research in the future is the identification of trends towards and away from globalisation, to which Peng (2004) added that future studies need to have a focus on the factors affecting the success and failure of firms in international markets. From what this chapter has presented it is possible to argue that the combination of external factors (industry-based view), internal factors (resource-based view), and ownership/funding types (institutional-based view), and how this combination has an impact on the internationalisation process of EE-based firms, is all affecting globalisation; and as a consequence, the internationalisation of firms in ways which have yet to be understood.

REFERENCES

[1] Barney, J. (1991). Firm resources and sustained competitive advantage. *Journal of Management, 17*, 99-120.

[2] Boisot, M., & Child, J. (1996). From fiefs to clans and network capitalism: Explaining China's emerging economic order. *Administrative Science Quarterly, 41*, 600-628.

[3] Boisot, M., & Meyer, M. (2008). Which Way through the Open Door? Reflections on the Internationalization of Chinese Firms. *Management and Organization Review, 4*(3), 349-365.

[4] Bonaccorsi, A. (1992). On the relationship between firm size and export intensity. *Journal of International Business Studies, 23*(4), 605-635.

[5] Buckley, P. (2002). Is the international business research agenda running out of steam? *Journal of International Business Studies, 33*(2), 365-374.

[6] Buckley, P., & Casson, M. (1976). *The Future of the Multinational Enterprise*. London: Macmillan.

[7] Buckley, P., Clegg, J., Cross, A., Liu, X., Voss, H., & Zheng, P. (2007). The determinants of Chinese outward foreign direct investment. *Journal of International Business Studies, 38*(4), 499-518.

[8] Cai, K. (1999). Outward foreign direct investment: a novel dimension of China's integration into the regional and global economy. *China Quarterly, 160*, 836-880.

[9] Calof, J. (1994). The relationship between firm size and export behaviour revisited. *Journal of International Business Studies, 25*(2), 367-387.

[10] Cardoza, G. (1997). Learning, innovation, and growth: A comparative policy approach to East Asia and Latin America. *Science and Public Policy, 24*(6).

[11] Cardoza, G., & Fornes, G. (2008). *National and International Expansion of SMEs from China.* Paper presented at the Academy of International Business, Milan.

[12] Child, J., & Rodrigues, S. (2005). The internationalization of Chinese firms: a case for theoretical extension? *Management and Organization Review, 1*(3), 381-410.

[13] Child, J., & Tse, D. (2001). China's transition and its implications for international business. *Journal of International Business Studies, 32*, 5-21.

[14] Dunning, J. (1977). Trade, location of economic activity, and the MNE: a search for an eclectic approach. In B. Ohlin, P. O. Hesselborn, & P. M. Wijkman (Eds.), *The international allocation of economic activity*. London: Macmillan.

[15] Filatotchev, I., Wright, M., Hoskisson, R., Uhlenbruck, K., & Tihanyi, L. (2003). Governance, organizational capabilities, and restructuring in transition economies. *Journal of World Business, 38*, 331-347.

[16] Fornes, G. (2008). *Foreign Exchange Exposure in Emerging Markets. A Holistic Approach to Minimising Its Effects on Multinational Enterprises.* Paper presented at the Academy of Management Conference Best Paper Proceedings, Anaheim.
[17] Fornes, G. (2009). *Foreign Exchange Exposure in Emerging Markets. How Companies Can Minimize It.* Basingstoke: Palgrave Macmillan.
[18] Fornes, G., & Butt-Philip, A. (2009). Chinese companies' outward internationalisation to emerging countries: The case of Latin America. *Chinese Business Review, 7*(1), 13-28.
[19] Fornes, G., & Cardoza, G. (2009). Foreign exchange exposure in emerging markets. A study of Spanish companies in Latin America. *International Journal of Emerging Markets, 4*(1), 6-25.
[20] Ge, G., & Ding, D. (2008). A strategic analysis of sourcing Chinese manufacturers: the case of Galanz. *Asia Pacific Journal of Management, 25*(4), 667-683.
[21] Guillen, M. F. (2000). Business groups in emerging economies: A resource-based view. *Academy of Management Journal, 43*(3), 362-380.
[22] Hoskisson, R. E., Eden, L., Lau, C. M., & Wright, M. (2000). Strategy in emerging economies. *Academy of Management Journal, 43*(3), 249-267.
[23] Johanson, J., & Wiedersheim-Paul, F. (1975). The internationalization of the firm. Four Swedish cases. *Journal of Management Studies, 12*, 305-322.
[24] Khanna, T., & Palepu, K. (1997). Why focused strategies may be wrong for emerging markets. *Harvard Business Review, 4*(75), 3-10.
[25] Khanna, T., & Palepu, K. (2000). The future of business groups in emerging markets: Long-run evidence from Chile. *Academy of Management Journal, 43*(3), 268-285.
[26] Leonidou, L. (2004). An analysis of the barriers hindering small business export development. *Journal of Small Business Management, 42*(3), 279-302.
[27] Li, P., Fornes, G., & Cardoza, G. (2009). The Internationalisation of Emerging Markets-based SMEs: Evidence from China's Shandong Province (Unpublished Working Paper).
[28] Liu, X., Xiao, W., & Huang, X. (2008). Bounded entrepreneurship and internationalisation of Indigenous private-owned firms. *International Business Review, 17*(4), 488-508.
[29] Mathews, J. (2006). Dragon multinationals: new players in 21st century globalization. *Asia Pacific Journal of Management, 23*(1), 5-27.
[30] Meyer, K., & Peng, M. (2005). Probing theoretically into Central and Eastern Europe: Transactions, resources, and institutions. *Journal of International Business Studies, 36*(6), 600-621.
[31] Ministry of Commerce of the People's Republic of China (2008a). China allocates $512 mln to support small enterprises Retrieved 21/8/08, from http://english.mofcom.gov.cn/aarticle/counselorsreport/asiareport/200808/20080805736435.html
[32] Ministry of Commerce of the People's Republic of China (2008b). China doubles ceiling for company small mortgage loans Retrieved 21/8/08, from http://english.mofcom.gov.cn/aarticle/counselorsreport/westernasiaandafricareport/200808/20080805735188.html
[33] Ministry of Commerce of the People's Republic of China (2008c). China to scrap administrative fees for small businesses Retrieved 24/8/2008, from

http://english.mofcom.gov.cn/aarticle/counselorsreport/westernasiaandafricareport/200808/20080805740063.html

[34] National Bureau of Statistics of China (2009). Retrieved 20/6/09, from http://www.stats.gov.cn/english/

[35] Nolan, P. (2001). *China and the Global Economy*. Basingstoke: Palgrave.

[36] North, D. (1990). *Institutions, Institutional Change, and Economic Performance*. New York: Cambridge University Press.

[37] Peng, M. (2003). Institutional transitions and strategic choices. *Academy of Management Review, 28*, 275-296.

[38] Peng, M. (2004). Identifying the big question in international business research. *Journal of International Business Studies, 35*(2), 99-108.

[39] Peng, M., Wang, D., & Jiang, Y. (2008). An Institution-based view of international business strategy: A focus on emerging economies. *Journal of International Business Studies, 39*, 920-936.

[40] Penrose, E. (1959). *The Theory of the Growth of the Firm*. White Plains NY: Sharpe.

[41] Porter, M. (1980). *Competitive Strategy*. New York: Free Press.

[42] Rugman, A., Collinson, S., & Hodgetts, R. (2006). *International Business* (4th Ed.). Harlow: Pearson.

[43] Rugman, A., & Li, J. (2007). *Can China's Multinationals Succeed Globally?* Paper presented at the Internationalisation of Indian and Chinese Firms, Brunel University – London.

[44] Santiso, J. (2005a). America Latina y Asia: bailando con los tigres y los dragones asiaticos. *Anuario Elcano: America Latina 2004-2005,* 275-298.

[45] Santiso, J. (2005b). La emergencia de China y su impacto en America Latina. *Politica Exterior, 19*(107), 97-112.

[46] Williamson, O. (1975). *Markets and Hierarchies Analysis and Antitrust Implications*. New York: Free Press.

[47] Wright, M., Filatotchev, I., Hoskisson, R. E., & Peng, M. W. (2005). Strategy research in emerging economies: Challenging the conventional wisdom. *Journal of Management Studies, 42*(1), 1-33.

[48] Xu, N., Fornes, G., & Cardoza, G. (2009). *The Internationalisation of Emerging Markets-based SMEs: Evidence from China's Jiangsu Province.* Paper presented at the China Goes Global conference, Harvard University – Boston.

[49] Xu, S., Fornes, G., & Cardoza, G. (2009). The Internationalisation of Emerging Markets-based SMEs: Evidence from China's Anhui Province (Unpublished Working Paper).

[50] Yamakawa, Y., Peng, M., & Deeds, D. (2008). What drives new ventures to internationalize from emerging to developed economies? *Entrepreneurship Theory and Practice, 32*(1), 59-82.

[51] Zeng, M., & Williamson, J. (2003). The hidden dragons. *Harvard Business Review, October 2003, 92-99.*

[52] Zhang, J., & Van Den Bulcke, D. (1996). International management strategies of Chinese multinational firms. In J. Child, & Y. Lu (Eds.), *Management Issues in China: International Enterprises*. London: Routledge.

In: Thirty Years of China's Economic Reform
Editors: Yue Wang and Prem Ramburuth
ISBN: 978-1-60876-908-7
© 2010 Nova Science Publishers, Inc.

Chapter 12

ECONOMIC COOPERATION BETWEEN CHINA AND ASEAN OVER THE LAST 30 YEARS: A HISTORICAL ACCOUNT OF BI-LATERAL TRADE AND THE ROLE OF GOVERNMENTS

*William K. W. Choy**
Policy and Leadership Studies Academic Group, National Institute of Education, Nanyang Technological University, Singapore

ABSTRACT

The chapter reviews the historical development of bilateral trade and foreign direct investment between China and the Association of the Southeast Asian Nations (ASEAN) from the 1970s to the present day. The author describes China's economic reform from 1979, which has served as a great incentive for the ASEAN member countries to engage in continuous political and economic dialogues with the economic giant. As a matter of fact, it is the extensive political and economic efforts initiated by the ASEAN and Chinese governments that have played a pivotal role in promoting bilateral trade and foreign direct investment. The institutional building at the macro-level between Chinese and ASEAN governments, which shape the pattern of economic cooperation, is different from those observed between China and Hong Kong/Taiwan. The case of Sino-Singapore Suzhou Industrial Park (SIP) illustrates the central roles of governments in driving the process of bilateral cooperation between China and the ASEAN member countries, leading to micro-level cooperation and business networking between firms.

Keywords: China; ASEAN, Bilateral trade; Economic-political relationship; Government-driven initiatives (interventions).

* Email: dr.william.choy@gmail.com

INTRODUCTION

Since the People's Republic of China started the market-oriented economic reform in 1979, the country has greatly expanded its trade and investment links with Western economies as well as the major economies in the Asia-Pacific region. Not surprisingly, China's entry into the WTO in 2001 further heightened the regional countries' need to foster greater bilateral trade agreements to improve economic cooperation with the rising giant (Ministry of Commerce of the People's Republic of China, 2008a; 2008b). One such region that has benefited from the latest developments in China's economic development is the Southeast Asian region. The economic cooperation between China and the Association of the Southeast Asian Nations (ASEAN) member countries can be traced back to the 1970s. This chapter provides a historical account of the economic relationship between China and ASEAN, and systematically charts the development of bilateral trade between the two partners over the last three decades.

The author explains that the development of the economic relationship between China and ASEAN has been largely shaped by the institutional-building between Chinese and ASEAN governments. Unlike the economic links between China and Hong Kong/Taiwan, where private sectors led the development of bilateral trade and FDI, economic cooperation between China and ASEAN was largely driven by government initiatives. China's policies directed towards the ASEAN countries have been closely associated with its domestic and foreign priorities (Lieberthal, 1988). Broadly speaking, China has been involved in a proactive and constructive role in the Southeast Asian region, in which the Chinese government has been readily increasing its diplomatic contacts and economic ties with the ASEAN states. Such efforts have focused primarily on attracting investment from, as well as increasing trade with, the overseas Chinese in the region, and beyond (Lieberthal, 1988). As a matter of fact, the extensive political and economic efforts initiated both by the ASEAN and Chinese governments have played a pivotal role in promoting bilateral trade between China and the ASEAN member countries.

In 1996, when China was accorded full Dialogue Partner status at the 29th ASEAN Ministerial Meeting (AMM) in Jakarta, cooperation between China and the ASEAN broadened and deepened, ensuring a more stable development of the China-ASEAN trade and investment ties. The relationship has been elevated to a higher level with the adoption of the Joint Declaration of the Heads of State/Government of the ASEAN and China on Strategic Partnership for Peace and Prosperity at the ASEAN-China Summit on 8 October 2003 in Bali (ASEAN Secretariat, 2007a; 2007b). The recent years have witnessed further rapid and comprehensive growth of China-ASEAN relations, yielding favorable outcomes through extensive and in-depth exchanges and cooperation between the two sides in political, economic, trade, social and cultural areas, among others (Ministry of Foreign Affairs {PRC}, 1998-2005).

The rest of the chapter is organised as follows. Section 2 provides an overview of the political and economic agenda of ASEAN to enhance development in the region. Section 3 examines the ASEAN external policies on international engagements, especially the bilateral trading arrangements that are being forged between ASEAN member countries such as Japan, Korea and, most importantly, China. Section 4 reviews the progressive development of

China's economic policy and efforts in establishing an economic relationship with ASEAN. Section 5 cites the case of the Sino-Singapore Suzhou Industrial Park (SIP) to illustrate the extent of governmental involvement between China and Singapore (a member country of ASEAN) in a concerted effort to build trade relations. Section 6 concludes with a broad discussion on the interventionist efforts by the Chinese and ASEAN leadership and policy-makers to enhance closer bilateral trade relationships and the implication for the future China-ASEAN economic collaboration.

The Southeast Asian Region and its Engagement with China

The ASEAN was established on 8 August 1967 in Bangkok by the five original member countries, namely Indonesia, Malaysia, Philippines, Singapore, and Thailand. Brunei Darussalam joined on 8 January 1984; Vietnam on 28 July 1995; Lao PDR and Myanmar on 23 July 1997; and Cambodia on 30 April 1999. Over the past few decades, the Southeast Asian region has achieved a combined gross domestic product of almost US$1,100 billion, and a total trade of about US$1,400 billion. The strong growth was a result of a committed aim and purpose of the Association, that sought: (1) to accelerate economic growth, social progress and cultural development in the region and (2) to promote regional peace and stability through abiding respect for justice and the rule of law in the relationships among countries in the region, and adherence to the principles of the United Nations Charter (ASEAN Secretariat, 2008).

Drawing upon the close cooperation between member countries, the ASEAN leaders have determined that key ASEAN communities are to be established to oversee three initiatives in the region. These initiatives include (1) political and security cooperation, (2) economic integration measures, and (3) socio-cultural development. These initiatives have come under the respective purview of the following communities, namely, the ASEAN Security Community, ASEAN Economic Community and ASEAN Socio-Cultural Community (ASEAN Secretariat, 2008). The goal of the *ASEAN Economic Community* is to create a stable, prosperous and highly competitive Southeast Asia economic region in which there would be greater trade liberalization - such that there is a free flow of goods, services, investment and a greater flow of capital – and equitable economic development, with an emphasis on reducing poverty and socio-economic disparities by the year 2020. The Community has sought to establish Southeast Asia as a single market and production base, capitalizing on the diversity that characterises ASEAN into opportunities for business investment, and making the region a more dynamic and stronger segment of the global supply chain. Thus, in order to enhance ASEAN's economic competitiveness through greater strategic integration between member countries, agreements have been formulated, for example, instituting new mechanisms and measures to strengthen the implementation of its existing economic initiatives, such as the ASEAN Free Trade Area (AFTA) (ASEAN Secretariat, 2008).

ASEAN External Policies, and Implications for China-ASEAN Trade Relations

Given the extensive political and economic efforts initiated by the ASEAN member countries, a long-term ASEAN initiative, known as the ASEAN Vision 2020, was established which would affirm an outward-looking ASEAN playing a pivotal role in the international community and advancing ASEAN's common interests. The ASEAN Vision 2020, adopted by the ASEAN Leaders on the 30th Anniversary of ASEAN, agreed on a shared vision of ASEAN as a concert of Southeast Asian nations; outward looking, living in peace, stability and prosperity, bonded together in partnership in dynamic development and in a community of caring societies. Building on the Joint Statement on East Asia Cooperation, collaboration between the Southeast and Northeast Asian countries has accelerated with the holding of an annual summit among the leaders of ASEAN, China, Japan, and the Republic of Korea within the ASEAN Plus Three cooperation (ASEAN Secretariat, 2007c, 2007d). Historically, the ASEAN Plus Three cooperation began in December 1997 with the convening of an informal summit among the leaders of ASEAN and their counterparts from East Asia, namely China, Japan and the Republic of Korea (ROK) ASEAN. As a result, the ASEAN Plus Three process was institutionalised in 1999 when the leaders issued a joint statement on East Asia Cooperation at their 3rd ASEAN Plus Three Summit in Manila (ASEAN Secretariat, 2007c, 2007d). Subsequently, bilateral trading arrangements have been or are being forged between ASEAN member countries, Japan, Korea and, most importantly, China. These arrangements have served as the building blocks of an East Asian Free Trade Area as a long term goal (ASEAN Secretariat, 2008). The inclusion of the East Asian counterparts was due to the fact that the leaders have expressed greater resolve and confidence in further strengthening and deepening East Asia collaboration at various levels and in various areas, particularly in economic, social, political, and other fields. There was a great deal of potential in multilevel benefits in trade and investments for the parties involved.

China-ASEAN Trade Relations Developments from the 1970s to the Present Day

China's economic system was undergoing fundamental changes, which would have significant impact on China's own economic future, as well as other countries'. The purpose of China's economic reform was to improve its overall economic efficiency by establishing a socialist commodity economy in place of the existing command economy (Yeh, 1988). China had previously been operating an economic system based on centralised planning by the government. This has resulted in an inward perspective in managing the economy, as reflected in part by the diverse resource base and large domestic market of its continental economy (Chia, 1988). However, China has recognised that it can no longer be isolated from the globalised economy and thus has sought to take proactive measures in order to build close partnerships with regional countries, and to expand its trade links and investment opportunities.

As China's economic development progressed, an evolution of bilateral economic relationship between China and the ASEAN occurred. Chia (1988) pointed out that such a relation had been long-standing, involving early Chinese commercial activities with Southeast Asia (or previously, known as Nanyang) based on a traditional tribute system. The trade that existed was due to the fact that there had been a steady flow of Chinese immigrants into the Southeast Asian region, that is, the commercial dealings involving the overseas Chinese communities of Singapore, Malaysia and Indonesia. The network of Chinese migrants played an important role in the economic development of their host countries, which would eventually serve as a key factor in the future political and economic relations between China and ASEAN (Chia, 1988).

Chia (1988) remarked that foreign economic interactions amongst nation-states based on similar political and economic systems are seldom shaped by economic factors alone. This is even more true of the economic association between the capitalistic nature of the market economy of ASEAN and the centrally-planned economic system of China, where the economic transactions of the latter are subject to a high degree of state intervention. In the evolving trade relations between China and ASEAN, it is apparent that such economic fundamentals and success cannot be divorced from political underpinnings. With an economic, and to some extent political focus, this paved the way for three distinguishable stages of trade relations between China and the ASEAN.

The first stage covered the post-1949 years up to the normalization of relations. Liberation in 1949 enabled China to achieve political independence, culminating in the establishment of diplomatic relations with many countries, thus allowing the country to embark on economic engagements with potential partners (Cheng & Zhang, 1987). The outcomes through which China interacted with the ASEAN are highlighted in their respective trade patterns, as tabulated and illustrated in Table 1, and Figures 1 & 2, respectively. The result of the earlier economic reform, and developments in China, created relatively limited impact on the ASEAN member countries (Wong, 1987; Chia, 1988). In fact, the extent of economic trade between China and the ASEAN was somewhat minimal. There are scant records of bilateral trade between China and the ASEAN up to 1978 (UNCTAD, 2008). The dismal trade outcomes stemmed from the fact that the ASEAN nation-states were still coming to terms with the "New China", marked by a strong revolutionary impulse and a proselytizing Marxist ideology, which a number of ASEAN members perceived as a threat - real or imagined - to their own security (Wong, 1987). The differing political and economic systems inevitably led to some misunderstanding between the potential partners. This resulted in a less-than-warm relationship between China and the ASEAN, with a constrained form of contact. However, it is was not till the early 1970s, with a desire to pursue a policy of détente, signaled by US President's Nixon's visit to Beijing, that the ASEAN member-states commenced their long and arduous course of normalization with China. Incidentally, on 27 November 1971, at a meeting held in Kuala Lumpur, Malaysia, comprised of the foreign ministers of the ASEAN nation-states, a declaration was issued for building a Zone of Peace, Freedom and Neutrality (ZOPFAN) in Southeast Asia. This was strongly supported by China (ASEAN Secretariat, 2004). This attracted positive reactions from the ASEAN members such as Indonesia, Malaysia, Philippines, Thailand and Singapore, thus leading to future diplomatic exchanges.

Table 1. China – ASEAN Bilateral Trade: Imports & Exports (1978 – 2006) (US Dollars at current prices in millions)

	1978	1979	1980	1981	1982	1983	1984	1985	1986	1987	1988
Exports of China to partner ASEAN	584.4	814.5	1195.5	1425.4	1315.5	1175.0	1992.0	2842.2	1918.5	2385.1	2958.5
Imports of China from partner ASEAN	329.4	424.4	653.5	592.3	918.7	678.1	838.7	1182.8	1547.5	2161.8	3197.8
Total Trade	913.8	1238.9	1849.0	2017.7	2234.2	1853.1	2830.7	4025.0	3466.0	4546.9	6156.3
Growth (%)											
Export	-	39.4	46.8	19.2	-7.7	-10.7	69.5	42.7	-32.5	24.3	24.0
Import	-	28.8	54.0	-9.4	55.1	-26.2	23.7	41.0	30.8	39.7	47.9
Total	-	35.6	49.2	9.1	10.7	-17.1	52.8	42.2	-13.9	31.2	35.4

	1989	1990	1991	1992	1993	1994	1995	1996	1997	1998	1999
Exports of China to partner ASEAN	3205.6	4150.7	4456.2	4667.8	5342.9	7165.8	10474.6	10319.0	12703.1	11032.4	12274.8
Imports of China from partner ASEAN	3766.5	3133.1	3943.8	4413.7	6283.7	7169.8	9896.2	10870.2	12357.5	12637.3	14927.0
Total Trade	6972.0	7283.8	8400.0	9081.5	11626.6	14335.6	20370.9	21189.2	25060.6	23669.6	27201.8
Growth (%)											
Export	8.4	29.5	7.4	4.7	14.5	34.1	46.2	-1.5	23.1	-13.2	11.3
Import	17.8	-16.8	25.9	11.9	42.4	14.1	38.0	9.8	13.7	2.3	18.1
Total	13.3	4.5	15.3	8.1	28.0	23.3	42.1	4.0	18.3	-5.6	14.9

	2000	2001	2002	2003	2004	2005	2006
Exports of China to partner ASEAN	17341.3	18571.2	23574.0	30925.5	42902.2	55478.8	55478.8
Imports of China from partner ASEAN	22180.7	23229.6	31193.3	47327.0	62977.5	75016.8	89548.7
Total Trade	39522.0	41800.8	54767.3	78252.4	105879.7	130495.6	145027.6
Growth (%)							
Export	41.3	7.1	26.9	31.2	38.7	29.3	0.0
Import	48.6	4.7	34.3	51.7	33.1	19.1	19.4
Total	45.3	5.8	31.0	42.9	35.3	23.2	11.1

Source: United Nations Conference on Trade and Development (UNCTAD) (2008)

The second stage covered the years of normalization of relations from 1974-76, up to 1984. This entailed a period of cool but improving economic relations, as a result of favorable domestic developments in China. After the fall of the "Gang of Four" in 1975, the Chinese government proceeded to focus on economic growth by launching the Four Modernization Programme, and by introducing economic and social liberalization initiatives. In addition, China brought forth its "open-door" economic policy so as to engage in greater interactions with the world economy in terms of foreign trade and investment (Wong, 1987). Not only that, Mr. Deng Xiaoping's return to power in 1978 intensified economic liberalization, culminating in the introduction of further vital economic reforms in late 1984. An important initiative undertaken by the Chinese government was the establishment and expansion of the Special Economic Zones (SEZ) within China, which included Shenzhen, Zhuhai, Shantou and Xiamen (Cheng & Zhang, 1987). Special administrative systems were instituted along with special economic policies for the SEZs. Preferential treatment was given to foreign investors

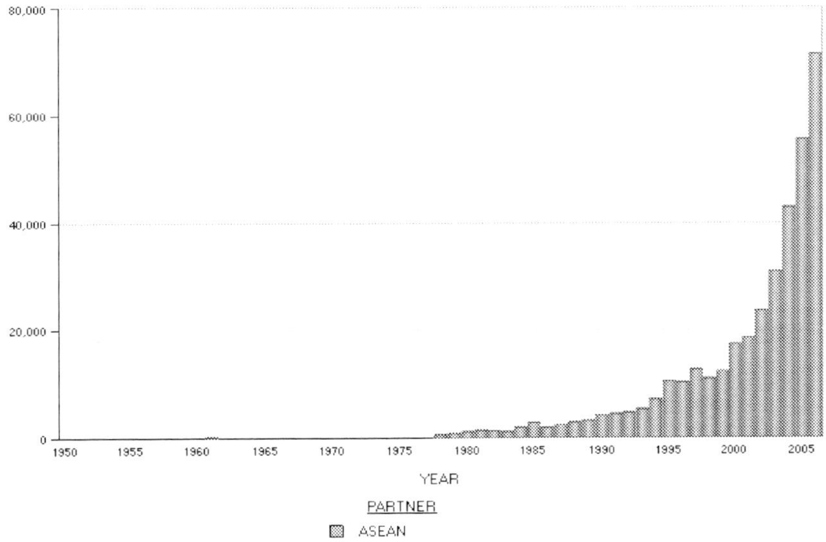

Source: United Nations Conference on Trade and Development (UNCTAD) (2008)

Figure 1. China – ASEAN Bilateral Trade: Export (1978 – 2006) (US Dollars at current prices in millions)

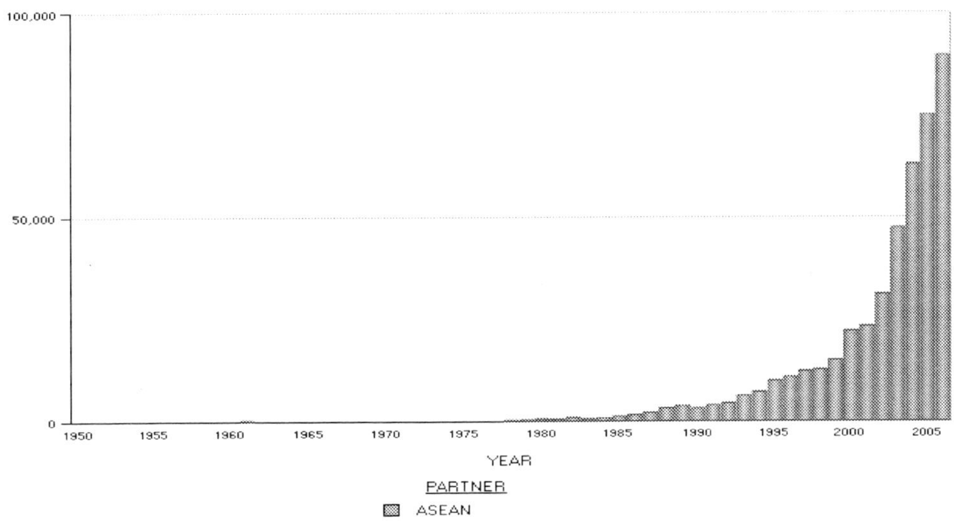

Source: United Nations Conference on Trade and Development (UNCTAD) (2008)

Figure 2. China – ASEAN Bilateral Trade: Import (1978 – 2006) (US Dollars at current prices in millions)

in terms of tax relief and circulation of capital (Ministry of Commerce {PRC}, 1984a). Further developments were institutionalised which included greater market orientation for the industries, so that export-oriented industries were required to complement import-substituting ones (Ministry of Commerce {PRC}, 1984b). The trade developments are highlighted in Table 1 and Figures 1 & 2, where there is a steady upward trend in terms of trade between China and the ASEAN countries. Between 1978 and 1983, the average export figure for China was US$1.09 billion, whereas the average import figure was US$3.6 billion. The starting export amount was US$584.4 million in 1978, and by the end of 1983 a total of US$1.17 billion was achieved. On the other hand, the import figure for China was US$329.4 million from 1978, and by 1983 the amount was recorded at US$678.1 million (UNCTAD, 2008). Following the success and experiences of the above SEZs, China initiated other SEZs to complement its economic progress. The new zones included Shanghai, Tianjin, Guangzhou and Dalian among others.

The third stage, starting from 1984, marked further improvement in the economic relationship between China and the ASEAN (Chia, 1988). China has sought to explore the possibility of greater international cooperative forms in various economic sectors (Cheng & Zhang, 1987). As previously discussed, China's economic reform involved three main thrusts: enterprise invigoration, market nurturing and macro-economic control improvement. Eventually, enterprises in China were permitted to engage in direct foreign markets dealings, such that there were extensive transformations of Chinese businesses. As a consequence of the economic progress, Chinese commodity producers and managers were given relative autonomy, accorded sole responsibility for profits and losses. Not surprisingly, Chinese enterprises were motivated to increase the degree of outward orientation in their commercial activities and expand international market access (Yang, Yu & Shen, 1989). With the improvement in China's economic policies, China's trade activities were more stable and predictable. This, undoubtedly, contributed to the expansion of trade between China and the ASEAN. From 1984 to the end of the 1980s, the average export figure for China was US$19.5 billion, whereas the average import figure was US$15.8 billion. The following decade, the 1990s, the Chinese export figure was US$95.8 billion, while the import figure amounted to US$104.7 billion (see Table 1, and Figures 1 & 2) (UNCTAD, 2008). The early 2000s marked a turning point in the trade relationship between China and the ASEAN. The successes and experiences of the past two decades have paved the way for further renewal of an interest in deeper cooperation and commitment between the trading partners. Highly reliant on exports, the ASEAN member states viewed China's 1.3 billion population and its fast developing economy as one of the most important markets in the world. For example, (starting) in 2001, trade volume between China and the ASEAN countries totalled US$41.8 billion, rising 5 percent over the previous year despite the worldwide economic recession. ASEAN member exports were worth US$23.2 billion to China, representing a growth of 4.7 percent over the previous year and resulting in a trade surplus of US$4.8 billion (China Internet Information Center, 2002). All in all, between the period of 2001 and 2006, the average Chinese export was US$37.8 billion and the average import was US$54.9 billion.

As such, China and the ASEAN reached a landmark agreement to establish a China-ASEAN Free Trade Area within 10 years at a recent ASEAN summit held in Brunei (China Internet Information Center, 2001a; Ministry of Foreign Affairs {PRC} 2001; ASEAN Secretariat, 2007e). The objectives of the Agreement are to: a) strengthen and enhance economic, trade and investment cooperation between the parties; b) progressively liberalise and promote trade in goods and services, as well as create a transparent, liberal and facilitative investment regime; c) explore new areas and develop appropriate measures for closer economic cooperation between the parties; and d) facilitate the more effective economic integration of newer ASEAN Member States and bridge the development gap among the parties (ASEAN Secretariat, 2007e). The framework will serve to progressively eliminate tariffs and non-tariff barriers in, substantially, all trade in goods; to expedite the expansion of trade in services and progressively liberalise trade in services with substantial sectoral coverage; and to promote investments and to create a liberal, facilitative, transparent and competitive investment regime. Other aspects of economic cooperation in the Agreement include the strengthening of cooperation in five priority sectors - agriculture; information and communications technology; human resources development; investment; and Mekong River basin development. In addition, cooperation is also extended to other areas, including, but not limited to, banking, finance, tourism, industrial cooperation, transport, telecommunications, intellectual property rights, small and medium enterprises (SMEs), environment, bio-technology, fishery, forestry and forestry products, mining, energy and sub-regional development. Last but not least, the economic partners have agreed to implement capacity-building programmes and technical assistance, particularly for the newer ASEAN member states, in order to adjust their economic structures and expand their trade and investment with China (ASEAN Secretariat, 2007e). Concurrently, the Chinese Premier Zhu Rongji has stressed that China's accession to the WTO would provide other countries, especially the ASEAN countries, with an alternative venue for investment and more business opportunities. Furthermore, the developments would create more favourable conditions for Chinese corporations to invest and set up businesses in neighbouring countries, including ASEAN members (China Internet Information Center, 2001b). This has definitely extended the horizon of China's regional economic cooperation, thus serving as a catalyst for greater East Asian economic dealings. ASEAN Secretary-General Rodolfo C. Severino has reaffirmed the ASEAN's support for China's entry into the World Trade Organization. He stressed the fact that it was certainly in the interest of ASEAN countries as it would create more business opportunities for ASEAN countries. He emphasised that China's participation in the world trade system not only represent a competitive challenge, but also an opportunity for ASEAN investors and for ASEAN products to enter the Chinese market more freely, since the development of China's economy represented a larger market and a source of investment (China Internet Information Center, 2001c). All in all, it is projected that by 2010, the average duty within the China-ASEAN FTA, if realised, would vary between zero and five percent, and internal trade and investment barriers would be eliminated. The free trade area would then possess 40 percent of the world's foreign exchange reserves and more than US$2 trillion in gross domestic product, 10 per cent of the world's total (China Internet Information Center, 2001a).

THE CASE OF SINO-SINGAPORE SUZHOU INDUSTRIAL PARK PROJECT (SIP)

What is definitely clear is that the past years of trade growth and development have served as an important turning point for the Chinese and ASEAN governments. The respective government leadership and policy-makers have been intervening strongly in their macro-economic control efforts to bring about closer ties between the countries. The strong pro-growth initiatives have injected symbiotic processes aimed at bilateral economic integration. One of the key dynamic consequences of such a relationship is the case of the China-Singapore Suzhou Industrial Park Project (CS-SIP; 中国--新加坡苏州工业园区) (Suzhou Industrial Park Administrative Committee, 2004).

Since 1997, China has been Singapore's top direct foreign investment location. Over the past 3 years, bilateral trade has been growing by more than 25%, thus making Singapore the eighth largest investor in China. The entry of China into the WTO and the start of the China-ASEAN tariff reduction plan on 20 July 2005 have further opened up the Chinese market (Ministry of Commerce {PRC}, 2005). This provided greater opportunity for Singapore to improve its bilateral trade relationship with China, which led to the formulation of the China-Singapore Suzhou Industrial Park Project.

The development of the industrial park was a result of China's modernization drive in the late 1980s, which has brought many Chinese political and industrial leaders to visit Singapore to learn about Singaporean management methods and business experiences. Incidentally, Singapore was also planning an economic regionalization, which focused on expanding overseas trade and investment. In 1992, the plan to develop a modern industrial township with Singapore experience was proposed. Following a series of discussions and site surveys, both countries formalised the proposal of the China-Singapore Suzhou Industrial Park on 26 February 1994 when the Chinese Vice Premier Li Lanqing and Singapore Senior Minister Lee Kuan Yew signed the Agreement on the Joint Development of Suzhou Industrial Park in Shanghai (Suzhou Industrial Park Administrative Committee, 2004). Without a doubt, Singaporean corporations have been encouraged to invest in the Suzhou industrial park, especially in the service outsourcing, logistics and water and environmental services. This is because China is considered an increasingly popular destination for business process outsourcing (BPO) operations, and because the Suzhou industrial park, being designated as a BPO demonstration base, has served to be a very attractive platform for Singapore companies wanting to ride the BPO wave in China (Ministry of Commerce {PRC}, 2007).

All in all, Singapore's trade with China reached S$67.08 billion in 2005, an increase of 28.7% over the corresponding period in 2004. A seven-fold growth in Sino-Singapore trade was registered in the last decade, from S$7.6 billion in 1994 to S$53.3 billion in 2004. Presently, China is Singapore's fourth-largest trading partner, accounting for a 9.4% share of Singapore's total trade - after Malaysia, the European Union and the US. With a cumulative contractual investment value of US$52.98 billion in 2005, Singapore is China's seventh-largest investor. The number of Chinese firms in Singapore also grew from 509 (in 1999) to 1,161 (in 2003). As of October 2005, there are also 89 Chinese companies listed in Singapore (International Enterprise Singapore, 2007).

Table 2. China – Singapore Bilateral Trade (2003 - 2006)

Trade	2003	2004	2005	Jan-2006
Total Trade	S$36.9b (+31.3%)	S$53.33b (+44.5%)	S$67.08b (+25.8%)	S$6.08b (+28.7%)
Import from China	S$19.2b (+21.6%)	S$27.36b (+41.9%)	S$34.17b (+24.9%)	S$3.20b (+32.2%)
Export to China	S$17.6b (+43.8%)	S$25.97b (+47.2%)	S$32.91b (+26.7%)	S$2.93b (+25.0%)
Re-Exports	S$7.6b (+47.4%)	S$11.78b (+54.6%)	S$15.31b (+30.0%)	S$1.47b (+48.1%)
Share of Singapore Total Trade	7.16%	8.48%	9.37%	10.19%
Balance of Trade	-S$1.6b	-S$1.38b	-S$1.26b	-S$0.23b
Ranking 2005	China is Singapore's 4th largest trading partner			

Source : International Enterprise Singapore, 2007

All in all, it can be said that both the Chinese and Singaporean leaders and senior officials have strongly steered the favourable trade relationships of both respective countries as a consequence of global realities and necessities in politics and economics. Not surprisingly, the similarities in sociocultural background (that is, a predominantly Chinese population and common ancestral links) have further helped to facilitate a progressive bilateral economic relationship and provide the essential foundations for the private sectors' involvement in establishing closer business networks between China and Singapore.

DISCUSSION AND CONCLUSION

The bilateral trade relationship between China and the ASEAN member countries is firmly established, with the promise of an enduring future. There is much promise as the China-ASEAN relations enter a new phase, as both sides are emphasizing continuous and mutually-enriching trade agreements. The respective leaders and policy makers of China and the ASEAN have recognised the fact that the booming industries and political/economic initiatives have provided immense opportunities for greater China-ASEAN networking and collaboration. The state-centric priorities of both governments toward expanding trade have motivated the leaders and other senior officials to serve in greater drive-and-steer roles and initiatives. Over time, state-led, government-to-government crafted trade dialogues, agreements and other developmental interventions have paved the way for business enterprises to establish global business networks, and thus flourish. A number of milestones in the development of the China-ASEAN relationship have ensured long-term benefits, which include further cooperation in the areas of political, security, economic and sociocultural improvement, with the signing of respective MOUs (Sheng, 2007). The rationale for the close relationship stems from the fact that China's expanding market is a drawing point for the ASEAN countries who want to continue doing business with the economic giant. Not only that, the competitive advantages in logistics, transportation and distribution networks within the ASEAN region, as well as potential in areas of port construction, logistics, tourism, telecommunication and industrial parks development, have served to affirm mutual commitments (Chang, 2007).

For instance, from December 2001 to September 2005, China's annual import average was reported as US$500 billion and created about 10 million employment opportunities for other countries and regions. China-ASEAN trade is estimated to reach over US$200 billion by 2010 as the China-ASEAN Free Trade Agreement eventuates. There is no doubt that there will be an increase in potential bilateral inter/intra-industrial trade within and between the corporations in China and the Southeast Asian region, and that the huge demand for imports by the Chinese market will provide strong incentives for the ASEAN to secure such lucrative trade. In addition, Beijing's proactive economic option to maintain trade deficits, in order to maintain a good working relationship with the ASEAN (note that ASEAN has benefited from a trade surplus of about US$20 billion with China), reveals its strong intentions to engage in pragmatic foreign policy and economic diplomacy to promote global integration, and signals a willingness to create stability and equilibrium, not only for its own economic and political developments, but for others within the region as well.

In view of the successful relationship between the trading partners, intense strategies and efforts must be put in place to enhance the partnership. The member states of the ASEAN and China must continue to coordinate their mutual interests and formulate a collective position with one another, for existing and future trade investment agreements (Chen, 2006). Preferential treatment and special attention could be accorded towards the negotiation of favourable terms and conditions in trade and investment agreements covering issues such as the elimination of import duties, progressive elimination of tariffs and non-tariff barriers, reaffirming the important role and contribution of the business sector, recognizing the different stages of economic development among ASEAN member states and the need for flexibility in facilitating the participation of the newer members of the China-ASEAN cooperation, endorsing the rights, obligations and undertakings of the respective parties under the World Trade Organisation (WTO), and other multilateral, regional and bilateral agreements and arrangements (ASEAN Secretariat, 2007d). No doubt, the challenges of a globalised economy and market-driven processes have urged the respective government leaderships to recognise the need for institutionalising measures of policy-driven cooperation between China and the ASEAN member countries. Eventually, by fulfilling such political and economic pre-conditions, regional prosperity would be achieved for the world's largest economic bloc, China and the ASEAN.

References

[1] Association of Southeast Asian Nations (ASEAN) Secretariat (2004). Zone of Peace, Freedom and Neutrality Declaration. Kuala Lumpur, Malaysia, 27 November 1971, http://www.aseansec.org/1215.htm, accessed 15 May 2009.

[2] Association of Southeast Asian Nations (2007a). Joint Declaration of the Heads of State/Government of the Association of Southeast Asian Nations and the People's Republic of China on Strategic Partnership for Peace and Prosperity, http://www.aseansec.org/15265.htm, accessed 15 May 2009.

[3] Association of Southeast Asian Nations (2007b). ASEAN-China Dialogue Relations, http://www.aseansec.org/5874.htm, accessed 15 May 2009.

[4] Association of Southeast Asian Nations (2007c). Joint Statement on East Asia Cooperation. Manila, Philippines, 28 November 1999, http://www.aseansec.org/5469.htm, accessed 15 May 2009.

[5] Association of Southeast Asian Nations (2007d). ASEAN Plus Three Cooperationhttp://www.aseansec.org/16580.htm, accessed 15 May 2009.

[6] Association of Southeast Asian Nations (2007e). Framework Agreement on Comprehensive Economic Co-Operation Between ASEAN and the People's Republic of China, Phnom Penh, 5 November 2002, http://www.aseansec.org/13196.htm, accessed 15 May 2009.

[7] Association of Southeast Asian Nations (2008). ASEAN Secretariat, Indonesia, http://www.aseansec.org/, accessed 1 July 2008.

[8] Chang, C. Y (2007). ASEAN-China economic relations: Moving towards service. In S-H Saw (Ed). ASEAN-China Economic Relations. Singapore: Institute of Southeast Asian Studies, 146 – 165.

[9] Chen, H. (2006). China-ASEAN FTA: An investment perspective. In J. Wong, K. Zou, & H. Zeng (Eds). China-ASEAN Relations: Economic and Legal Dimensions. Singapore: World Scientific Publishing Co. Pte. Ltd, 133-157.

[10] Cheng, B., & Zhang, N. (1987). Institutional factors in China-ASEAN economic relations. In S-Y. Chia, & B. Cheng (Eds.). ASEAN-China Economic Relations: Trends and Patterns. Singapore: Institute of Southeast Asian Studies, 21 – 37.

[11] Chia, S-Y (1988). China's economic relations with ASEAN countries. In J. K. Kallgren, N. Sopiee, & S. Djiwandono (Eds.). ASEAN and China: An Evolving Relationship. Berkeley, California: Institute of East Asian Studies, University of California, 189-214.

[12] China Internet Information Center (2001a). China/ASEAN Agree on Free Trade Zone, China Daily, November 7, http://www.china.org.cn/english/2001/Nov/21720.htm, accessed 15 May 2009.

[13] China Internet Information Center (2001b). China Hopes Sino-ASEAN Free Trade Area Talk, People's Daily, November 6, http://www.china.org.cn/english/FR/21677.htm, accessed 15 May 2009.

[14] China Internet Information Center (2001c). ASEAN Reaffirms Support for China's WTO Accession, Xinhua News Agency, July 27, http://www.china.org.cn/english/2001/Jul/16701.htm, accessed 15 May 2009.

[15] China Internet Information Center (2002). ASEAN-China FTA Benefits Both Sides, China Daily, April 3, http://www.china.org.cn/english/FR/30000.htm, accessed 15 May 2009.

[16] Feng, Y., & Chen, D. (1992). China joins the multilateral trade system: Impact on trade and economic cooperation between China and the ASEAN countries. In S-Y. Chia, & B. Cheng (Eds.). ASEAN-China Economic Relations: In the Context of Pacific Economic Development and Cooperation. Singapore: Institute of Southeast Asian Studies, 126-149.

[17] International Enterprise Singapore (2007). Singapore's Bilateral Trade with China. Singapore: International Enterprise.

[18] Lieberthal, K. (1988). Implications of China's Political Situation on ASEAN. In J. K. Kallgren, N. Sopiee, & S. Djiwandono (Eds.). ASEAN and China: An Evolving Relationship. Berkeley, California: Institute of East Asian Studies, University of California, 3-21.

[19] Ministry of Commerce of the People's Republic of China (1984a). Detailed rules for the implementation of registration and administration of enterprises in Shenzhen Special Economic Zone. China: Ministry of Commerce of the People's Republic of China.

[20] Ministry of Commerce of the People's Republic of China (1984b). Regulations on the import of technology to the Xiamen Special Economic Zone. China: Ministry of Commerce of the People's Republic of China.

[21] Ministry of Commerce of the People's Republic of China (2008a). Main Mandate of the Ministry of Commerce. Ministry of Commerce of the People's Republic of China.

[22] Ministry of Commerce of the People's Republic of China (2008b). Ministry of Commerce of the People's Republic of China, http://english.mofcom.gov.cn/, accessed 1 Nov 2008.

[23] Ministry of Foreign Affairs of the People's Republic of China (1998-2005). ASEAN-China Dialogue Relations – An Overview. Ministry of Foreign Affairs of the People's Republic of China.
[24] Ministry of Foreign Affairs of the People's Republic of China (2001). Working Together to Create a New Phase of China-ASEAN Cooperation. Address by Premier Zhu Rongji at 5th China-ASEAN Summit, Bandar Seri Begawan, November 6, http://asean-chinasummit.fmprc.gov.cn/eng/zywj/t270550.htm, accessed 15 May 2009.
[25] Sheng, L. (2007). China's economic relations with ASEAN: Developments and strategic intent. In S-H Saw (Ed). ASEAN-China Economic Relations. Singapore: Institute of Southeast Asian Studies, 295-317.
[26] Suzhou Industrial Park Administrative Committee (2004). China-Singapore Suzhou Industrial Park (CS-SIP), http://www.sipac.gov.cn/english/, accessed on 1 Aug 2009,
[27] United Nations Conference on Trade and Development (UNCTAD) (2008). Handbook of Statistics 2008, http://stats.unctad.org/handbook/ReportFolders/ReportFolders.aspx, accessed 1 Aug 2009.
[28] Wong, J. (1987). An overview of ASEAN-China economic relations. In S-Y. Chia, & B. Cheng (Eds). ASEAN-China Economic Relations: Trends and Patterns. Singapore: Institute of Southeast Asian Studies, 1 – 20.
[29] Wong, J. (2006). China-ASEAN relations: An economic perspective. In J. Wong, K. Zou, & H. Zeng (Eds). China-ASEAN Relations: Economic and Legal Dimensions. Singapore: World Scientific Publishing Co. Pte. Ltd, 17-32.
[30] Yang, D., Yu, Y., & Shen, H. (1989). Economic reforms in China and their impact on China-ASEAN economic relations. In S-Y. Chia, & B. Cheng (Eds.). ASEAN-China Economic Relations: Developments in ASEAN and China. Singapore: Institute of Southeast Asian Studies, 1 – 22.
[31] Yeh, K. C. (1988). China's economic reform. In J. K. Kallgren, N. Sopiee, & S. Djiwandono (Eds.). ASEAN and China: An Evolving Relationship. Berkeley, California: Institute of East Asian Studies, University of California, 35-52.

INDEX

A

B

C

D

H

I

J

K

L

M

S

T

U

V

W

X

Y

Z